Mel Bay Presents

The MUSICIAN'S ULTIMA
Picture Chord
ENCYCLOPEDIA

M000087222

compiled by David K. Atkinson

1 2 3 4 5 6 7 8 9 0

Visit us on the Web at www.melbay.com — E-mail us at email@melbay.com

Layout and design by David K. Atkinson

Photos and graphic constructions by David K. Atkinson

Graphic manipulations, scalings, and editing by Jeri Trgina

Contents

From the Author ---4

About this Book ---5

    Thumb chords --6

    Barre chords ---6

    Open chords & alternate fingerings --7

    Chord diagram descriptions ---8

    Key & diatonic scale chart descriptions -----------------------------------9

Music Theory Crash Course -- 10

    12 half steps -- 10

    Sharps & flats --- 11

    Major scales --- 11

    Harmony & thirds -- 11

    Chords & triads --- 12

    7th's, 9th's, 11th's, & 13th's--- 13

    4th's & 6th's --- 13

Chord Encyclopedia Table of Contents ------------------------------- 14

    Five basic chord forms --330

    Key signatures --332

    Modal chord - Scale chart ---333

About the Author--336

from the author...

The aspiring guitar player has been showered with a plethora of instructional materials and books since the 1960's. Because of this a reasonable question might be: why write another one? To answer that, I must confess I have always been attracted to instructional materials, especially the "self taught" or "learn at your own pace" stuff. Of the books I've acquired, some filled my expectations while others did not. Many of the guitar chord books brought about one of my biggest frustrations, the lack of a clear, thoughtful layout.

A good chord book should organize the fundamentals of chord construction in a simple straight forward, no nonsense manner so that a basic understanding of why chords are designated in the fashion that they are will be brought to light. In addition, the photographs need to be shot from the player's perspective so that when the eyes move from the photo on the page to the hand on the neck, the angle of view remains the same. This would (consciously or subconsciously) remove the anguish of twisting and reversing an image mentally and leave the mind with a cleared field of thought, unobstructed and primed for input.

It was the need for this book that brought me to the realization that I should create it myself and hence the answer to the query "Why write another one?"

I didn't stop there. I felt if I was going to tackle this problem, why not address another that has plagued musicians both old and new. In playing an instrument it is likely at some point in time you will play with another musician. This can be, and usually is, one of the most rewarding benefits of playing music. As with anything that is good, it doesn't come easily and becoming a band member is no exception. It requires a lot of dedication. One of the largest hurdles to overcome is communicating musically with other members in the band. Music theory and acquiring the ability to read and write music is of course the answer, but as life would have it you are not likely to be in a band where every one is equally proficient in music theory. The cross-references of standard music notation, keyboard graphics, guitar chord diagrams and photographs that this book provides, levels the playing field between the most schooled and least schooled musicians enough that they may enjoy performing music together. It takes the guess work out of playing chords and literally keeps you and the other bandmembers on the same page. This is accomplished not by dragging the accomplished musicians down but rather by pulling the less learned into a higher knowledge of music. This is achieved simply by making them aware of what they are playing.

David K. Atkinson

about this book...

CHORDS

Each page in the encyclopedia contains one chord displayed at different positions on the guitar. These are presented from left to right starting with the lowest neck position, which is usually an open chord.

Selecting the chords to be used in this book and creating their appropriate diagrams, fingerings and neck positions involved sifting through seemingly endless volumes of guitar and keyboard chord charts. The guitar chord diagrams which made the final cut had to satisfy at least two of the following criteria:

1) Ease of fingering
2) Root note included
3) Note count (how many notes are being played)

This proved to be a very grueling experience and took in excess of one year's time. This had to be completed before the actual construction of the keycharts, keyboard graphics and chord diagrams could begin, which of course had to be completed before the photos could be taken, all of which ended with the creation of the most versatile chord book available today.

PHOTOS

The photographs were taken using a state of the art digital camera with the lens angle and placement set in close proximity to the players eyes. This resulted in the player's view of the fretboard which is comfortable and familiar. The underlying mental anguish which usually accompanies comparing chord diagrams from a vertical perspective on the page to a horizontal guitar neck, has therefore been eliminated. These "player's view photos" create a mindframe which is conducive to immediate recognition and comprehension. There's truly nothing like it. It's a no brainer!

GRAPHICS

Each photograph is accompanied with a guitar chord diagram, keyboard layout graphic and a diatonic grid with standard music notation depicting the root, third, fifth, seventh, ninth, eleventh and thirteenth used for that particular chord.

The combination of all the above components creates a cross reference indispensable to all musicians. The communication afforded band members who use this book make it a must have. Say good bye to yelling notes across the room while trying to figure out chords. Here, the work has already been done for you, and it's in black and white and in your face.

THUMB CHORDS

Thumb chords utilize the thumb to sound notes in the lower register of the instrument that would physically be an impossibility using only the fingers.

The thumb adds fullness to a chord that would otherwise sound rather thin.

BARRE CHORDS

Barre chords requiring only two fingers in addition to the first finger barre utilize fingers 3 and 4. These guidelines allow the 2nd finger to provide additional support to the 1st finger barre.

The downward pressure achieved using the double finger affords a much cleaner sounding chord.

OPEN CHORDS

For open chords requiring no more than three fretted notes, utilize fingers 2, 3, and 4. This facilitates the chord to become a moveable barre chord simply by sliding the hand up the neck and adding the 1st finger barre.

ALTERNATE FINGERINGS

Throughout this book you will see evidence of the same chord being fingered with alternate fingers as in the augmented chords shown below. Of course one should use fingerings that are most comfortable to them individually. Experiment and find the one that is right for you.

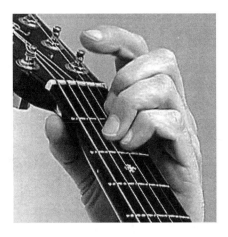

CHORD DIAGRAMS

Chord diagrams are graphic representations of a span of five frets on the fingerboard. The frets run horizontally. The strings run vertically.

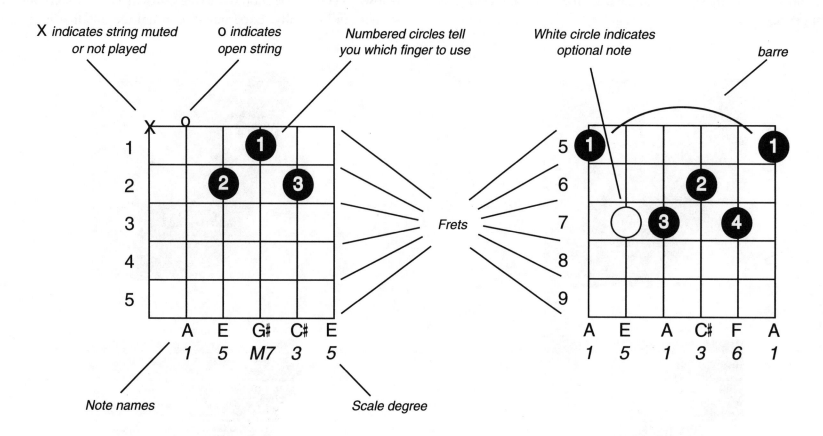

KEY & DIATONIC SCALE
CHARTS

Key Name

Key and Chord in closed position (The order the notes are built from the major scale.) 1, 3, 5, 7, 9 etc. displayed in standard music notation

Major Scale Notes

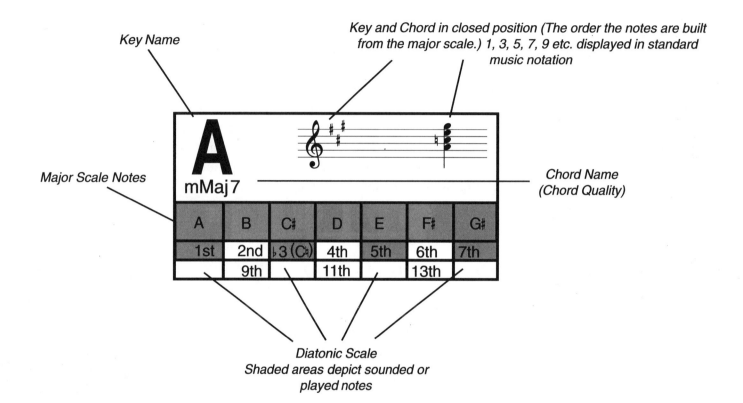

Chord Name (Chord Quality)

Diatonic Scale Shaded areas depict sounded or played notes

MUSIC THEORY CRASH COURSE

The next few pages are designed to bring about a basic awareness of music theory. There are a countless number of theory books that would serve you well should you wish to learn more. My plan is to have you at least understand how and why chords are constructed and labled the way they are. Please read thoroughly as this information has been boiled down to the essentials.

Our music system consists of a series of notes evenly divided into twelve half steps. Each of these half steps is an individual note. This span of twelve notes does not include the octave which is a repeat of the first note only higher in pitch (twice the wave frequency).

Although there are twelve notes we only use the first seven letters of the alphabet (A,B,C,D,E,F & G) to name them. We must travel two half steps to move from one note name to another. There are two exceptions to this rule, and that is when we are traveling from the 3rd scale degree (note 3) to the 4th scale degree (note 4), and when traveling from note 7 to the octave. At these two locations and only these two locations we travel one half step to reach the next note name. Guitars and keyboards are layed out in the key of C and as shown below there is no note between E (note 3) and F (note 4) also there is no note between B (note 7) and C (octave). These are the only two locations which have no note between them. Below you will see graphic layouts of our twelve note system.

* Fretted instruments such as guitars are layed out in these half steps.

* Keyboards are layed out so the half steps that fall between letter names are black keys.

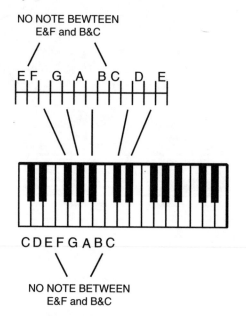

SHARPS and FLATS

The ♯ (sharp) sign indicates that a note is to be played 1/2 step higher. The ♭ (flat) sign indicates a note is to be played 1/2 step lower. A note that falls between two letter names is referred to as either a sharp (♯) or flat (♭) depending on the scale and following the rule listed below that a scale is to use all seven letter names.

MAJOR SCALES

A major scale is comprised of seven ascending consecutive letter notes. It is important to remember that each of these seven notes has a different letter name. For example in the major key of E you would not have an E♭ and an E because the letter E would have been used twice. They would have to be labeled D♯ and E, even though the notes D♯ and E♭ are the same as far as frequency and position on the instrument are concerned.

The format of steps (whole steps and half steps) is as illustrated on the previous page. This pattern or sequence of whole step, whole step, half step, whole step, whole step, whole step, half step is always the same regardless of which of the twelve notes is chosen to be the key name. A pneumonic aid is to remember just as the numeral 2 comes before 3 so the two whole step sequence comes before the three whole step sequence. Again this pattern is whole step, whole step, half step, whole step, whole step, whole step, half step. The two single half step intervals fall between notes 3 & 4 and after 7.

HARMONY AND THIRDS

Thirds are what harmony is all about. A third is found by counting up three letter notes using the originating note as number one. In other words start on a given letter note skip a letter note and land on a third. Because of the sequence of whole steps and half steps described in the above major scale text, you will see that depending on where you originate the thirds will fall into one of two categories:

1. **MAJOR THIRDS** - two whole steps (4 half steps).

Example 1. C to E   Major 3rd.

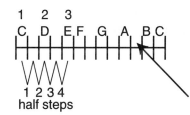

Notes that fall between the letter names are refered to as sharps (♯'s) or flats (♭'s).
This note would be called either an A♯ or a B♭ depending on the scale and following the rule that a scale is to use all seven letter names.

2. **MINOR THIRDS** - one whole step plus a half step (3 half steps).

Example 2. D to F   minor 3rd.

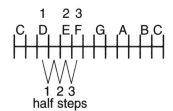

CHORDS and TRIADS

When you skip a note and land on a third (as described in the previous paragraph on harmony and thirds) and continue skipping over the next note and landing, (choosing every other note) you are stacking thirds. This is how chords are built. A simple chord of two thirds stacked on top of each other is called a triad and is comprised of scale degrees 1, 3, & 5 or root, third & fifth.

Different combinations of major and minor thirds result in four types of triads or chords. They are as follows:

MAJOR + MINOR = **MAJOR**

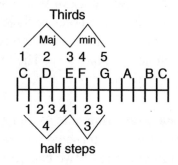

MINOR + MAJOR = **MINOR**

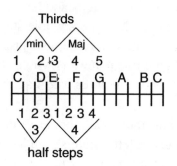

MINOR + MINOR = **DIMINISHED**

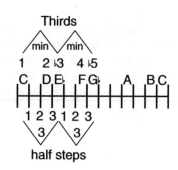

MAJOR + MAJOR = **AUGMENTED**

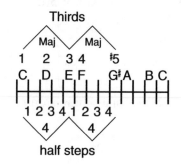

7th's, 9th's, 11th's, & 13th's

If you continue stacking thirds on top of the 5th by repeating the method of playing every other note you will be building the more complex chords of 7th's, 9th's, 11th's, & 13th's. In most cases a chord labeled with one of these will include all the triads up to that point. In other words, an 11th chord would usually include the root, third, fifth, seventh and the eleventh. The thirteenth chord sometimes falls outside this rule in that it does not always incude the eleventh.

4th's & 6th's

By now you should have the idea that chords are called as they are seen. The fourth chord and the sixth chord are no exception. If the chord name includes the term fourth or sixth then it of course sounds that scale note in the chord. There is, however, a clash between these notes being sounded with neighboring notes in the chord when they do not fall into the triad theory of every other note we just learned. It is for that reason that a chord with a fourth included would not have the third sounded and is called a suspended fourth. It is again for that very same reason that a sixth chord will not have the seventh note sounded.

Chord Encyclopedia Table of Contents

A Maj --------------------------------18	B♭ Maj ------------------------------44	B Maj -------------------------------70
A 6 ----------------------------------19	B♭ 6 --------------------------------45	B 6 ---------------------------------71
A 6/9 --------------------------------20	B♭ 6/9 ------------------------------46	B 6/9 -------------------------------72
A Maj 7 ----------------------------- 21	B♭ Maj 7 ----------------------------47	B Maj 7 ----------------------------- 73
A mMaj7 ---------------------------- 22	B♭ mMaj7 ---------------------------48	B mMaj7 ---------------------------- 74
A Maj 9 ----------------------------- 23	B♭ Maj 9 ----------------------------49	B Maj 9 ----------------------------- 75
A 7 ---------------------------------- 24	B♭ 7 --------------------------------50	B 7 ---------------------------------- 76
A 7♭5 ------------------------------- 25	B♭ 7♭5 ------------------------------51	B 7♭5 ------------------------------- 77
A 7♯5 ------------------------------- 26	B♭ 7♯5 ------------------------------52	B 7♯5 ------------------------------- 78
A 7♭9 ------------------------------- 27	B♭ 7♭9 ------------------------------53	B 7♭9 ------------------------------- 79
A 7♯9 ------------------------------- 28	B♭ 7♯9 ------------------------------54	B 7♯9 ------------------------------- 80
A 9 ---------------------------------- 29	B♭ 9 --------------------------------55	B 9 ---------------------------------- 81
A 9♭5 ------------------------------- 30	B♭ 9♭5 ------------------------------56	B 9♭5 ------------------------------- 82
A 9♯5 ------------------------------- 31	B♭ 9♯5 ------------------------------57	B 9♯5 ------------------------------- 83
A 11 --------------------------------- 32	B♭ 11 -------------------------------58	B 11 --------------------------------- 84
A 13 --------------------------------- 33	B♭ 13 -------------------------------59	B 13 --------------------------------- 85
A 13♭5♭9 --------------------------- 34	B♭ 13♭5♭9 ------------------------- 60	B 13♭5♭9 --------------------------- 86
A minor ----------------------------- 35	B♭ minor ---------------------------- 61	B minor ----------------------------- 87
A m6 -------------------------------- 36	B♭ m6 ------------------------------- 62	B m6 -------------------------------- 88
A m7 -------------------------------- 37	B♭ m7 ------------------------------- 63	B m7 -------------------------------- 89
A m7♭5 ----------------------------- 38	B♭ m7♭5 ---------------------------- 64	B m7♭5 ----------------------------- 90
A m 9 -------------------------------- 39	B♭ m 9 ------------------------------ 65	B m 9 -------------------------------- 91
A dim7 ------------------------------- 40	B♭ dim7 ----------------------------- 66	B dim7 ------------------------------- 92
A aug -------------------------------- 41	B♭ aug ------------------------------- 67	B aug -------------------------------- 93
A sus 4 ------------------------------ 42	B♭ sus 4 ----------------------------- 68	B sus 4 ------------------------------ 94
A 7 sus4 ----------------------------- 43	B♭ 7 sus4 --------------------------- 69	B 7 sus4 ----------------------------- 95

Chord Encyclopedia Table of Contents

C Maj ----------96	C# Maj ----------122	D Maj ----------148
C 6 ----------97	C# 6 ----------123	D 6 ----------149
C 6/9 ----------98	C# 6/9 ----------124	D 6/9 ----------150
C Maj 7 ---------- 99	C# Maj 7 ----------125	D Maj 7 ----------151
C mMaj7 ----------100	C# mMaj7 ----------126	D mMaj7 ----------152
C Maj 9 ----------101	C# Maj 9 ----------127	D Maj 9 ----------153
C 7 ----------102	C# 7 ----------128	D 7 ----------154
C 7b5 ---------- 103	C# 7b5 ----------129	D 7b5 ----------155
C 7#5 ----------104	C# 7#5 ----------130	D 7#5 ----------156
C 7b9 ----------105	C# 7b9 ----------131	D 7b9 ----------157
C 7#9 ----------106	C# 7#9 ----------132	D 7#9 ----------158
C 9 ----------107	C# 9 ----------133	D 9 ----------159
C 9b5 ----------108	C# 9b5 ----------134	D 9b5 ----------160
C 9#5 ----------109	C# 9#5 ----------135	D 9#5 ----------161
C 11 ----------110	C# 11 ----------136	D 11 ----------162
C 13 ----------111	C# 13 ----------137	D 13 ----------163
C 13b5b9 ----------112	C# 13b5b9 ----------138	D 13b5b9 ----------164
C minor ----------113	C# minor ----------139	D minor ----------165
C m6 ----------114	C# m6 ----------140	D m6 ----------166
C m7 ----------115	C# m7 ----------141	D m7 ----------167
C m7b5 ----------116	C# m7b5 ----------142	D m7b5 ----------168
C m 9 ----------117	C# m 9 ----------143	D m 9 ----------169
C dim7 ----------118	C# dim7 ----------144	D dim7 ----------170
C aug ----------119	C# aug ----------145	D aug ----------171
C sus 4 ----------120	C# sus 4 ----------146	D sus 4 ----------172
C 7 sus4 ----------121	C# 7 sus4 ----------147	D 7 sus4 ----------173

E♭ Maj	174	E Maj	200	F Maj	226
E♭ 6	175	E 6	201	F 6	227
E♭ 6/9	176	E 6/9	202	F 6/9	228
E♭ Maj 7	177	E Maj 7	203	F Maj 7	229
E♭ mMaj7	178	E mMaj7	204	F mMaj7	230
E♭ Maj 9	179	E Maj 9	205	F Maj 9	231
E♭ 7	180	E 7	206	F 7	232
E♭ 7♭5	181	E 7♭5	207	F 7♭5	233
E♭ 7♯5	182	E 7♯5	208	F 7♯5	234
E♭ 7♭9	183	E 7♭9	209	F 7♭9	235
E♭ 7♯9	184	E 7♯9	210	F 7♯9	236
E♭ 9	185	E 9	211	F 9	237
E♭ 9♭5	186	E 9♭5	212	F 9♭5	238
E♭ 9♯5	187	E 9♯5	213	F 9♯5	239
E♭ 11	188	E 11	214	F 11	240
E♭ 13	189	E 13	215	F 13	241
E♭ 13♭5♭9	190	E 13♭5♭9	216	F 13♭5♭9	242
E♭ minor	191	E minor	217	F minor	243
E♭ m6	192	E m6	218	F m6	244
E♭ m7	193	E m7	219	F m7	245
E♭ m7♭5	194	E m7♭5	220	F m7♭5	246
E♭ m 9	195	E m 9	221	F m 9	247
E♭ dim7	196	E dim7	222	F dim7	248
E♭ aug	197	E aug	223	F aug	249
E♭ sus 4	198	E sus 4	224	F sus 4	250
E♭ 7 sus4	199	E 7 sus4	225	F 7 sus4	251

F♯ Maj ------------------------252
F♯ 6 --------------------------253
F♯ 6/9 ------------------------254
F♯ Maj 7 ----------------------255
F♯ mMaj7 ----------------------256
F♯ Maj 9 ----------------------257
F♯ 7 --------------------------258
F♯ 7♭5 ------------------------259
F♯ 7♯5 ------------------------260
F♯ 7♭9 ------------------------261
F♯ 7♯9 ------------------------262
F♯ 9 --------------------------263
F♯ 9♭5 ------------------------264
F♯ 9♯5 ------------------------265
F♯ 11 -------------------------266
F♯ 13 -------------------------267
F♯ 13♭5♭9 ---------------------268
F♯ minor ----------------------269
F♯ m6 -------------------------270
F♯ m7 -------------------------271
F♯ m7♭5 -----------------------272
F♯ m 9 ------------------------273
F♯ dim7 -----------------------274
F♯ aug ------------------------275
F♯ sus 4 ----------------------276
F♯ 7 sus4 ---------------------277

G Maj -------------------------278
G 6 ---------------------------279
G 6/9 -------------------------280
G Maj 7 -----------------------281
G mMaj7 -----------------------282
G Maj 9 -----------------------283
G 7 ---------------------------284
G 7♭5 -------------------------285
G 7♯5 -------------------------286
G 7♭9 -------------------------287
G 7♯9 -------------------------288
G 9 ---------------------------289
G 9♭5 -------------------------290
G 9♯5 -------------------------291
G 11 --------------------------292
G 13 --------------------------293
G 13♭5♭9 ----------------------294
G minor -----------------------295
G m6 --------------------------296
G m7 --------------------------297
G m7♭5 ------------------------298
G m 9 -------------------------299
G dim7 ------------------------300
G aug -------------------------301
G sus 4 -----------------------302
G 7 sus4 ----------------------303

A♭ Maj ------------------------304
A♭ 6 --------------------------305
A♭ 6/9 ------------------------306
A♭ Maj 7 ----------------------307
A♭ mMaj7 ----------------------308
A♭ Maj 9 ----------------------309
A♭ 7 --------------------------310
A♭ 7♭5 ------------------------311
A♭ 7♯5 ------------------------312
A♭ 7♭9 ------------------------313
A♭ 7♯9 ------------------------314
A♭ 9 --------------------------315
A♭ 9♭5 ------------------------316
A♭ 9♯5 ------------------------317
A♭ 11 -------------------------318
A♭ 13 -------------------------319
A♭ 13♭5♭9 ---------------------320
A♭ minor ----------------------321
A♭ m6 -------------------------322
A♭ m7 -------------------------323
A♭ m7♭5 -----------------------324
A♭ m 9 ------------------------325
A♭ dim7 -----------------------326
A♭ aug ------------------------327
A♭ sus 4 ----------------------328
A♭ 7 sus4 ---------------------329

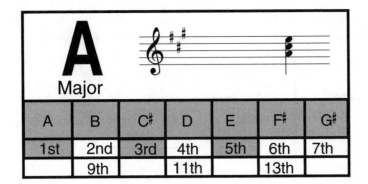

A Major						
A	B	C#	D	E	F#	G#
1st	2nd	3rd	4th	5th	6th	7th
	9th		11th		13th	

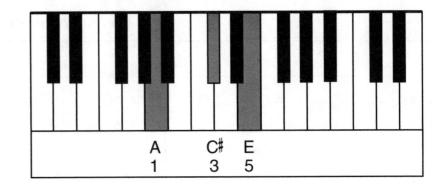

A 1   C# 3   E 5

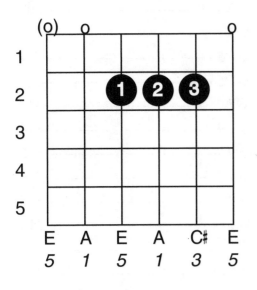

E	A	E	A	C#	E
5	1	5	1	3	5

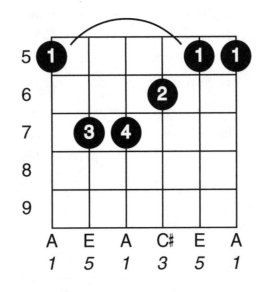

A	E	A	C#	E	A
1	5	1	3	5	1

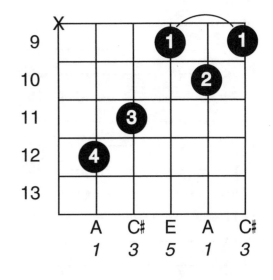

A	C#	E	A	C#
1	3	5	1	3

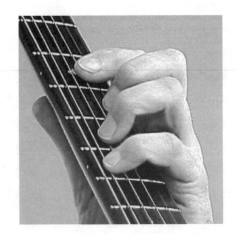

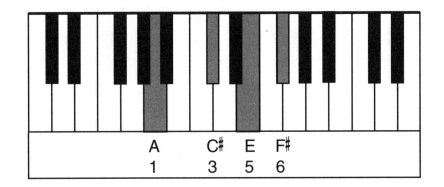

A E C# F#
1 3 5 6

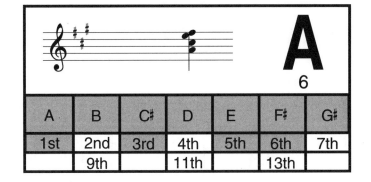

A

6

A	B	C#	D	E	F#	G#
1st	2nd	3rd	4th	5th	6th	7th
	9th		11th		13th	

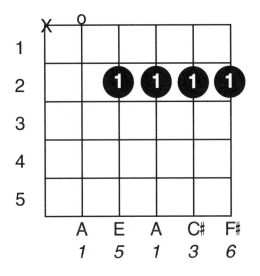

A E A C# F#
1 5 1 3 6

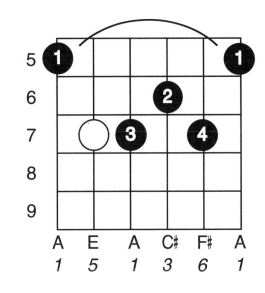

A E A C# F# A
1 5 1 3 6 1

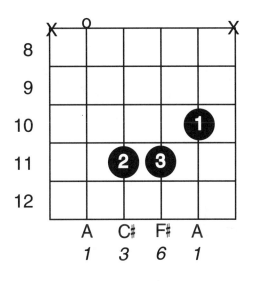

A C# F# A
1 3 6 1

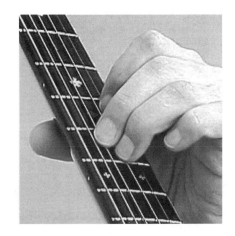

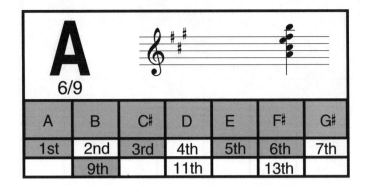

A
6/9

A	B	C#	D	E	F#	G#
1st	2nd	3rd	4th	5th	6th	7th
	9th		11th		13th	

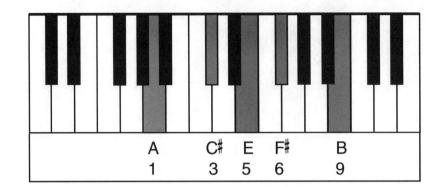

A	C#	E	F#	B
1	3	5	6	9

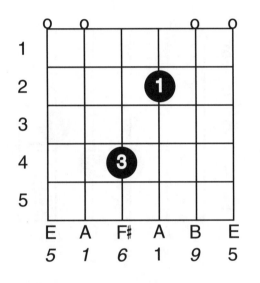

E	A	F#	A	B	E
5	*1*	*6*	*1*	*9*	*5*

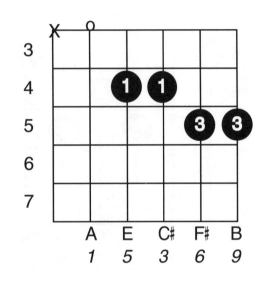

A	E	C#	F#	B
1	*5*	*3*	*6*	*9*

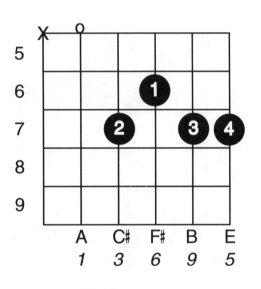

A	C#	F#	B	E
1	*3*	*6*	*9*	*5*

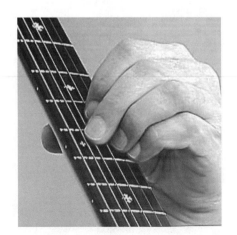

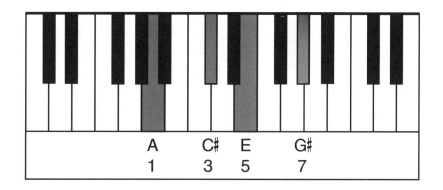

A 1 · C# 3 · E 5 · G# 7

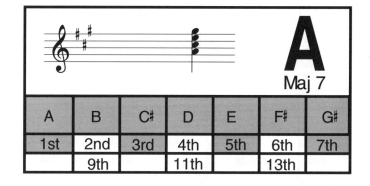

A
Maj 7

A	B	C#	D	E	F#	G#
1st	2nd	3rd	4th	5th	6th	7th
	9th		11th		13th	

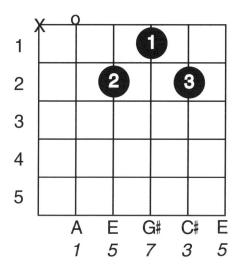

X O

1 — ①
2 — ② ③
3
4
5

A E G# C# E
1 5 7 3 5

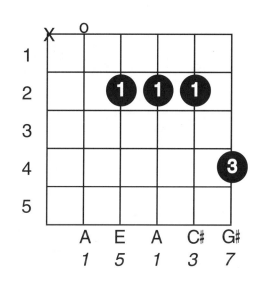

X O

1
2 — ① ① ①
3
4 — ③
5

A E A C# G#
1 5 1 3 7

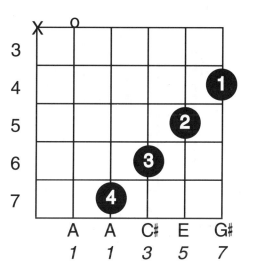

X O

3
4 — ①
5 — ②
6 — ③
7 — ④

A A C# E G#
1 1 3 5 7

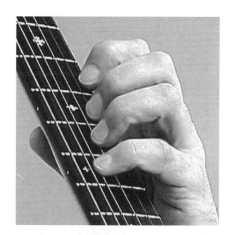

A
mMaj7

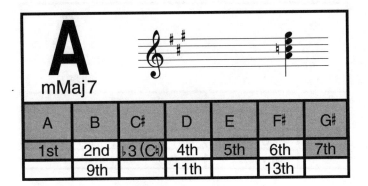

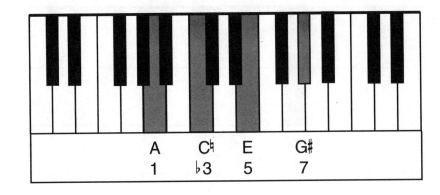

A	B	C#	D	E	F#	G#
1st	2nd	♭3 (C♮)	4th	5th	6th	7th
	9th		11th		13th	

A   C♮   E   G#
1   ♭3   5   7

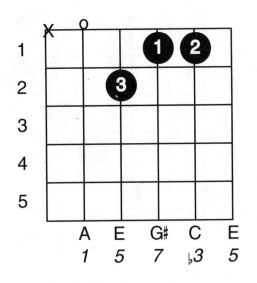

```
1
2    ①  ②
3  ③
4
5
```
A   E   G#   C   E
1   5   7   ♭3   5

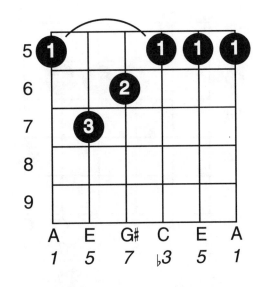

```
5  ①        ①  ①  ①
6      ②
7    ③
8
9
```
A   E   G#   C   E   A
1   5   7   ♭3   5   1

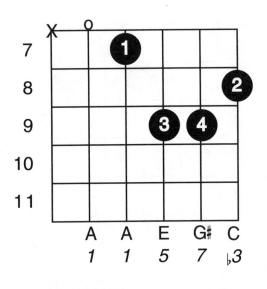

```
7      ①
8                ②
9          ③  ④
10
11
```
A   A   E   G#   C
1   1   5   7   ♭3

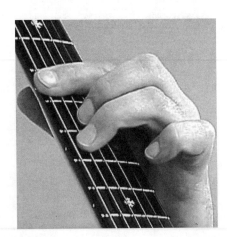

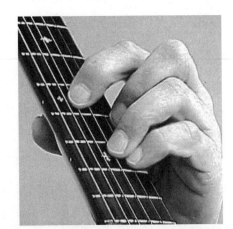

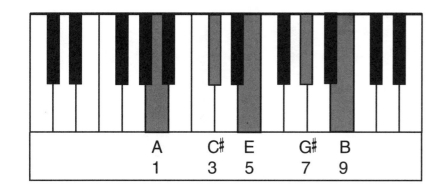

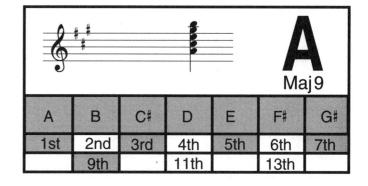

A Maj9

	A	B	C#	D	E	F#	G#
	1st	2nd	3rd	4th	5th	6th	7th
		9th		11th		13th	

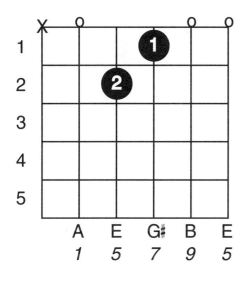

x o o o

1
2
3
4
5

A	E	G#	B	E
1	5	7	9	5

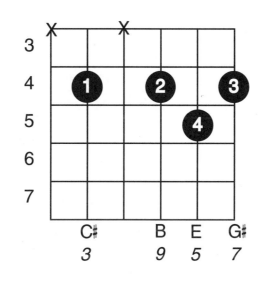

x x

3
4
5
6
7

C#		B	E	G#
3		9	5	7

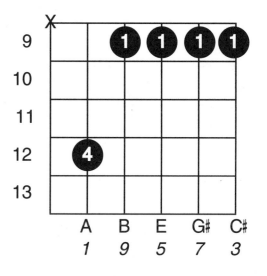

x

9
10
11
12
13

A	B	E	G#	C#
1	9	5	7	3

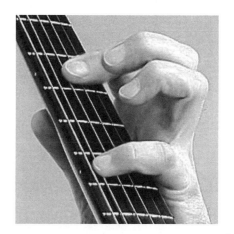

A 7

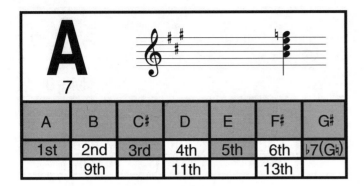

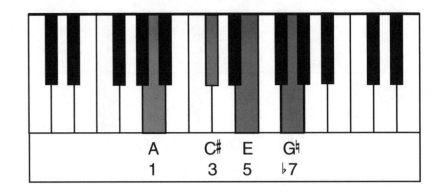

A	B	C#	D	E	F#	G#
1st	2nd	3rd	4th	5th	6th	♭7(G♮)
	9th		11th		13th	

A   C#   E   G♮
1   3   5   ♭7

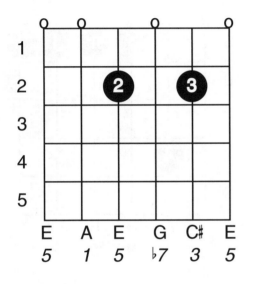

E	A	E	G	C#	E
5	*1*	*5*	*♭7*	*3*	*5*

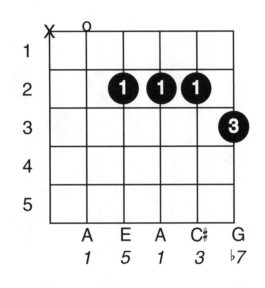

A	E	A	C#	G
1	*5*	*1*	*3*	*♭7*

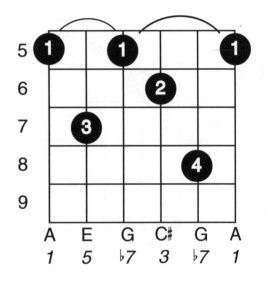

A	E	G	C#	G	A
1	*5*	*♭7*	*3*	*♭7*	*1*

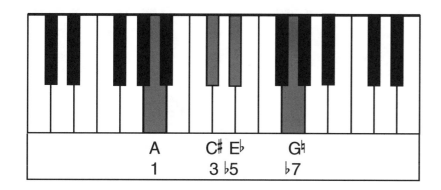

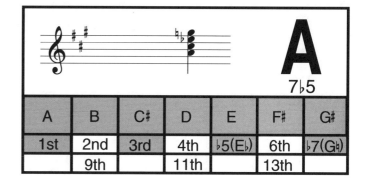

A	B	C#	D	E	F#	G#
1st	2nd	3rd	4th	♭5(E♭)	6th	♭7(G♮)
	9th		11th		13th	

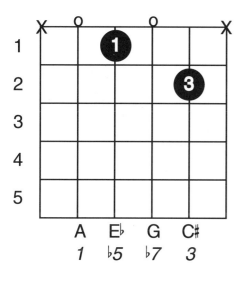

A　E♭　G　C#
1　*♭5*　*♭7*　*3*

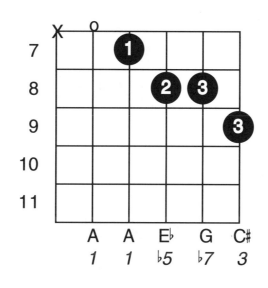

A　A　E♭　G　C#
1　*1*　*♭5*　*♭7*　*3*

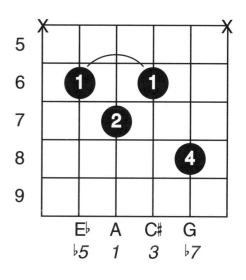

E♭　A　C#　G
♭5　*1*　*3*　*♭7*

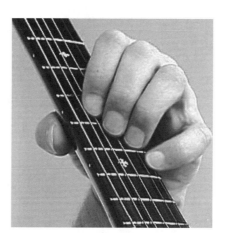

A

7#5

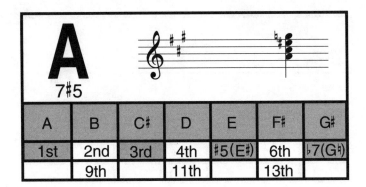

A	B	C#	D	E	F#	G#
1st	2nd	3rd	4th	#5(E#)	6th	♭7(G♮)
	9th		11th		13th	

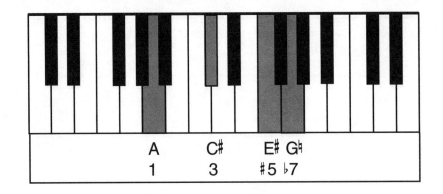

A   C#   E# G♮
1   3   #5 ♭7

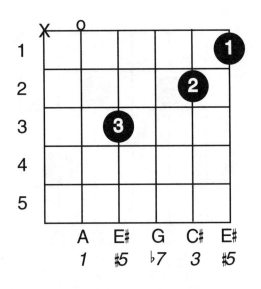

A E# G C# E#
1 #5 ♭7 3 #5

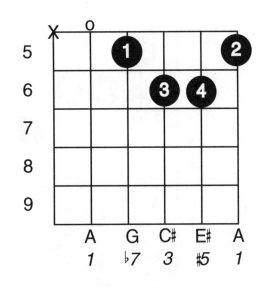

A G C# E# A
1 ♭7 3 #5 1

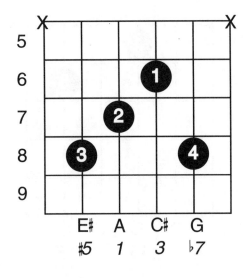

E# A C# G
#5 1 3 ♭7

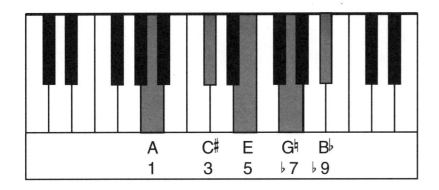

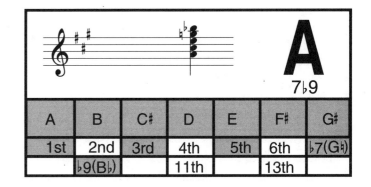

A 7♭9

A	B	C#	D	E	F#	G#
1st	2nd	3rd	4th	5th	6th	♭7(G♮)
	♭9(B♭)		11th		13th	

Keyboard notes: A (1), C# (3), E (5), G♮ (♭7), B♭ (♭9)

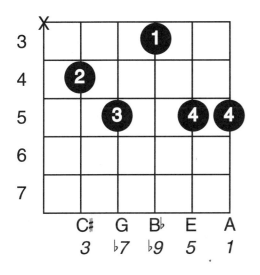

C# G B♭ E A
3 ♭7 ♭9 5 1

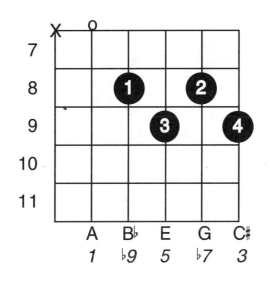

A B♭ E G C#
1 ♭9 5 ♭7 3

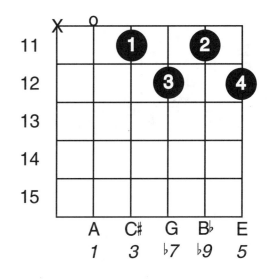

A C# G B♭ E
1 3 ♭7 ♭9 5

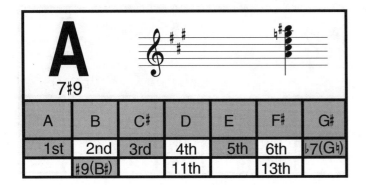

A
7#9

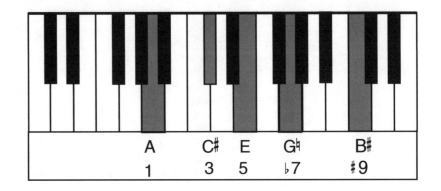

A	B	C#	D	E	F#	G#
1st	2nd	3rd	4th	5th	6th	♭7(G♭)
	#9(B#)		11th		13th	

A — 1
C# — 3
E — 5
G♮ — ♭7
B# — #9

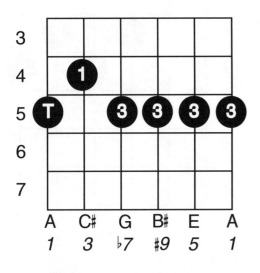

A C# G B# E A
1 *3* *♭7* *#9* *5* *1*

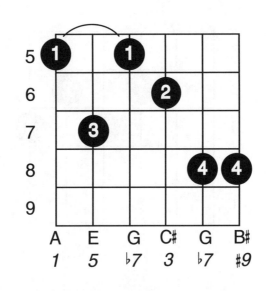

A E G C# G B#
1 *5* *♭7* *3* *♭7* *#9*

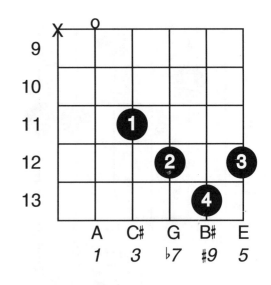

A C# G B# E
1 *3* *♭7* *#9* *5*

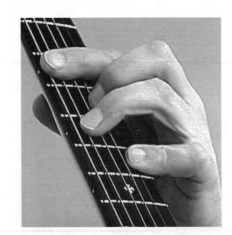

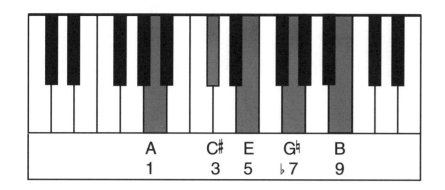

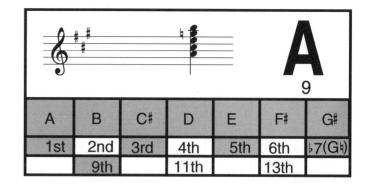

A

9

A	B	C#	D	E	F#	G#
1st	2nd	3rd	4th	5th	6th	♭7 (G♮)
	9th		11th		13th	

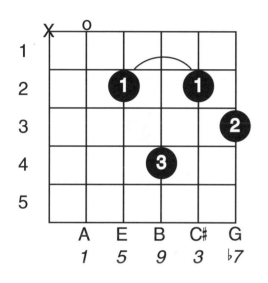

A E B C# G
1 5 9 3 ♭7

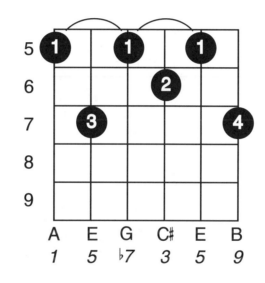

A E G C# E B
1 5 ♭7 3 5 9

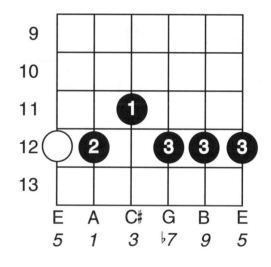

E A C# G B E
5 1 3 ♭7 9 5

29

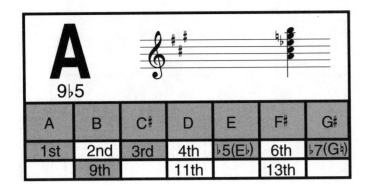

A

9♭5

A	B	C#	D	E	F#	G#
1st	2nd	3rd	4th	♭5(E♭)	6th	♭7(G♮)
	9th		11th		13th	

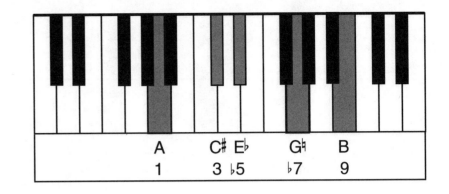

A		C#	E♭		G♮		B
1		3	♭5		♭7		9

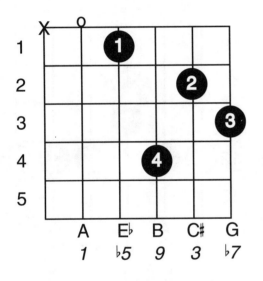

A	E♭	B	C#	G
1	*♭5*	*9*	*3*	*♭7*

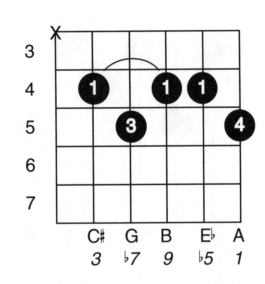

C#	G	B	E♭	A
3	*♭7*	*9*	*♭5*	*1*

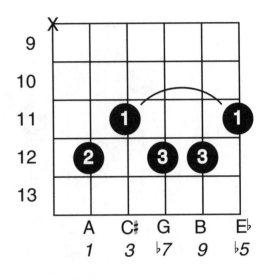

A	C#	G	B	E♭
1	*3*	*♭7*	*9*	*♭5*

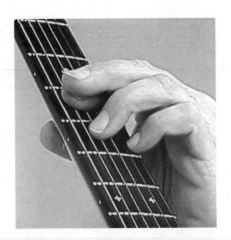

30

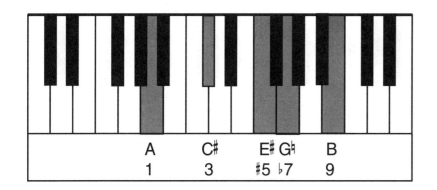

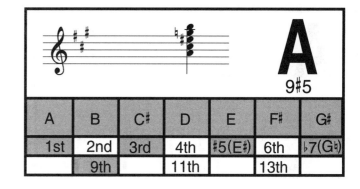

A
9#5

A	B	C#	D	E	F#	G#
1st	2nd	3rd	4th	#5(E#)	6th	♭7(G♮)
	9th		11th		13th	

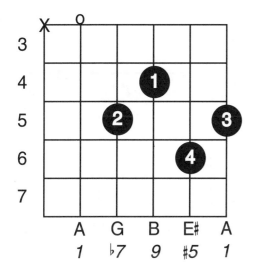

A	G	B	E#	A
1	*♭7*	*9*	*#5*	*1*

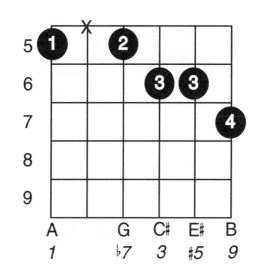

A	G	C#	E#	B
1	*♭7*	*3*	*#5*	*9*

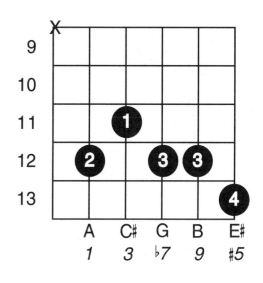

A	C#	G	B	E#
1	*3*	*♭7*	*9*	*#5*

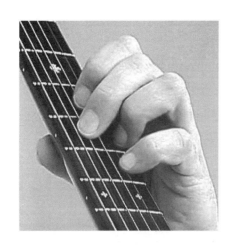

31

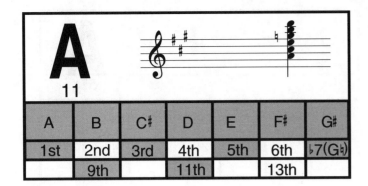

A
11

A	B	C#	D	E	F#	G#
1st	2nd	3rd	4th	5th	6th	♭7(G♮)
	9th		11th		13th	

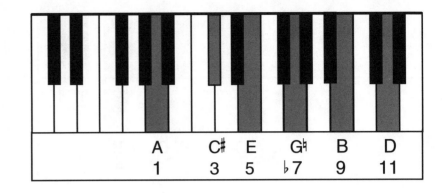

			A		C#	E	G♮	B	D
			1		3	5	♭7	9	11

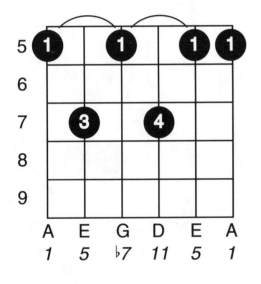

A	E	G	D	E	A
1	*5*	*♭7*	*11*	*5*	*1*

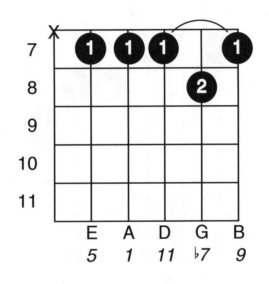

E	A	D	G	B
5	*1*	*11*	*♭7*	*9*

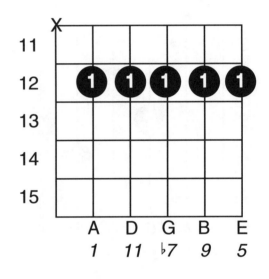

A	D	G	B	E
1	*11*	*♭7*	*9*	*5*

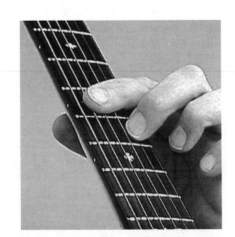

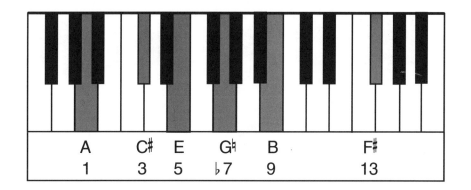

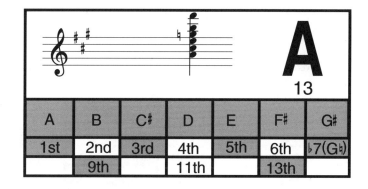

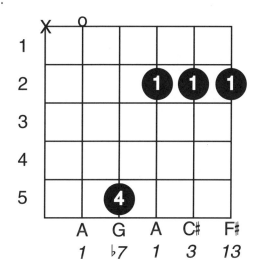

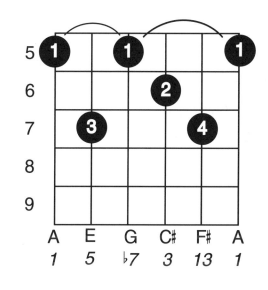

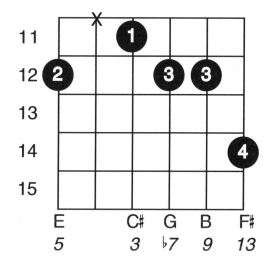

33

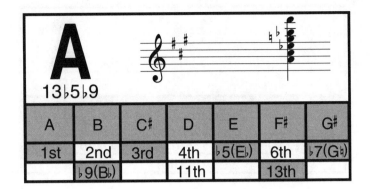

A
13♭5♭9

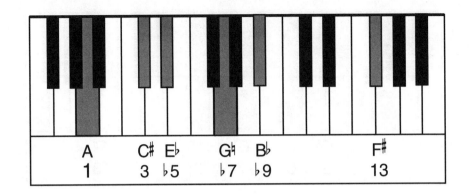

A	C#	E♭	G♮	B♭	F#
1	3	♭5	♭7	♭9	13

A	B	C#	D	E	F#	G#
1st	2nd	3rd	4th	♭5(E♭)	6th	♭7(G♮)
	♭9(B♭)		11th		13th	

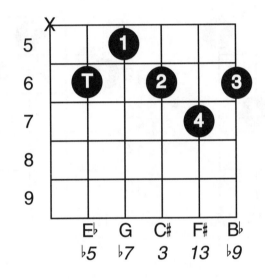

E♭	G	C#	F#	B♭
♭5	♭7	3	13	♭9

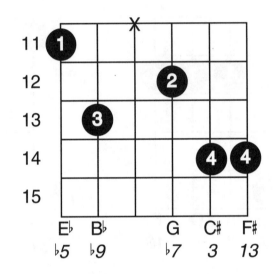

E♭	B♭		G	C#	F#
♭5	♭9		♭7	3	13

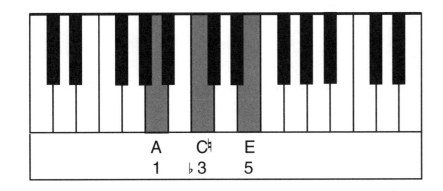

A C♮ E
1 ♭3 5

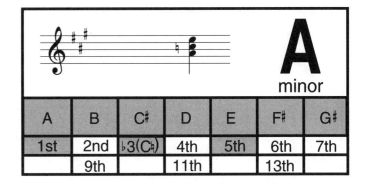

A
minor

A	B	C♯	D	E	F♯	G♯
1st	2nd	♭3(C♮)	4th	5th	6th	7th
	9th		11th		13th	

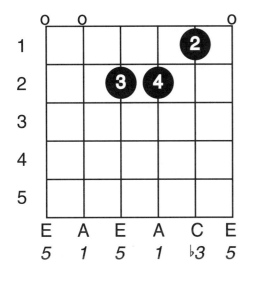

E A E A C E
5 1 5 1 ♭3 5

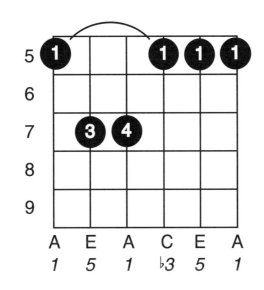

A E A C E A
1 5 1 ♭3 5 1

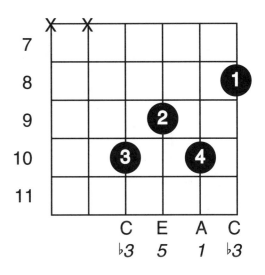

C E A C
♭3 5 1 ♭3

A
m6

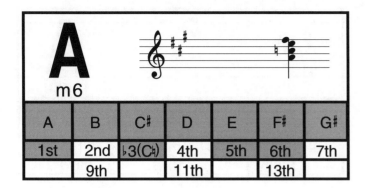

A	B	C#	D	E	F#	G#
1st	2nd	♭3(C♮)	4th	5th	6th	7th
	9th		11th		13th	

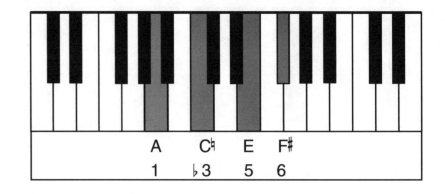

A   C♮   E   F#
1   ♭3   5   6

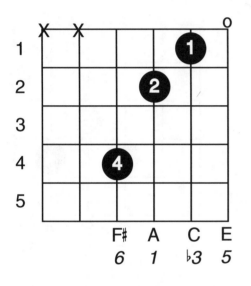

F#   A   C   E
6   *1*   *♭3*   *5*

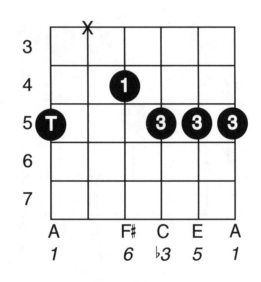

A   F#   C   E   A
1   *6*   *♭3*   *5*   *1*

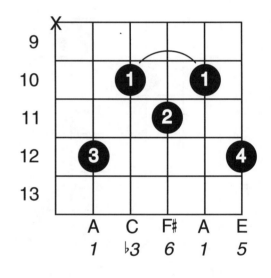

A   C   F#   A   E
1   *♭3*   *6*   *1*   *5*

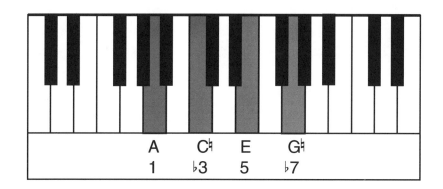

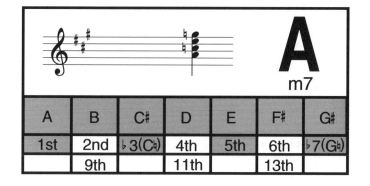

A m7

A	B	C#	D	E	F#	G#
1st	2nd	♭3(C♮)	4th	5th	6th	♭7(G♮)
	9th		11th		13th	

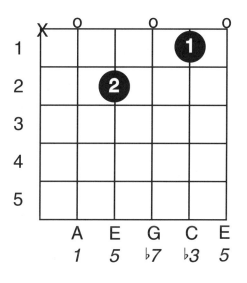

A	E	G	C	E
1	*5*	*♭7*	*♭3*	*5*

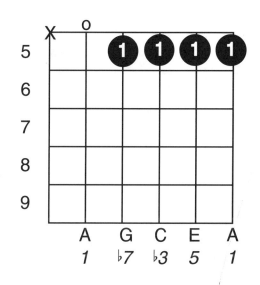

A	G	C	E	A
1	*♭7*	*♭3*	*5*	*1*

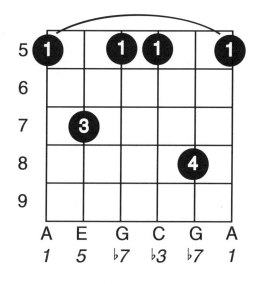

A	E	G	C	G	A
1	*5*	*♭7*	*♭3*	*♭7*	*1*

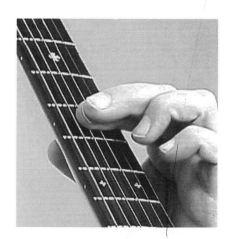

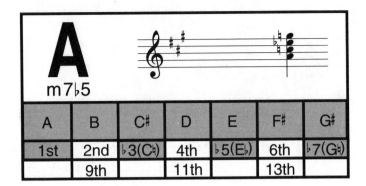

A
m7♭5

A	B	C#	D	E	F#	G#
1st	2nd	♭3(C♮)	4th	♭5(E♭)	6th	♭7(G♮)
	9th		11th		13th	

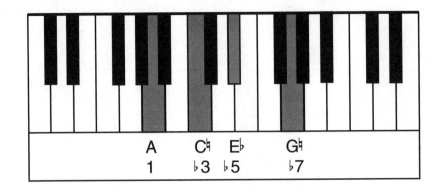

A	C#	E♭	G♮	
1	♭3	♭5	♭7	

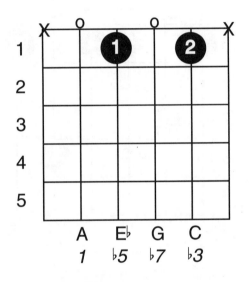

A	E♭	G	C
1	*♭5*	*♭7*	*♭3*

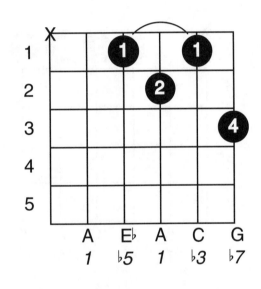

A	E♭	A	C	G
1	*♭5*	*1*	*♭3*	*♭7*

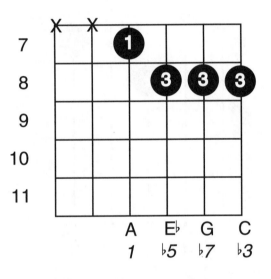

A	E♭	G	C
1	*♭5*	*♭7*	*♭3*

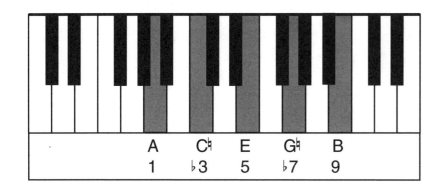

A C♮ E G♮ B
1 ♭3 5 ♭7 9

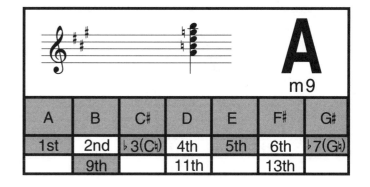

A
m9

A	B	C#	D	E	F#	G#
1st	2nd	♭3(C♮)	4th	5th	6th	♭7(G♮)
	9th		11th		13th	

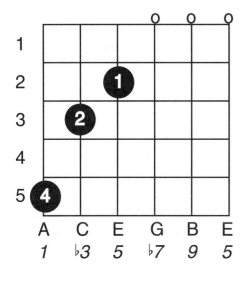

A C E G B E
1 *♭3* *5* *♭7* *9* *5*

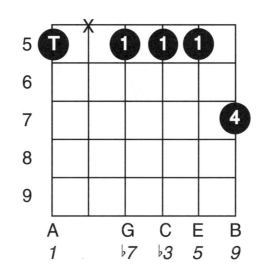

A G C E B
1 *♭7* *♭3* *5* *9*

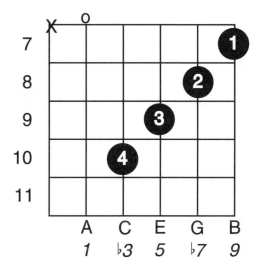

A C E G B
1 *♭3* *5* *♭7* *9*

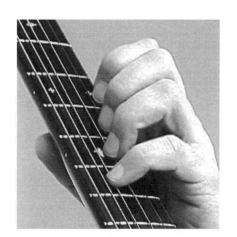

A
dim7

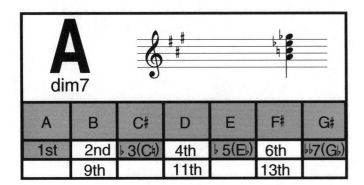

A	B	C#	D	E	F#	G#
1st	2nd	♭3(C♮)	4th	♭5(E♭)	6th	♭♭7(G♭)
	9th		11th		13th	

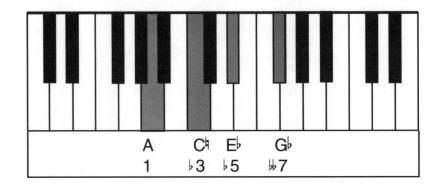

A | C♮ | E♭ | G♭
1 | ♭3 | ♭5 | ♭♭7

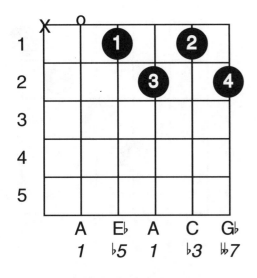

A   E♭   A   C   G♭
1 *♭5* *1* *♭3* *♭♭7*

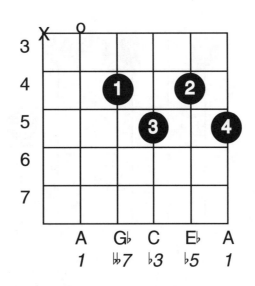

A   G♭   C   E♭   A
1 *♭♭7* *♭3* *♭5* *1*

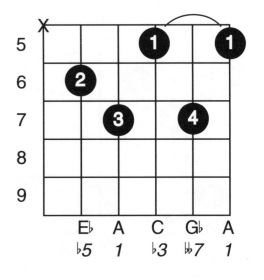

E♭   A   C   G♭   A
♭5 *1* *♭3* *♭♭7* *1*

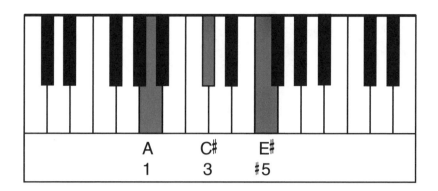

A
C#
E#
1
3
#5

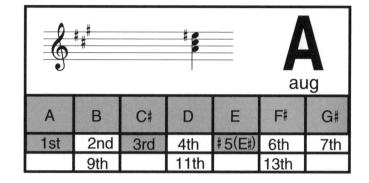

A
aug

A	B	C#	D	E	F#	G#
1st	2nd	3rd	4th	#5 (E#)	6th	7th
	9th		11th		13th	

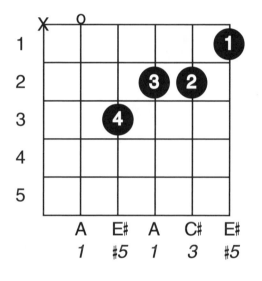

A	E#	A	C#	E#
1	#5	1	3	#5

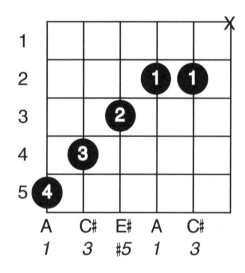

A	C#	E#	A	C#
1	3	#5	1	3

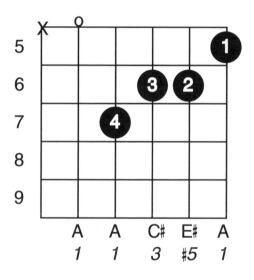

A	A	C#	E#	A
1	1	3	#5	1

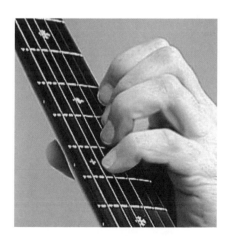

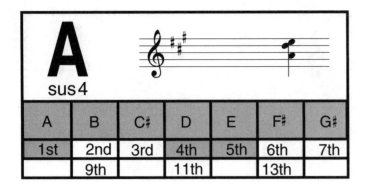

A sus4

A	B	C#	D	E	F#	G#
1st	2nd	3rd	4th	5th	6th	7th
	9th		11th		13th	

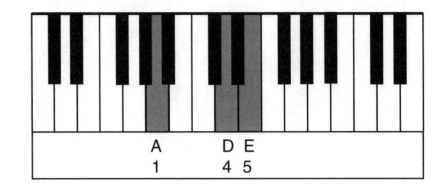

A   D E
1   4 5

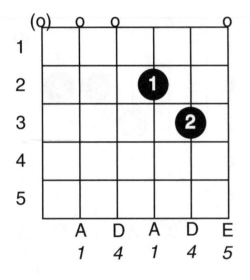

A D A D E
1 4 1 4 5

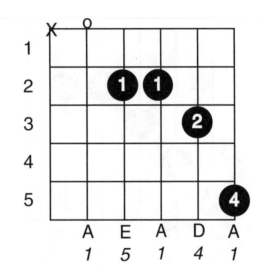

A E A D A
1 5 1 4 1

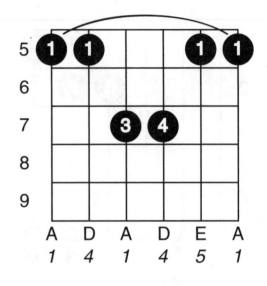

A D A D E A
1 4 1 4 5 1

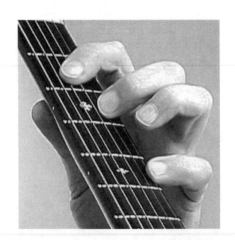

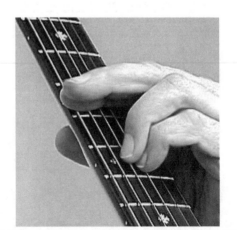

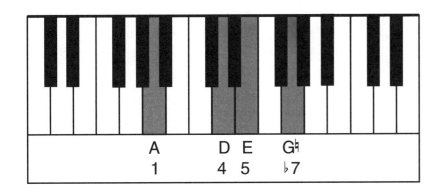

A D E G♮
1 4 5 ♭7

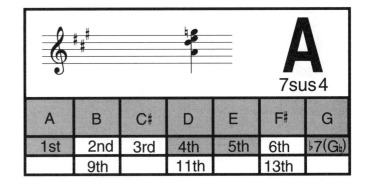

A
7sus4

A	B	C#	D	E	F#	G
1st	2nd	3rd	4th	5th	6th	♭7(G♭)
	9th		11th		13th	

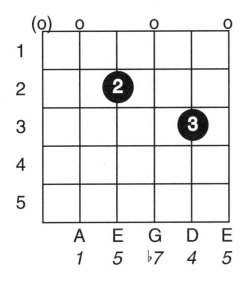

(o) o   o   o

A E G D E
1 5 ♭7 4 5

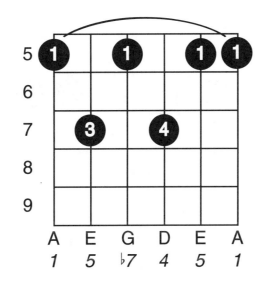

A E G D E A
1 5 ♭7 4 5 1

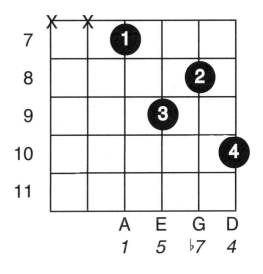

x x

A E G D
1 5 ♭7 4

43

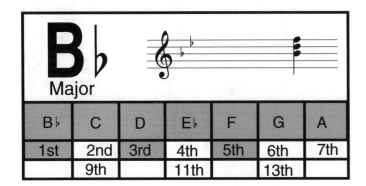

B♭

Major

B♭	C	D	E♭	F	G	A
1st	2nd	3rd	4th	5th	6th	7th
	9th		11th		13th	

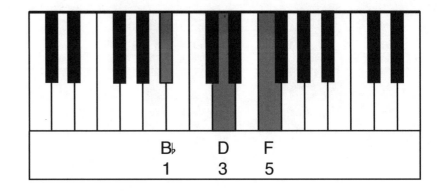

B♭   D   F
1   3   5

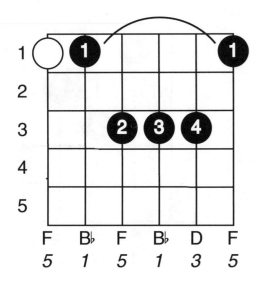

F B♭ F B♭ D F
5   1   5   1   3   5

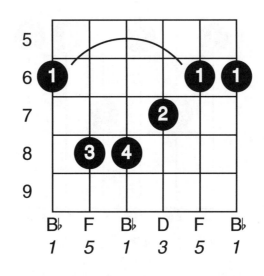

B♭ F B♭ D F B♭
1   5   1   3   5   1

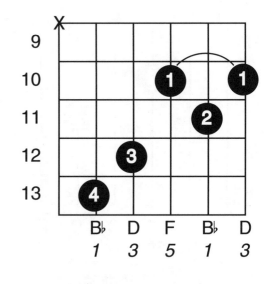

B♭ D F B♭ D
1   3   5   1   3

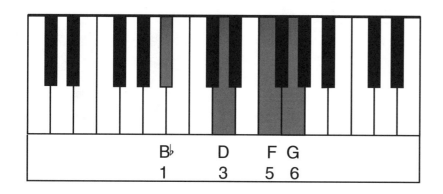

B♭ D F G
1 3 5 6

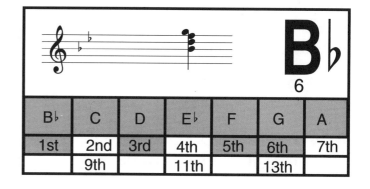

B♭
6

B♭	C	D	E♭	F	G	A
1st	2nd	3rd	4th	5th	6th	7th
	9th		11th		13th	

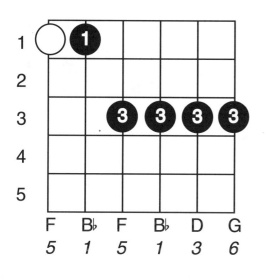

F B♭ F B♭ D G
5 1 5 1 3 6

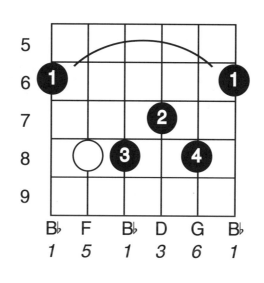

B♭ F B♭ D G B♭
1 5 1 3 6 1

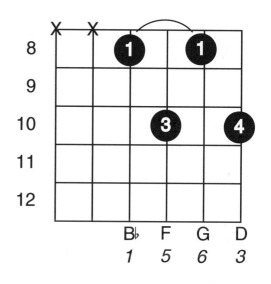

B♭ F G D
1 5 6 3

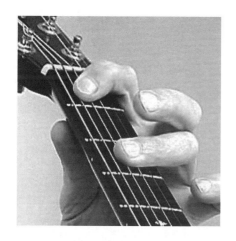

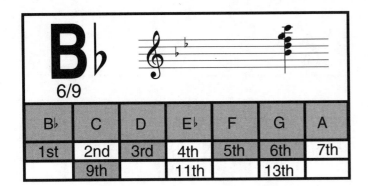

B♭
6/9

B♭	C	D	E♭	F	G	A
1st	2nd	3rd	4th	5th	6th	7th
	9th		11th		13th	

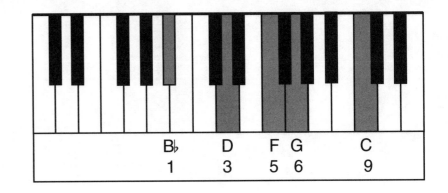

B♭ D F G C
1 · 3 · 5 6 · 9

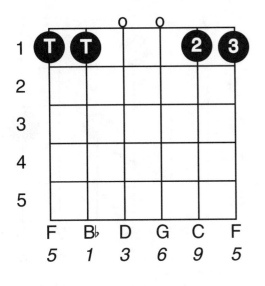

F B♭ D G C F
5 *1* *3* *6* *9* *5*

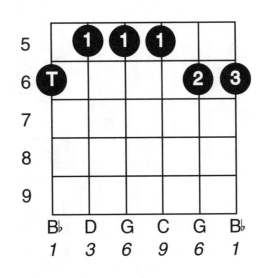

B♭ D G C G B♭
1 *3* *6* *9* *6* *1*

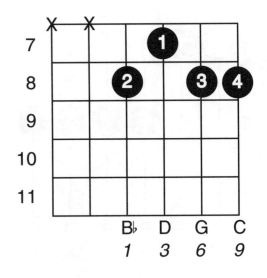

B♭ D G C
1 *3* *6* *9*

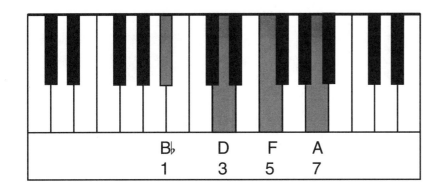

B♭   D   F   A
1   3   5   7

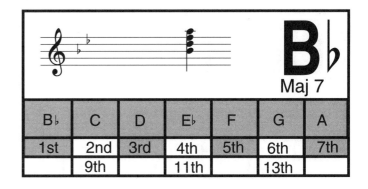

B♭

Maj 7

B♭	C	D	E♭	F	G	A
1st	2nd	3rd	4th	5th	6th	7th
	9th		11th		13th	

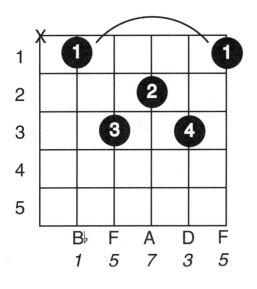

B♭   F   A   D   F
1   *5*   *7*   *3*   *5*

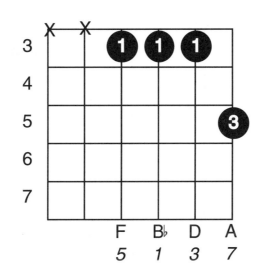

F   B♭   D   A
5   *1*   *3*   *7*

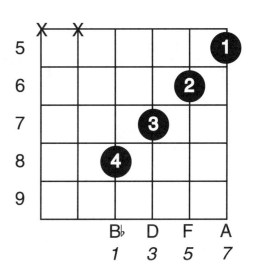

B♭   D   F   A
1   *3*   *5*   *7*

B♭

mMaj7

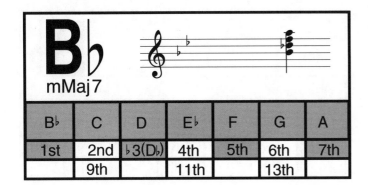

B♭	C	D	E♭	F	G	A
1st	2nd	♭3(D♭)	4th	5th	6th	7th
	9th		11th		13th	

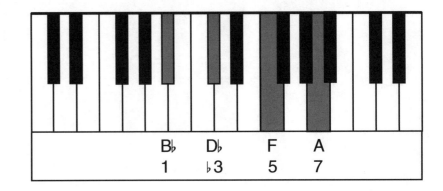

B♭   D♭   F   A
1   ♭3   5   7

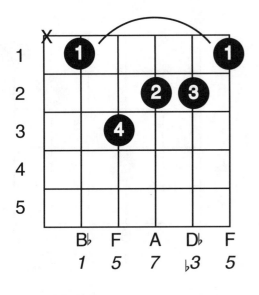

B♭ F A D♭ F
1 5 7 ♭3 5

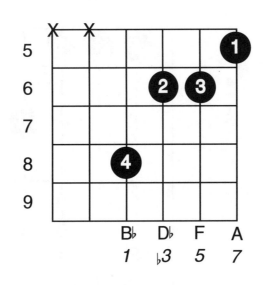

B♭ D♭ F A
1 ♭3 5 7

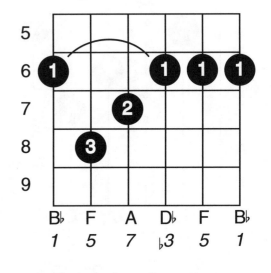

B♭ F A D♭ F B♭
1 5 7 ♭3 5 1

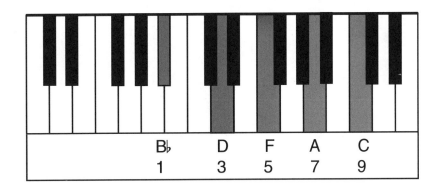

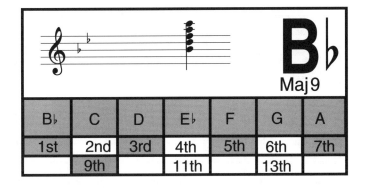

B♭	C	D	E♭	F	G	A
1st	2nd	3rd	4th	5th	6th	7th
	9th		11th		13th	

B♭
Maj9

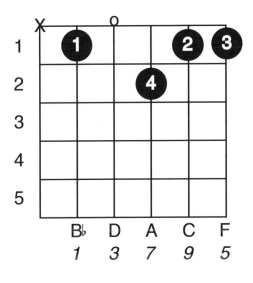

B♭ D A C F
1   3   7   9   5

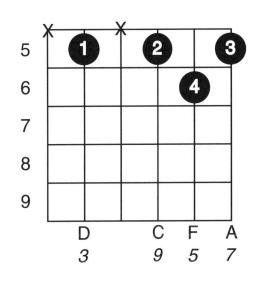

D   C F A
3   9   5   7

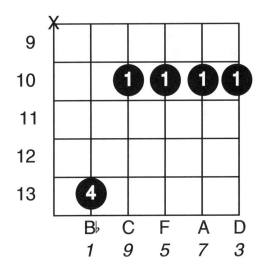

B♭ C F A D
1   9   5   7   3

49

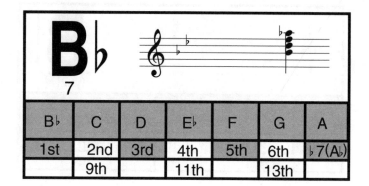

Bb	C	D	Eb	F	G	A
1st	2nd	3rd	4th	5th	6th	b7(Ab)
	9th		11th		13th	

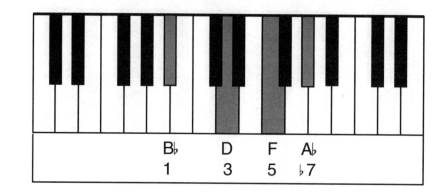

Bb   D   F   Ab
1   3   5   b7

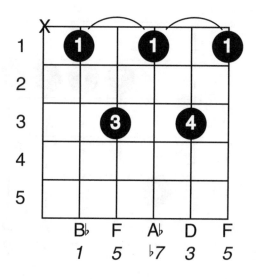

Bb   F   Ab   D   F
1   *5*   *b7*   *3*   *5*

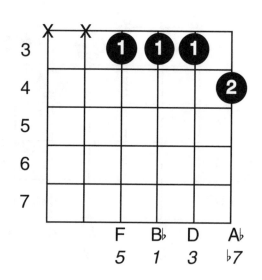

F   Bb   D   Ab
5   *1*   *3*   *b7*

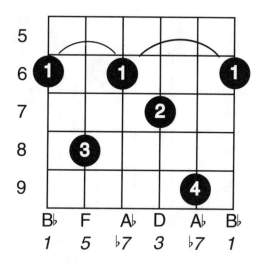

Bb   F   Ab   D   Ab   Bb
1   *5*   *b7*   *3*   *b7*   *1*

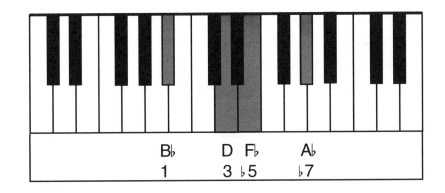

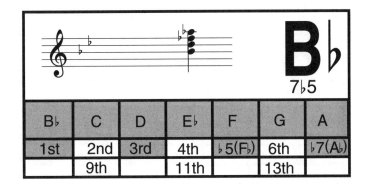

B♭
7♭5

B♭	C	D	E♭	F	G	A
1st	2nd	3rd	4th	♭5(F♭)	6th	♭7(A♭)
	9th		11th		13th	

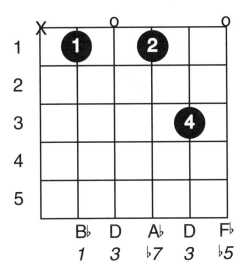

B♭	D	A♭	D	F♭
1	3	♭7	3	♭5

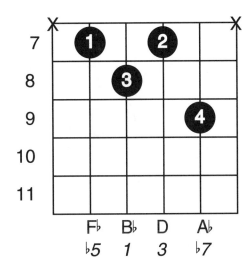

F♭	B♭	D	A♭
♭5	1	3	♭7

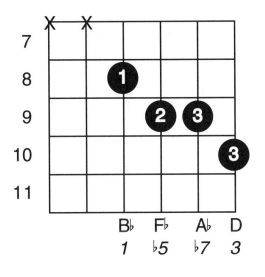

B♭	F♭	A♭	D
1	♭5	♭7	3

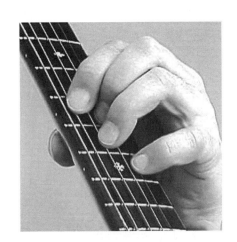

51

B♭

7♯5

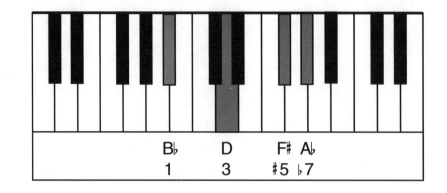

B♭	C	D	E♭	F	G	A
1st	2nd	3rd	4th	♯5(F♯)	6th	♭7(A♭)
	9th		11th		13th	

B♭   D   F♯ A♭
1   3   ♯5 ♭7

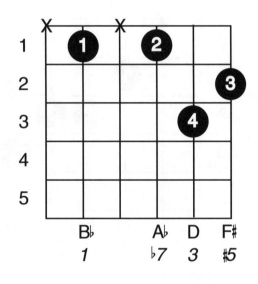

B♭   A♭ D F♯
1   *♭7* *3* *♯5*

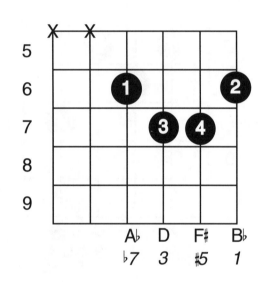

A♭ D F♯ B♭
♭7 *3* *♯5* *1*

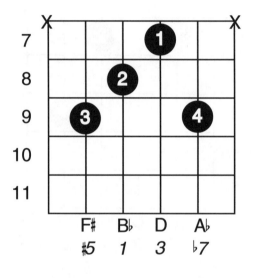

F♯ B♭ D A♭
♯5 *1* *3* *♭7*

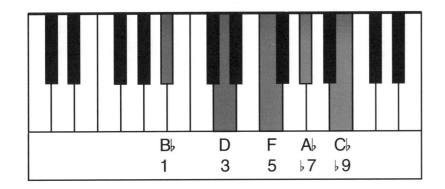

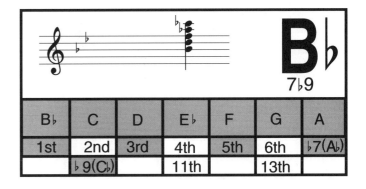

B♭7♭9

B♭	C	D	E♭	F	G	A
1st	2nd	3rd	4th	5th	6th	♭7(A♭)
	♭9(C♭)		11th		13th	

Keyboard notes:
B♭	D	F	A♭	C♭
1	3	5	♭7	♭9

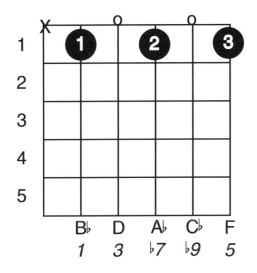

B♭	D	A♭	C♭	F
1	3	♭7	♭9	5

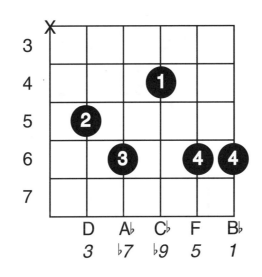

D	A♭	C♭	F	B♭
3	♭7	♭9	5	1

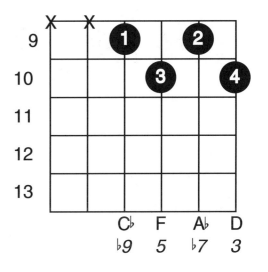

C♭	F	A♭	D
♭9	5	♭7	3

53

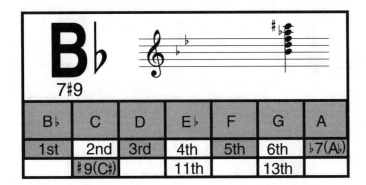

B♭	C	D	E♭	F	G	A
1st	2nd	3rd	4th	5th	6th	♭7(A♭)
	#9(C#)		11th		13th	

B♭ 7#9

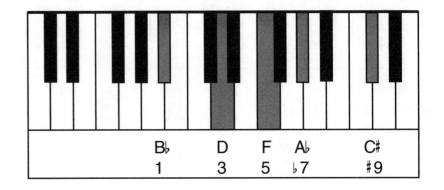

B♭	D	F	A♭	C#
1	3	5	♭7	#9

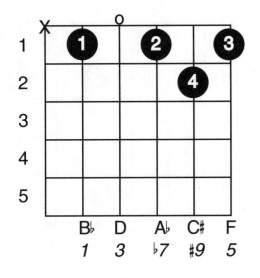

B♭	D	A♭	C#	F
1	3	♭7	#9	5

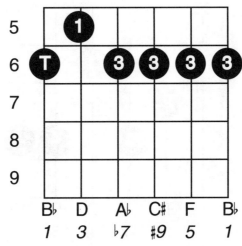

B♭	D	A♭	C#	F	B♭
1	3	♭7	#9	5	1

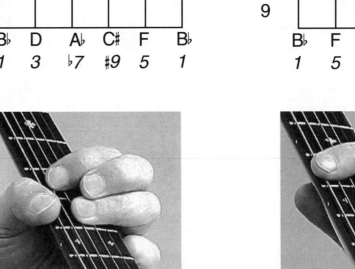

B♭	F	A♭	D	A♭	C#
1	5	♭7	3	♭7	#9

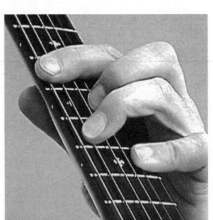

54

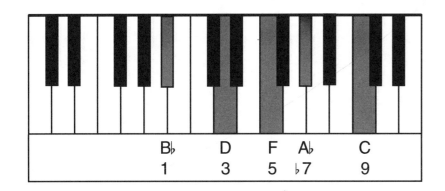

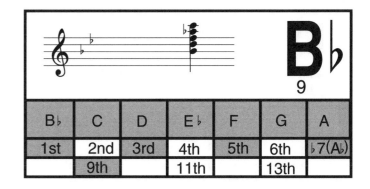

Bb	C	D	Eb	F	G	A
1st	2nd	3rd	4th	5th	6th	b7(Ab)
	9th		11th		13th	

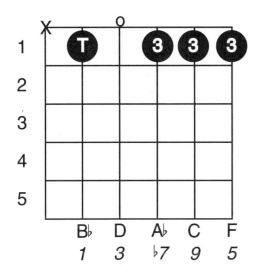

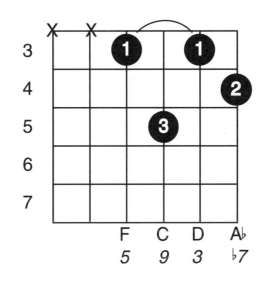

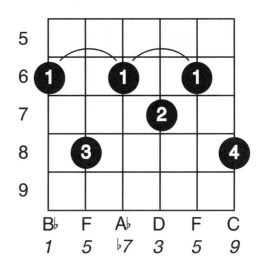

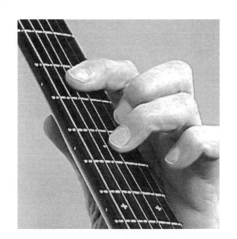

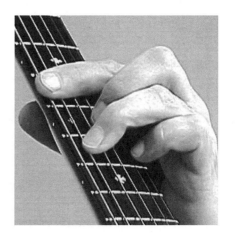

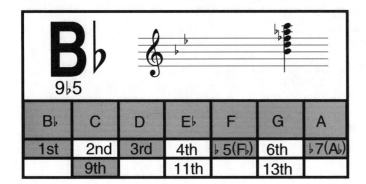

B♭	C	D	E♭	F	G	A
1st	2nd	3rd	4th	♭5(F♭)	6th	♭7(A♭)
	9th		11th		13th	

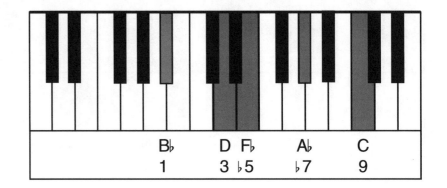

	B♭	D F♭	A♭	C
	1	3 ♭5	♭7	9

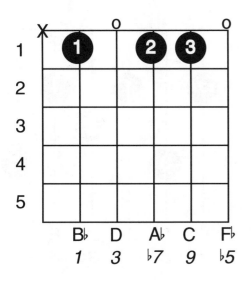

B♭	D	A♭	C	F♭
1	3	♭7	9	♭5

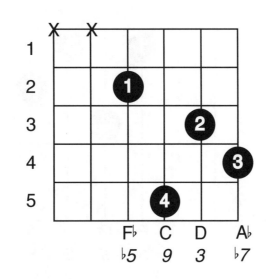

F♭	C	D	A♭
♭5	9	3	♭7

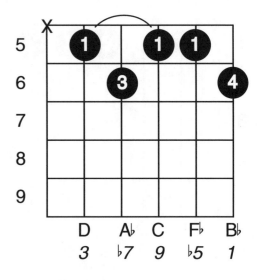

D	A♭	C	F♭	B♭
3	♭7	9	♭5	1

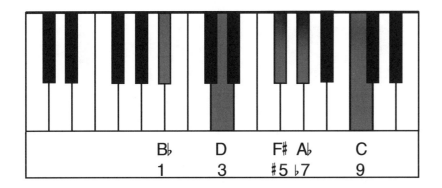

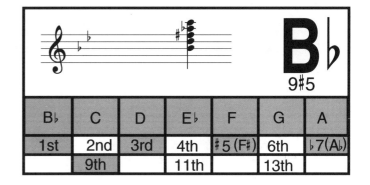

B♭
9♯5

B♭	C	D	E♭	F	G	A
1st	2nd	3rd	4th	♯5 (F♯)	6th	♭7 (A♭)
	9th		11th		13th	

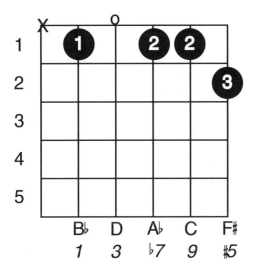

B♭ D A♭ C F♯
1 3 ♭7 9 ♯5

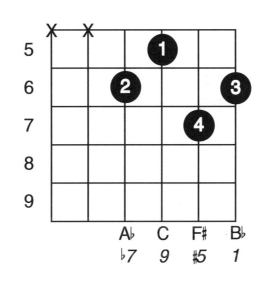

A♭ C F♯ B♭
♭7 9 ♯5 1

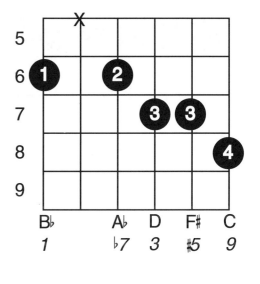

B♭   A♭ D F♯ C
1   ♭7 3 ♯5 9

57

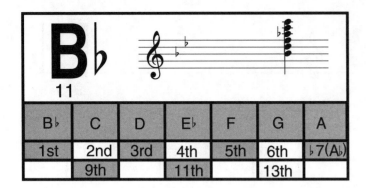

Bb	C	D	Eb	F	G	A
1st	2nd	3rd	4th	5th	6th	b7(Ab)
	9th		11th		13th	

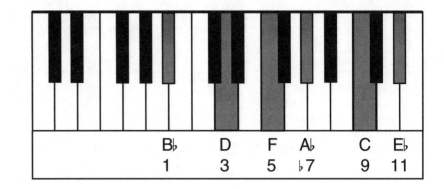

Bb D F Ab C Eb
1   3 5 b7 9 11

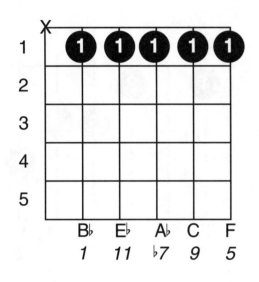

Bb Eb Ab C F
1   11 b7 9 5

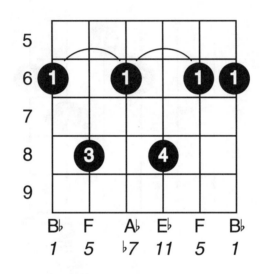

Bb F Ab Eb F Bb
1   5 b7 11 5 1

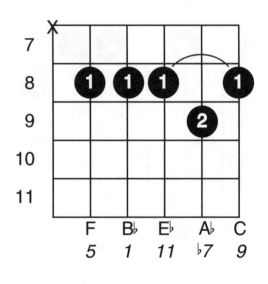

F Bb Eb Ab C
5 1   11 b7 9

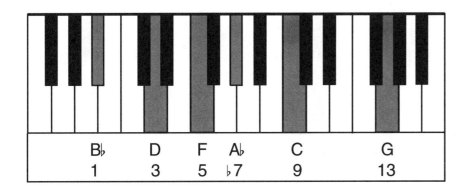

B♭ D F A♭ C G
1 3 5 ♭7 9 13

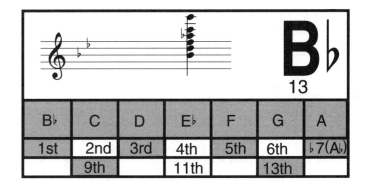

B♭ 13

B♭	C	D	E♭	F	G	A
1st	2nd	3rd	4th	5th	6th	♭7(A♭)
	9th		11th		13th	

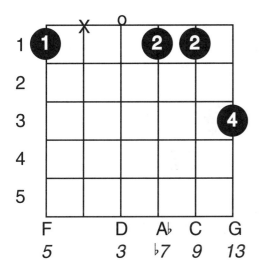

F D A♭ C G
5 *3* *♭7* *9* *13*

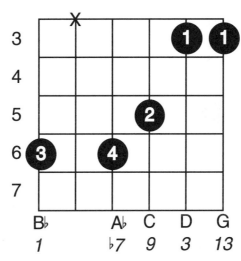

B♭ A♭ C D G
1 *♭7* *9* *3* *13*

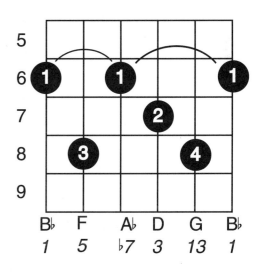

B♭ F A♭ D G B♭
1 *5* *♭7* *3* *13* *1*

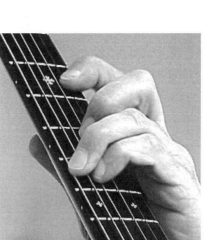

59

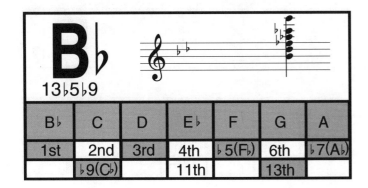

B♭	C	D	E♭	F	G	A
1st	2nd	3rd	4th	♭5(F♭)	6th	♭7(A♭)
	♭9(C♭)		11th		13th	

13♭5♭9

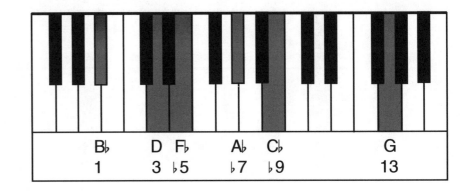

B♭		D	F♭		A♭	C♭		G
1		3	♭5		♭7	♭9		13

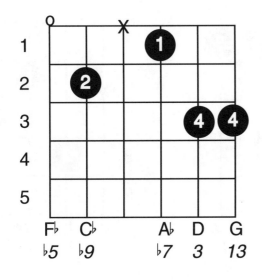

F♭	C♭		A♭	D	G
♭5	♭9		♭7	3	13

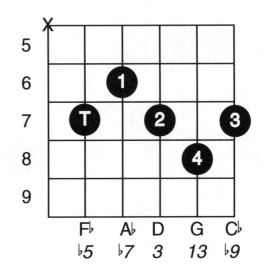

F♭	A♭	D	G	C♭
♭5	♭7	3	13	♭9

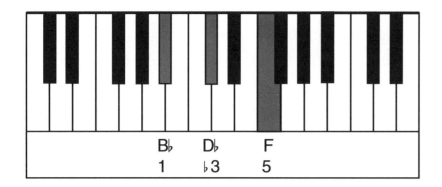

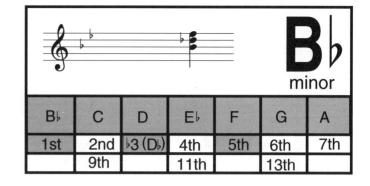

B♭	C	D	E♭	F	G	A
1st	2nd	♭3 (D♭)	4th	5th	6th	7th
	9th		11th		13th	

Keyboard notes:

B♭   D♭   F
1   ♭3   5

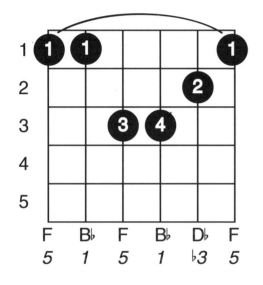

F	B♭	F	B♭	D♭	F
5	1	5	1	♭3	5

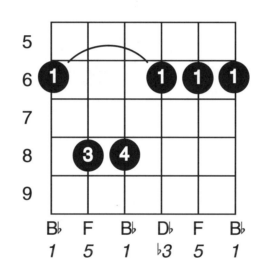

B♭	F	B♭	D♭	F	B♭
1	5	1	♭3	5	1

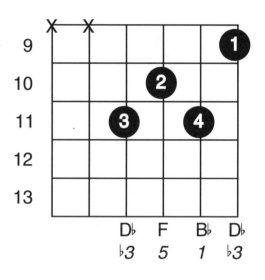

D♭	F	B♭	D♭
♭3	5	1	♭3

61

B♭

m6

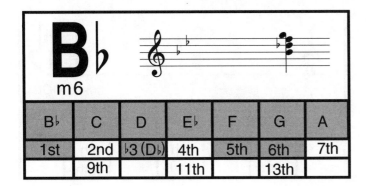

B♭	C	D	E♭	F	G	A
1st	2nd	♭3 (D♭)	4th	5th	6th	7th
	9th		11th		13th	

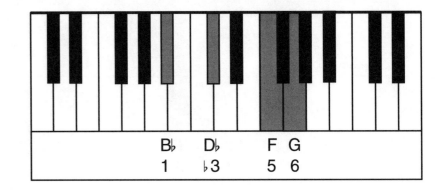

B♭   D♭   F   G
1   ♭3   5   6

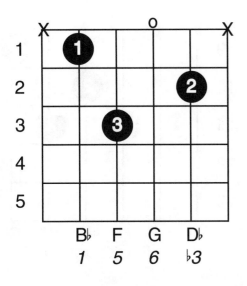

B♭   F   G   D♭
1   *5*   *6*   *♭3*

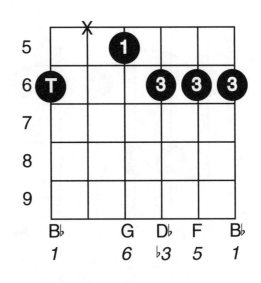

B♭   G   D♭   F   B♭
1   *6*   *♭3*   *5*   *1*

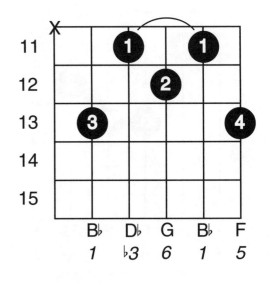

B♭   D♭   G   B♭   F
1   *♭3*   *6*   *1*   *5*

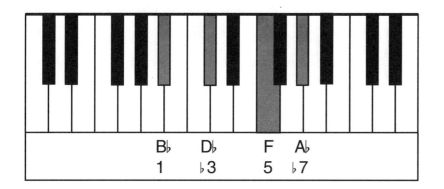

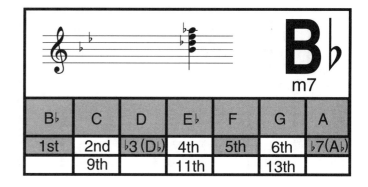

Bb	C	D	Eb	F	G	A
1st	2nd	b3 (Db)	4th	5th	6th	b7(Ab)
	9th		11th		13th	

Bb m7

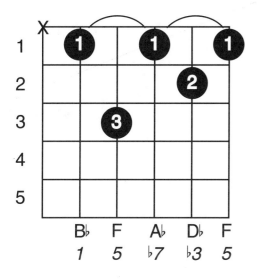

	Bb	F	Ab	Db	F
	1	5	b7	b3	5

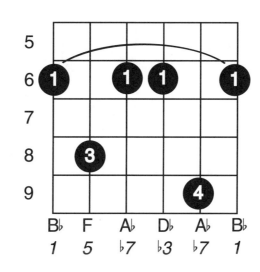

	Bb	F	Ab	Db	Ab	Bb
	1	5	b7	b3	b7	1

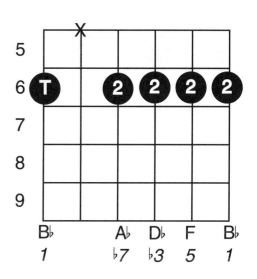

	Bb		Ab	Db	F	Bb
	1		b7	b3	5	1

63

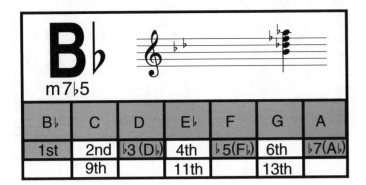

B♭

m7♭5

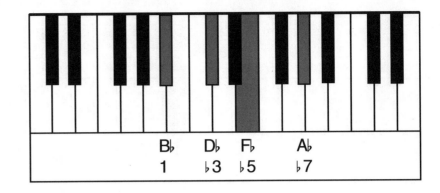

B♭	C	D	E♭	F	G	A
1st	2nd	♭3 (D♭)	4th	♭5(F♭)	6th	♭7(A♭)
	9th		11th		13th	

B♭   D♭   F♭   A♭
1   ♭3   ♭5   ♭7

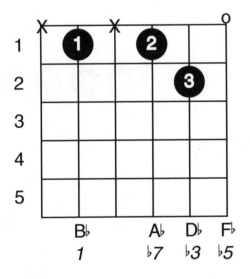

B♭   A♭   D♭   F♭
1   *♭7*   *♭3*   *♭5*

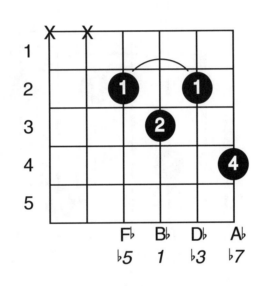

F♭   B♭   D♭   A♭
♭5   *1*   *♭3*   *♭7*

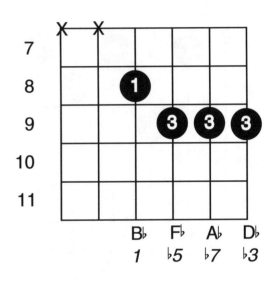

B♭   F♭   A♭   D♭
1   *♭5*   *♭7*   *♭3*

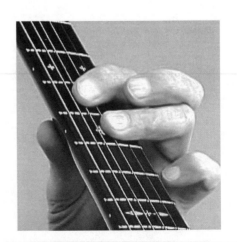

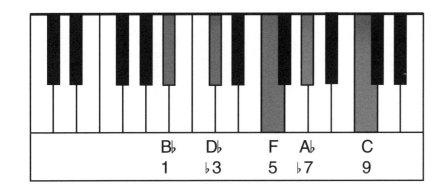

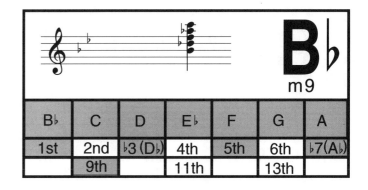

B♭	C	D	E♭	F	G	A
1st	2nd	♭3 (D♭)	4th	5th	6th	♭7(A♭)
	9th		11th		13th	

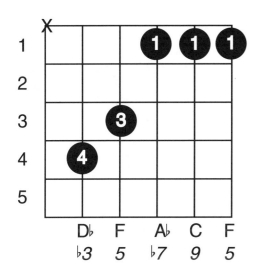

D♭ F A♭ C F
♭3 5 ♭7 9 5

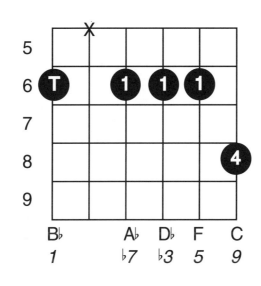

B♭ A♭ D♭ F C
1 ♭7 ♭3 5 9

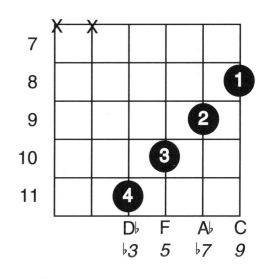

D♭ F A♭ C
♭3 5 ♭7 9

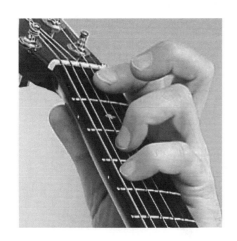

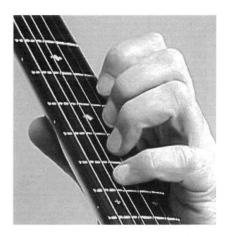

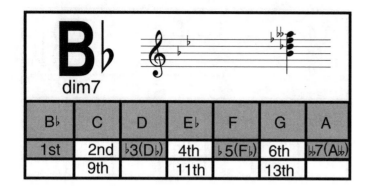

B♭ dim7

B♭	C	D	E♭	F	G	A
1st	2nd	♭3(D♭)	4th	♭5(F♭)	6th	♭♭7(A♭♭)
	9th		11th		13th	

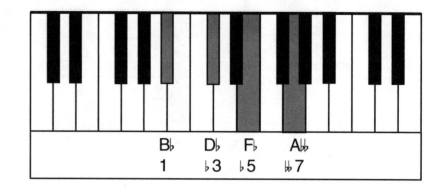

B♭	D♭	F♭	A♭♭
1	♭3	♭5	♭♭7

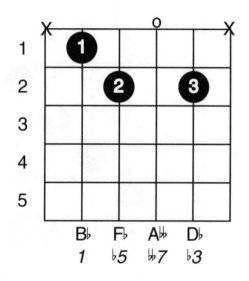

B♭	F♭	A♭♭	D♭
1	♭5	♭♭7	♭3

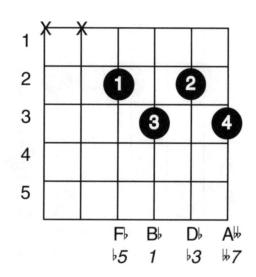

F♭	B♭	D♭	A♭♭
♭5	1	♭3	♭♭7

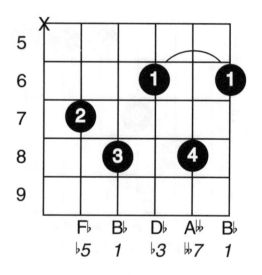

F♭	B♭	D♭	A♭♭	B♭
♭5	1	♭3	♭♭7	1

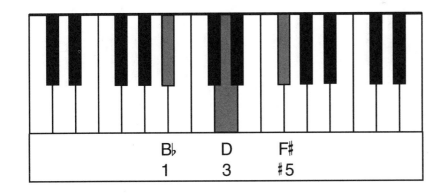

B♭   D   F#
1   3   #5

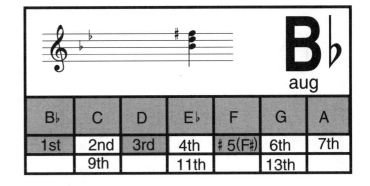

B♭ aug

B♭	C	D	E♭	F	G	A
1st	2nd	3rd	4th	#5(F#)	6th	7th
	9th		11th		13th	

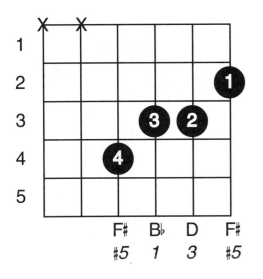

F#   B♭   D   F#
#5   1   3   #5

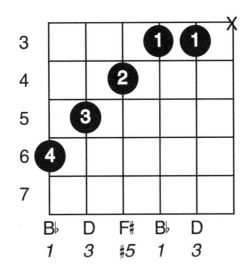

B♭   D   F#   B♭   D
1   3   #5   1   3

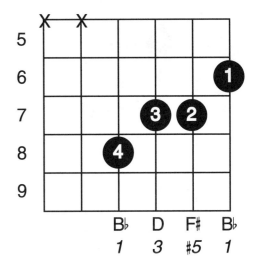

B♭   D   F#   B♭
1   3   #5   1

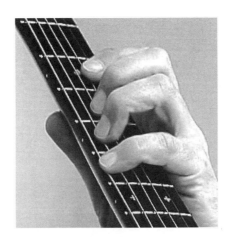

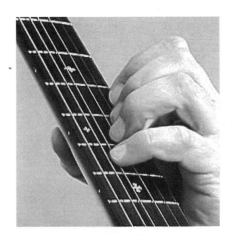

B♭
sus4

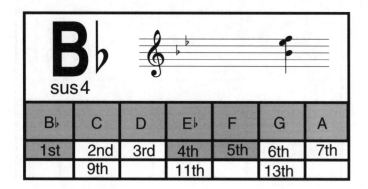

B♭	C	D	E♭	F	G	A
1st	2nd	3rd	4th	5th	6th	7th
	9th		11th		13th	

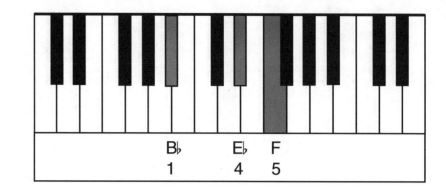

	B♭	E♭	F
	1	4	5

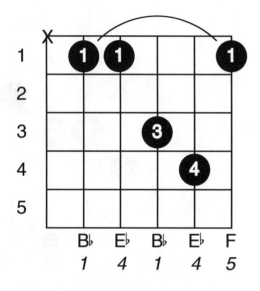

B♭	E♭	B♭	E♭	F
1	4	1	4	5

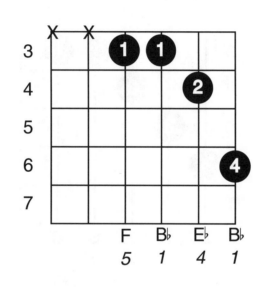

F	B♭	E♭	B♭
5	1	4	1

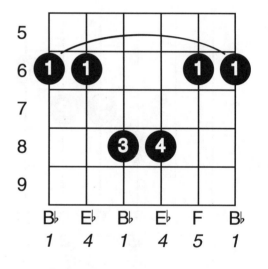

B♭	E♭	B♭	E♭	F	B♭
1	4	1	4	5	1

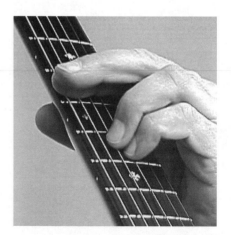

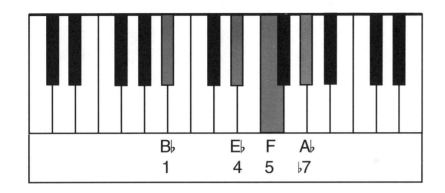

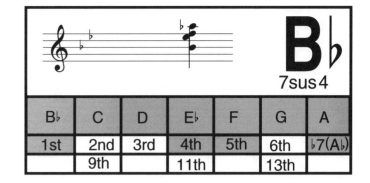

B♭	C	D	E♭	F	G	A
1st	2nd	3rd	4th	5th	6th	♭7(A♭)
	9th		11th		13th	

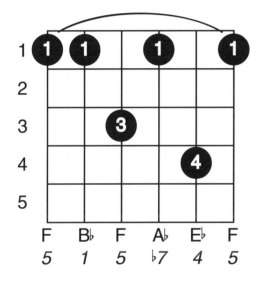

F B♭ F A♭ E♭ F
5 1 5 ♭7 4 5

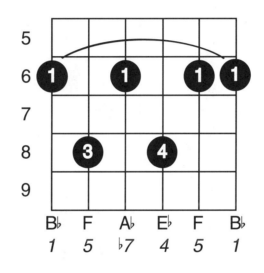

B♭ F A♭ E♭ F B♭
1 5 ♭7 4 5 1

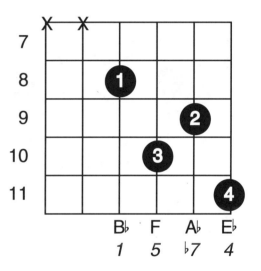

B♭ F A♭ E♭
1 5 ♭7 4

B
Major

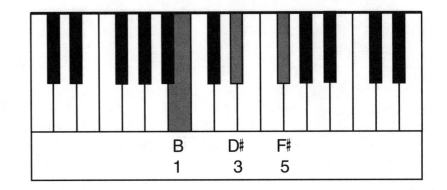

B	C#	D#	E	F#	G#	A#
1st	2nd	3rd	4th	5th	6th	7th
	9th		11th		13th	

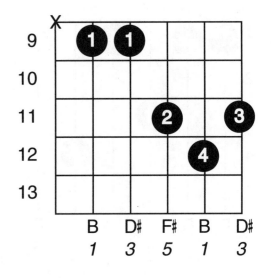

B · D# · F#
1 · 3 · 5

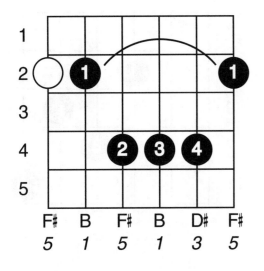

F#	B	F#	B	D#	F#
5	*1*	*5*	*1*	*3*	*5*

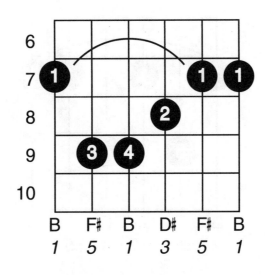

B	F#	B	D#	F#	B
1	*5*	*1*	*3*	*5*	*1*

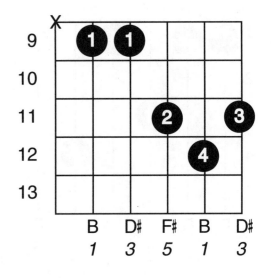

B	D#	F#	B	D#
1	*3*	*5*	*1*	*3*

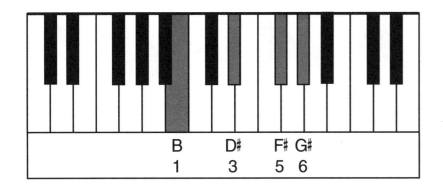

B | 1 | D# | 3 | F# | G# | 5 | 6

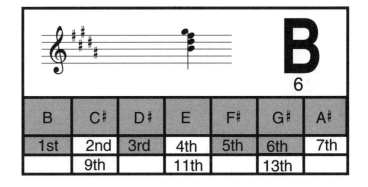

B

6

B	C#	D#	E	F#	G#	A#
1st	2nd	3rd	4th	5th	6th	7th
	9th		11th		13th	

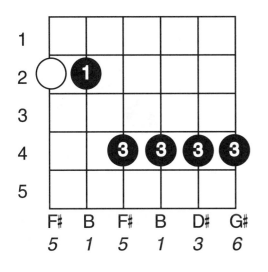

1						
2	◯	1				
3						
4			3	3	3	3
5						

F# | B | F# | B | D# | G#
5 | 1 | 5 | 1 | 3 | 6

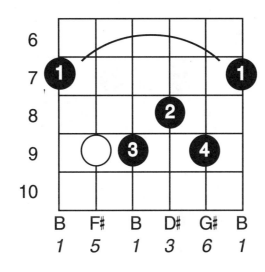

6						
7	1				1
8				2	
9		◯	3		4
10					

B | F# | B | D# | G# | B
1 | 5 | 1 | 3 | 6 | 1

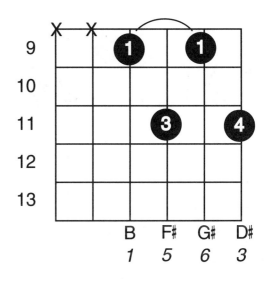

9	✕	✕	1		1	
10						
11				3		4
12						
13						

B | F# | G# | D#
1 | 5 | 6 | 3

71

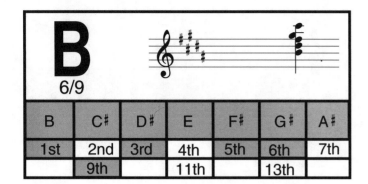

B

6/9

B	C#	D#	E	F#	G#	A#
1st	2nd	3rd	4th	5th	6th	7th
	9th		11th		13th	

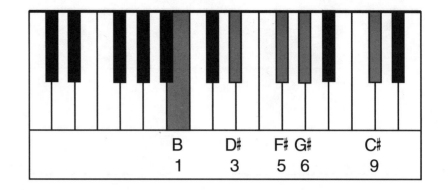

B	D#	F#	G#		C#
1	3	5	6		9

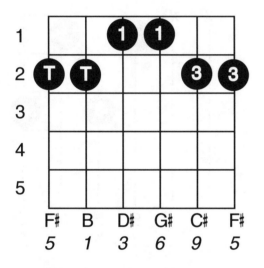

F#	B	D#	G#	C#	F#
5	1	3	6	9	5

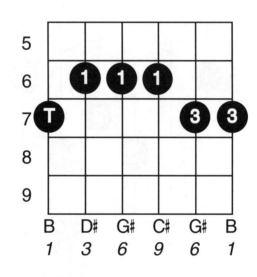

B	D#	G#	C#	G#	B
1	3	6	9	6	1

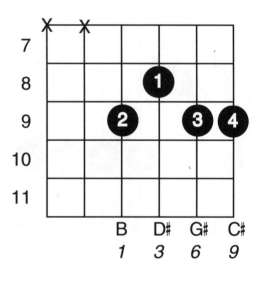

B	D#	G#	C#
1	3	6	9

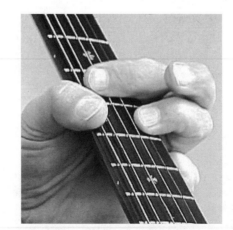

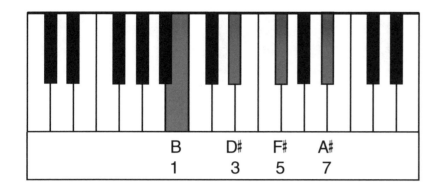

B
1

D#
3

F#
5

A#
7

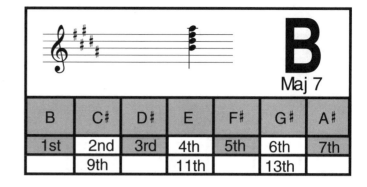

B
Maj 7

B	C#	D#	E	F#	G#	A#
1st	2nd	3rd	4th	5th	6th	7th
	9th		11th		13th	

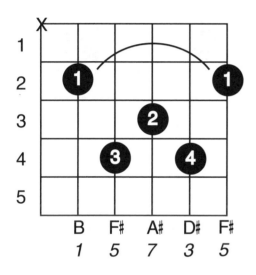

B   F#   A#   D#   F#
1 *5*   *7*   *3*   *5*

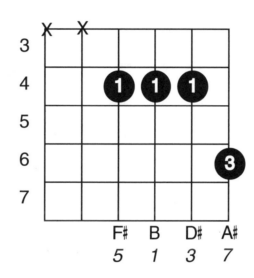

F#   B   D#   A#
5   *1*   *3*   *7*

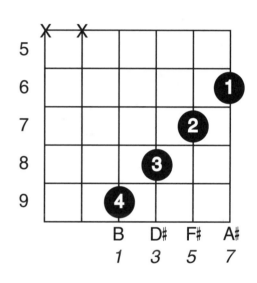

B   D#   F#   A#
1   *3*   *5*   *7*

B mMaj7

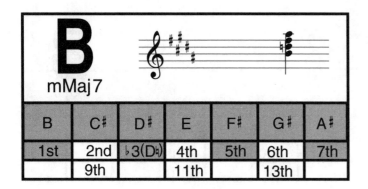

B	C#	D#	E	F#	G#	A#
1st	2nd	♭3(D♮)	4th	5th	6th	7th
	9th		11th		13th	

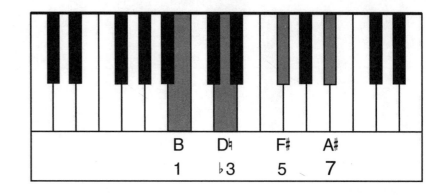

B   D♮   F#   A#
1   ♭3   5   7

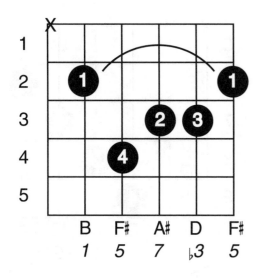

B   F#   A#   D   F#
1   5   7   ♭3   5

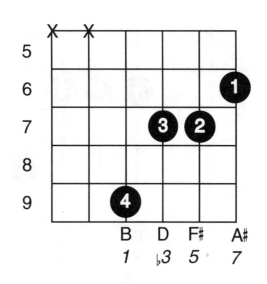

B   D   F#   A#
1   ♭3   5   7

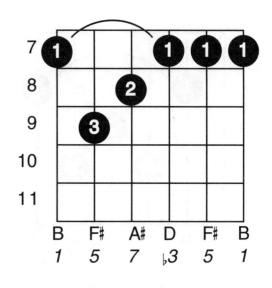

B   F#   A#   D   F#   B
1   5   7   ♭3   5   1

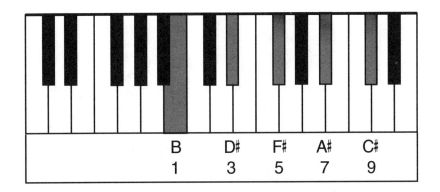

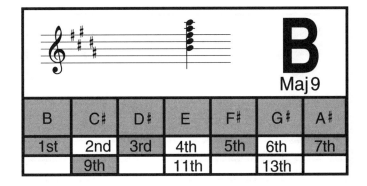

B	C#	D#	E	F#	G#	A#
1st	2nd	3rd	4th	5th	6th	7th
	9th		11th		13th	

B Maj9

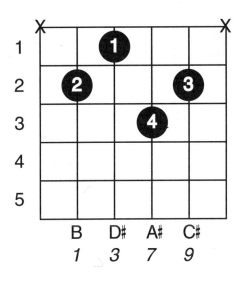

B D# A# C#
1 3 7 9

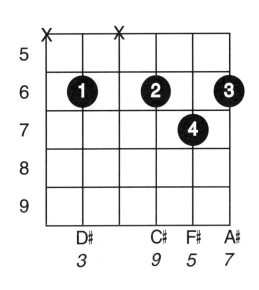

D# C# F# A#
3 9 5 7

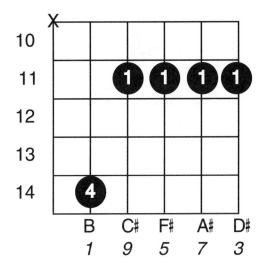

B C# F# A# D#
1 9 5 7 3

75

B

7th

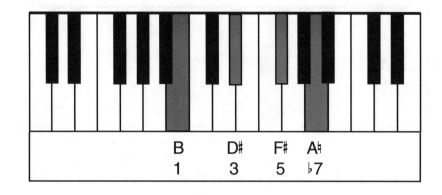

B	C#	D#	E	F#	G#	A#
1st	2nd	3rd	4th	5th	6th	♭7 (A♮)
	9th		11th		13th	

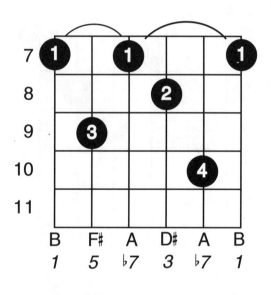

B   D#   F#   A♮
1   3   5   ♭7

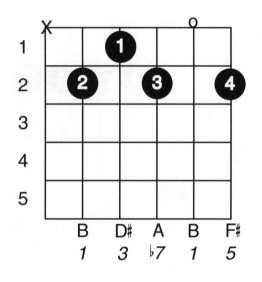

×   o

```
1
2
3
4
5
```

B   D#   A   B   F#
1   3   ♭7   1   5

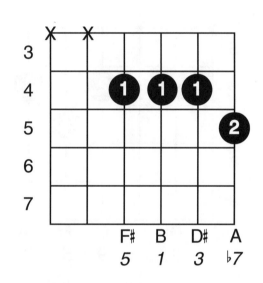

×   ×

```
3
4
5
6
7
```

F#   B   D#   A
5   1   3   ♭7

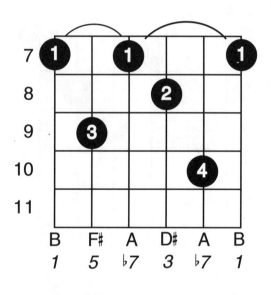

```
7
8
9
10
11
```

B   F#   A   D#   A   B
1   5   ♭7   3   ♭7   1

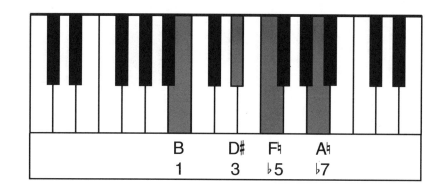

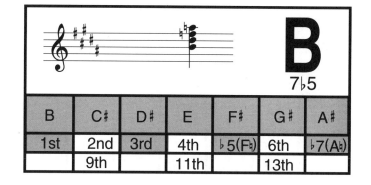

B	C#	D#	E	F#	G#	A#
1st	2nd	3rd	4th	♭5(F♮)	6th	♭7(A♮)
	9th		11th		13th	

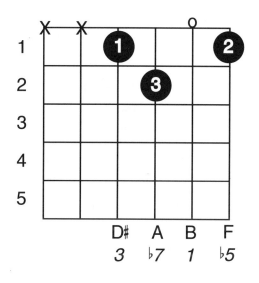

D# A B F
3 *♭7* *1* *♭5*

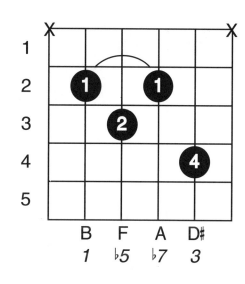

B F A D#
1 *♭5* *♭7* *3*

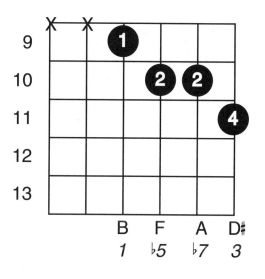

B F A D#
1 *♭5* *♭7* *3*

77

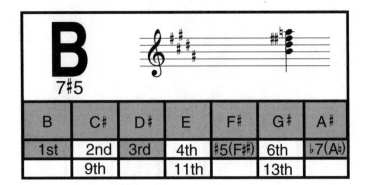

B
7#5

B	C#	D#	E	F#	G#	A#
1st	2nd	3rd	4th	#5(F##)	6th	♭7(A♮)
	9th		11th		13th	

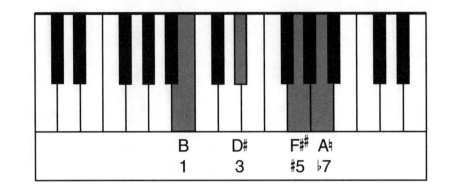

B · D# · F## · A♮
1 · 3 · #5 · ♭7

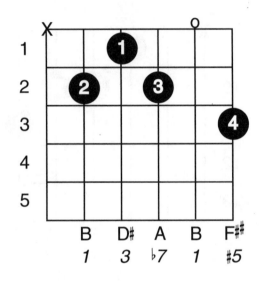

B D# A B F##
1 3 ♭7 1 #5

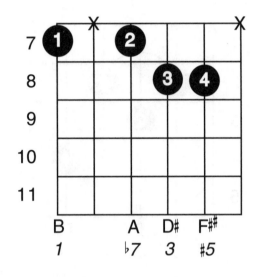

B A D# F##
1 ♭7 3 #5

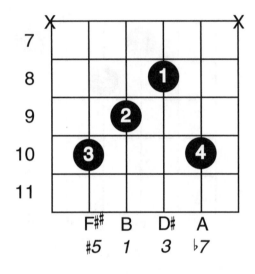

F## B D# A
#5 1 3 ♭7

78

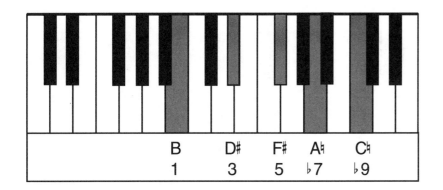

B7♭9

B	C♯	D♯	E	F♯	G♯	A♯
1st	2nd	3rd	4th	5th	6th	♭7(A♮)
	♭9(C♮)		11th		13th	

Keyboard notes:
B D♯ F♯ A♮ C♮
1 3 5 ♭7 ♭9

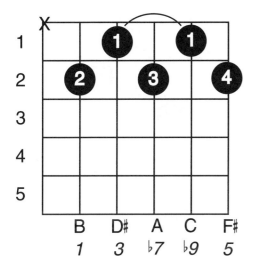

B D♯ A C F♯
1 3 ♭7 ♭9 5

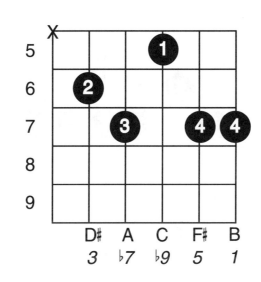

D♯ A C F♯ B
3 ♭7 ♭9 5 1

C F♯ A D♯
♭9 5 ♭7 3

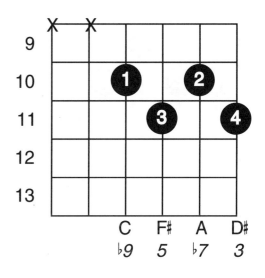

B
7#9

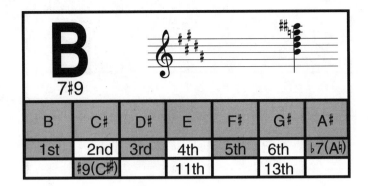

B	C#	D#	E	F#	G#	A#
1st	2nd	3rd	4th	5th	6th	♭7(A♮)
	#9(C##)		11th		13th	

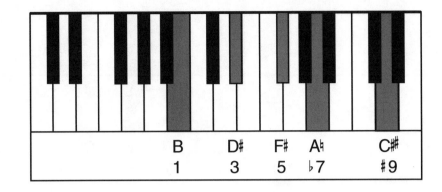

B		D#		F#		A♮		C##
1		3		5		♭7		#9

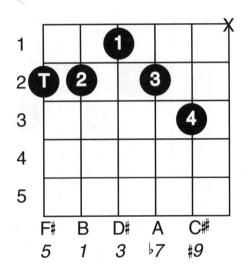

F#	B	D#	A	C#
5	*1*	*3*	*♭7*	*#9*

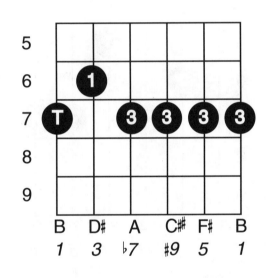

B	D#	A	C##	F#	B
1	*3*	*♭7*	*#9*	*5*	*1*

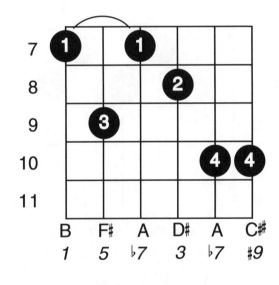

B	F#	A	D#	A	C##
1	*5*	*♭7*	*3*	*♭7*	*#9*

80

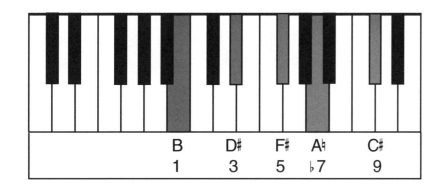

B D# F# A♮ C#
1 3 5 ♭7 9

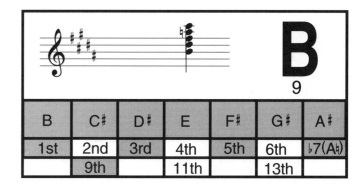

B

9

B	C#	D#	E	F#	G#	A#
1st	2nd	3rd	4th	5th	6th	♭7(A♮)
	9th		11th		13th	

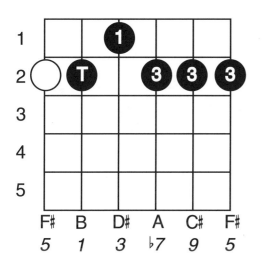

| 1 | | | | | | |
| 2 | | | | | | |

F# B D# A C# F#
5 1 3 ♭7 9 5

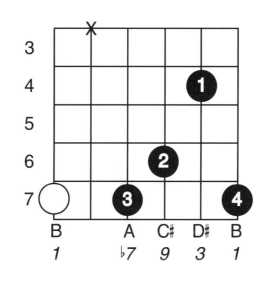

B A C# D# B
1 ♭7 9 3 1

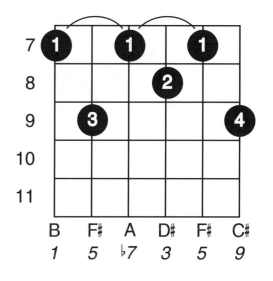

B F# A D# F# C#
1 5 ♭7 3 5 9

81

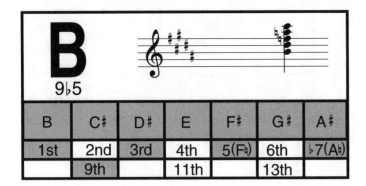

B

9♭5

B	C#	D#	E	F#	G#	A#
1st	2nd	3rd	4th	5(F♮)	6th	♭7(A♮)
	9th		11th		13th	

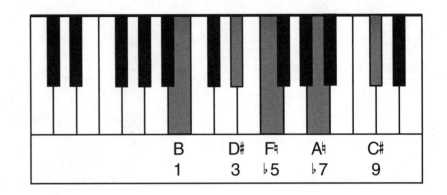

B	D#	F♮	A♮	C#
1	3	♭5	♭7	9

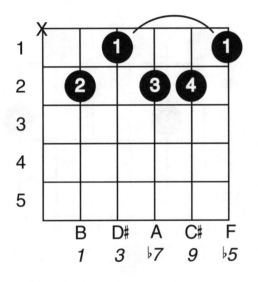

B	D#	A	C#	F
1	3	♭7	9	♭5

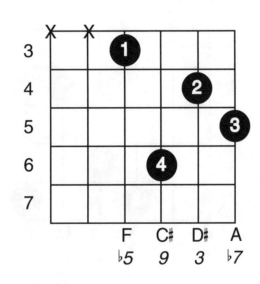

F	C#	D#	A
♭5	9	3	♭7

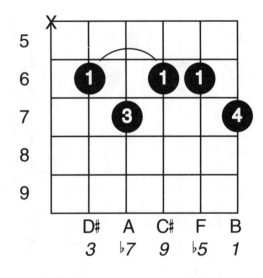

D#	A	C#	F	B
3	♭7	9	♭5	1

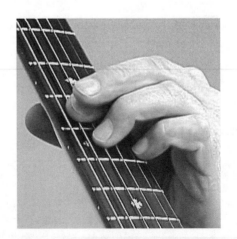

82

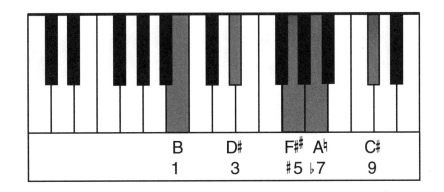

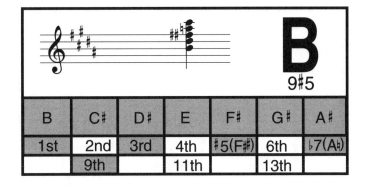

B 9#5

B	C#	D#	E	F#	G#	A#
1st	2nd	3rd	4th	#5(F##)	6th	♭7(A♮)
	9th		11th		13th	

Keyboard labels:
B 1, D# 3, F# #5, A♮ ♭7, C# 9

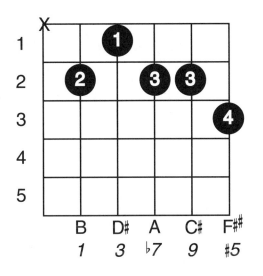

B 1   D# 3   A ♭7   C# 9   F## #5

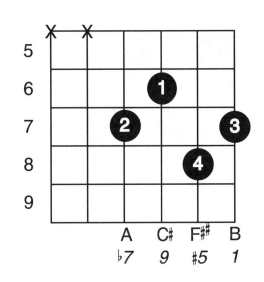

A ♭7   C# 9   F## #5   B 1

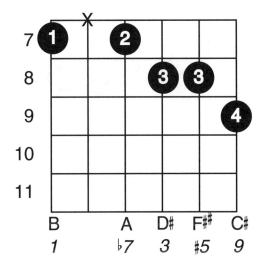

B 1   A ♭7   D# 3   F## #5   C# 9

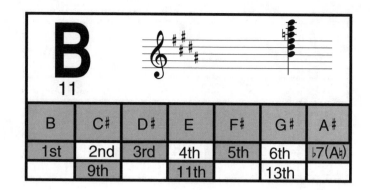

B

11

B	C#	D#	E	F#	G#	A#
1st	2nd	3rd	4th	5th	6th	♭7(A♮)
	9th		11th		13th	

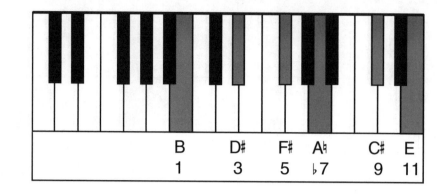

B	D#	F#	A♮	C#	E
1	3	5	♭7	9	11

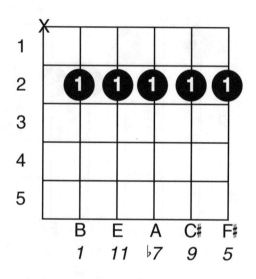

X

B	E	A	C#	F#
1	*11*	*♭7*	*9*	*5*

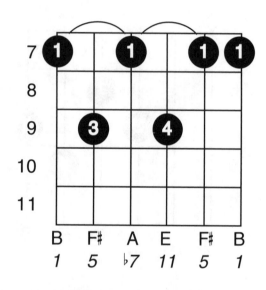

B	F#	A	E	F#	B
1	*5*	*♭7*	*11*	*5*	*1*

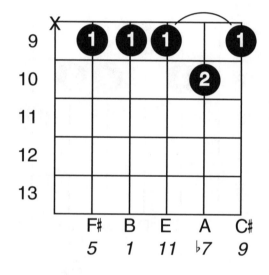

X

F#	B	E	A	C#
5	*1*	*11*	*♭7*	*9*

84

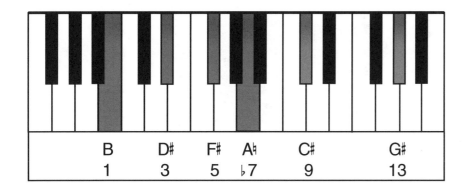

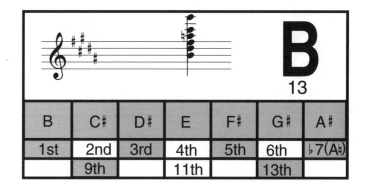

B

13

B	C#	D#	E	F#	G#	A#
1st	2nd	3rd	4th	5th	6th	♭7(A♮)
	9th		11th		13th	

Keyboard (left):

B	D#	F#	A♮	C#	G#
1	3	5	♭7	9	13

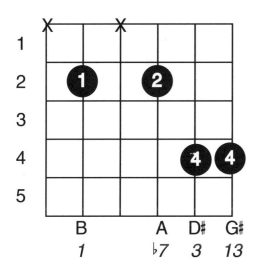

B		A	D#	G#
1		♭7	3	13

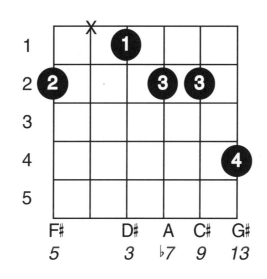

F#		D#	A	C#	G#
5		3	♭7	9	13

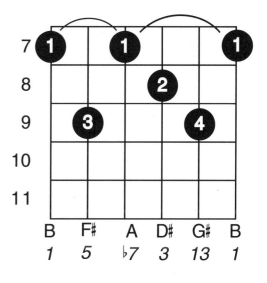

B	F#	A	D#	G#	B
1	5	♭7	3	13	1

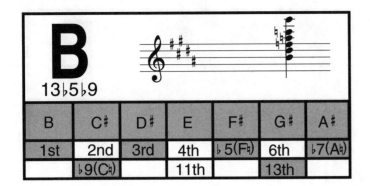

B 13♭5♭9

B	C#	D#	E	F#	G#	A#
1st	2nd	3rd	4th	♭5(F♮)	6th	♭7(A♮)
	♭9(C♮)		11th		13th	

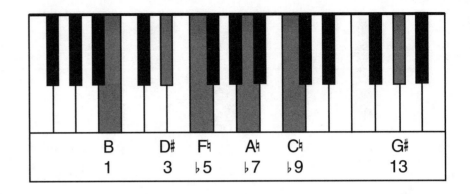

	B	D#	F♮	A♮	C♮	G#
	1	3	♭5	♭7	♭9	13

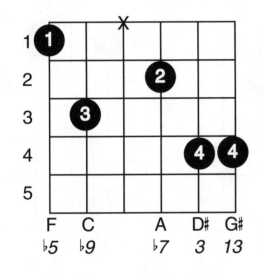

F	C		A	D#	G#
♭5	♭9		♭7	3	13

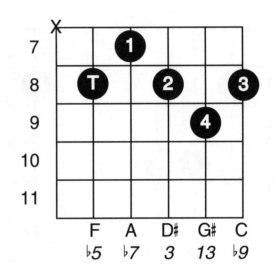

F	A	D#	G#	C
♭5	♭7	3	13	♭9

86

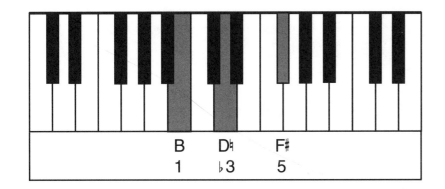

B D♮ F#
1 ♭3 5

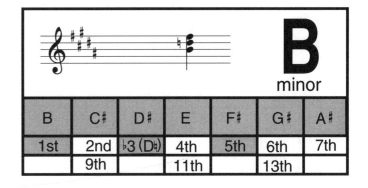

B
minor

B	C#	D#	E	F#	G#	A#
1st	2nd	♭3 (D♮)	4th	5th	6th	7th
	9th		11th		13th	

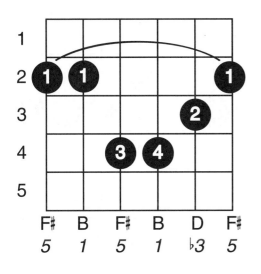

F# B F# B D F#
5 1 5 1 ♭3 5

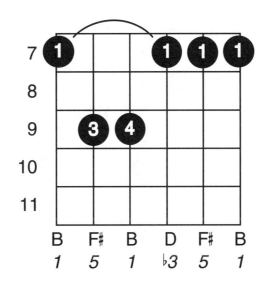

B F# B D F# B
1 5 1 ♭3 5 1

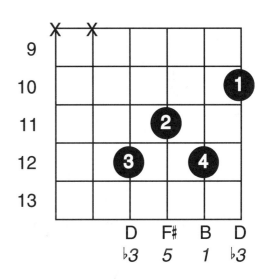

D F# B D
♭3 5 1 ♭3

B

m6

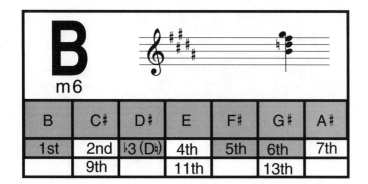

B	C#	D#	E	F#	G#	A#
1st	2nd	♭3 (D♮)	4th	5th	6th	7th
	9th		11th		13th	

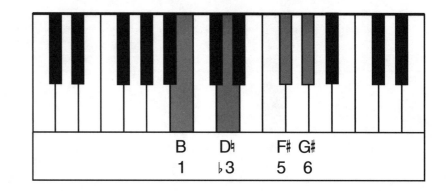

B   D♮   F# G#
1   ♭3   5 6

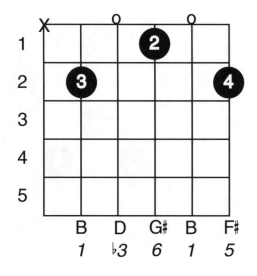

B   D   G# B   F#
1 *♭3* *6* *1* *5*

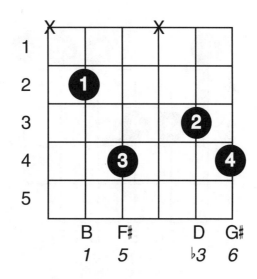

B   F#   D   G#
1 *5*   *♭3* *6*

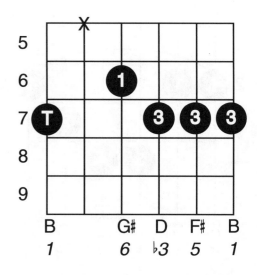

B   G# D F# B
1   *6* *♭3* *5* *1*

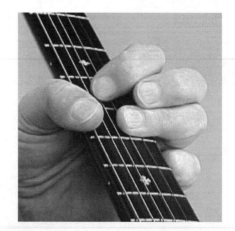

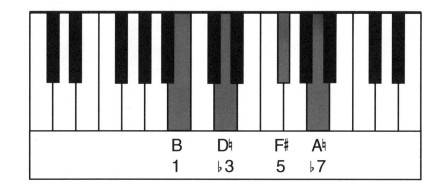

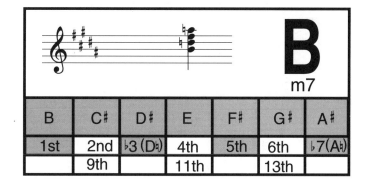

B	C#	D#	E	F#	G#	A#
1st	2nd	♭3 (D♮)	4th	5th	6th	♭7(A♮)
	9th		11th		13th	

B m7

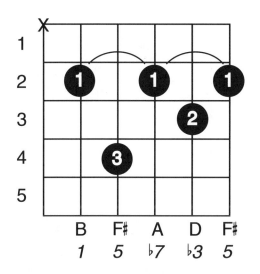

B F# A D F#
1 5 ♭7 ♭3 5

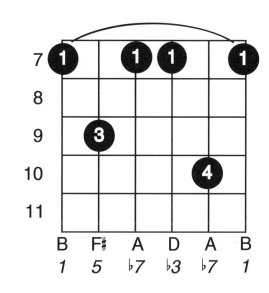

B F# A D A B
1 5 ♭7 ♭3 ♭7 1

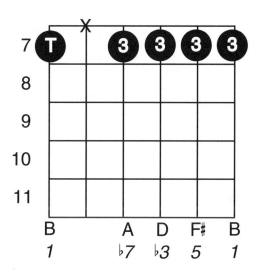

B A D F# B
1 ♭7 ♭3 5 1

B

m7♭5

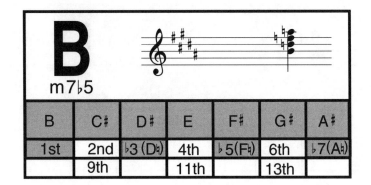

B	C#	D#	E	F#	G#	A#
1st	2nd	♭3 (D♮)	4th	♭5(F♮)	6th	♭7(A♮)
	9th		11th		13th	

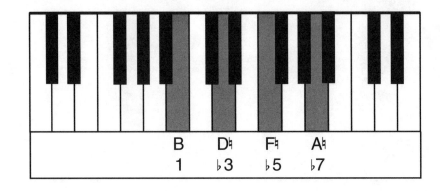

				B	D♮	F♮	A♮
				1	♭3	♭5	♭7

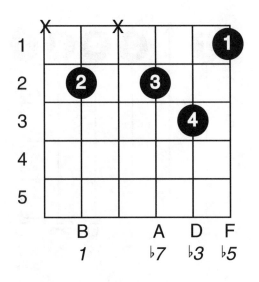

		B		A	D	F
		1		*♭7*	*♭3*	*♭5*

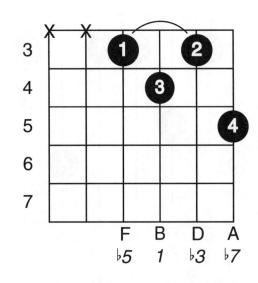

		F	B	D	A
		♭5	*1*	*♭3*	*♭7*

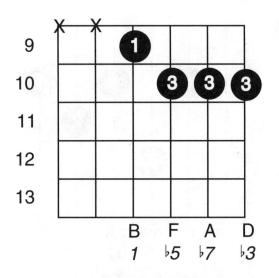

		B	F	A	D
		1	*♭5*	*♭7*	*♭3*

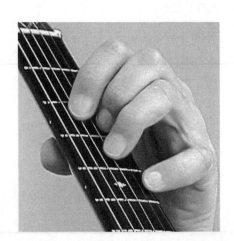

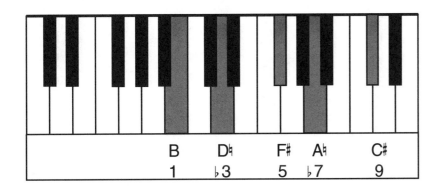

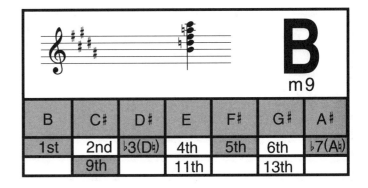

B	C#	D#	E	F#	G#	A#
1st	2nd	♭3(D♮)	4th	5th	6th	♭7(A♮)
	9th		11th		13th	

B on keyboard: B D♮ F# A♮ C#
1 ♭3 5 ♭7 9

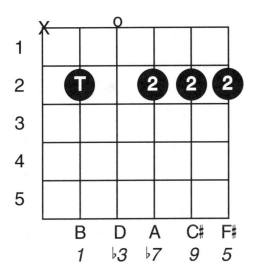

B   D   A   C#   F#
1   ♭3   ♭7   9   5

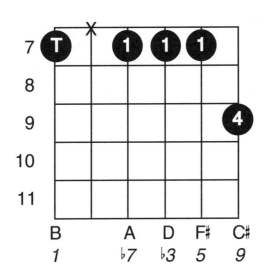

B   A   D   F#   C#
1   ♭7   ♭3   5   9

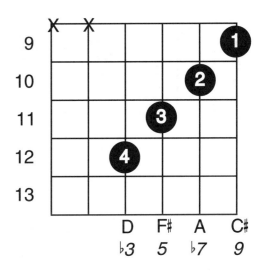

D   F#   A   C#
♭3   5   ♭7   9

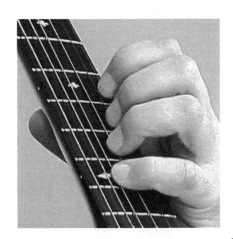

91

B

dim7

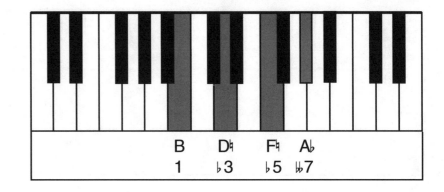

B	C#	D#	E	F#	G#	A#
1st	2nd	♭3 (D♮)	4th	♭5(F♮)	6th	♭♭7 (A♭)
	9th		11th		13th	

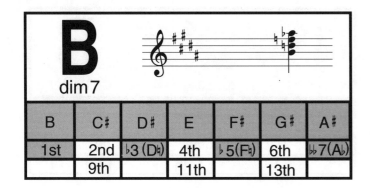

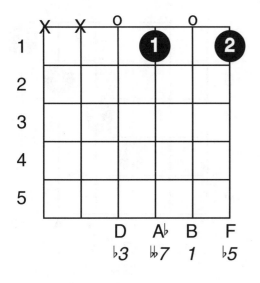

D | A♭ | B | F
♭3 | ♭♭7 | 1 | ♭5

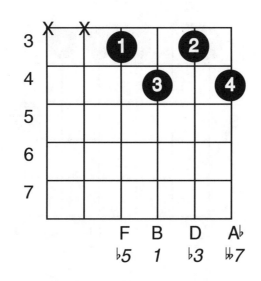

F | B | D | A♭
♭5 | 1 | ♭3 | ♭♭7

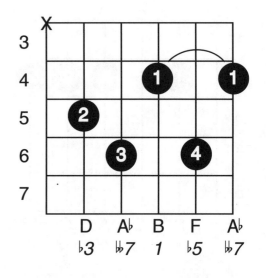

D | A♭ | B | F | A♭
♭3 | ♭♭7 | 1 | ♭5 | ♭♭7

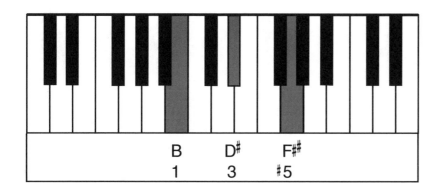

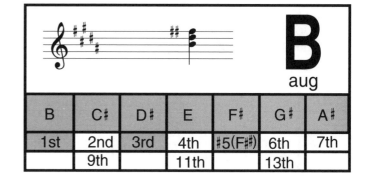

B	C♯	D♯	E	F♯	G♯	A♯
1st	2nd	3rd	4th	♯5(F♯♯)	6th	7th
	9th		11th		13th	

B aug

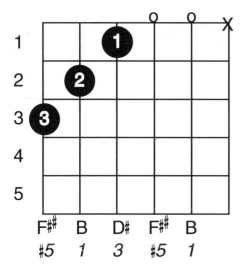

F♯♯ B D♯ F♯♯ B
♯5   1   3   ♯5   1

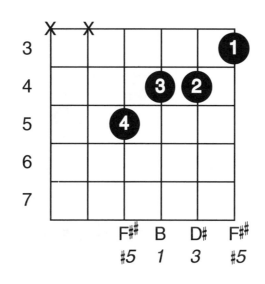

F♯♯ B D♯ F♯♯
♯5   1   3   ♯5

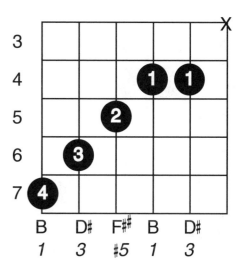

B D♯ F♯♯ B D♯
1   3   ♯5   1   3

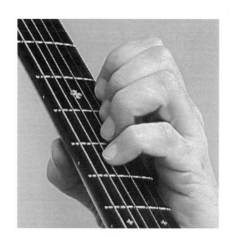

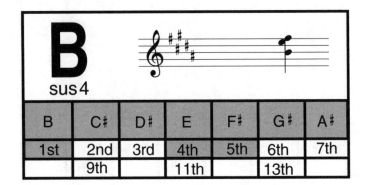

B sus 4

B	C#	D#	E	F#	G#	A#
1st	2nd	3rd	4th	5th	6th	7th
	9th		11th		13th	

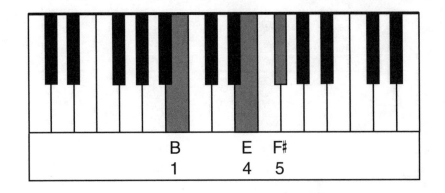

B   E   F#
1   4   5

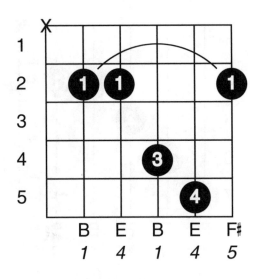

B   E   B   E   F#
1   4   1   4   5

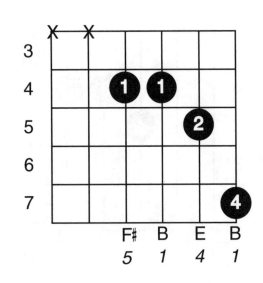

F#   B   E   B
5   1   4   1

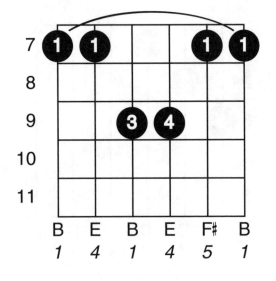

B   E   B   E   F#   B
1   4   1   4   5   1

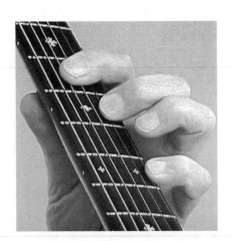

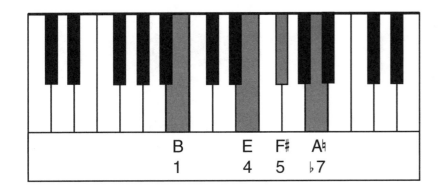

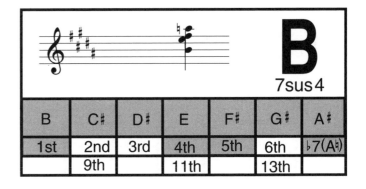
B	C#	D#	E	F#	G#	A#
1st	2nd	3rd	4th	5th	6th	b7(A♮)
	9th		11th		13th	

Keyboard (from photo):

B E F# A♮
1 4 5 b7

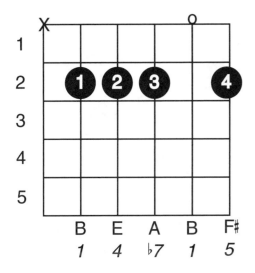

B E A B F#
1 4 b7 1 5

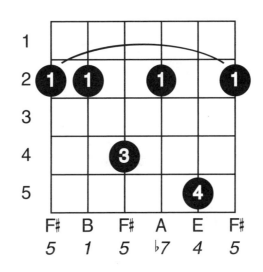

F# B F# A E F#
5 1 5 b7 4 5

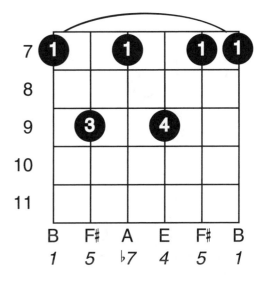

B F# A E F# B
1 5 b7 4 5 1

95

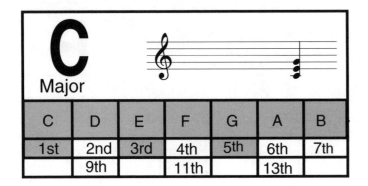

C
Major

C	D	E	F	G	A	B
1st	2nd	3rd	4th	5th	6th	7th
	9th		11th		13th	

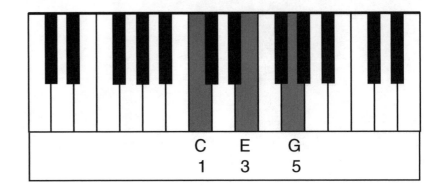

C   E   G
1   3   5

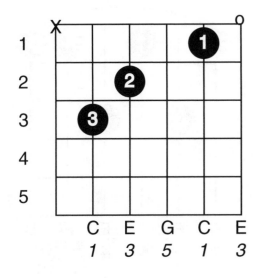

C   E   G   C   E
1   *3*   *5*   *1*   *3*

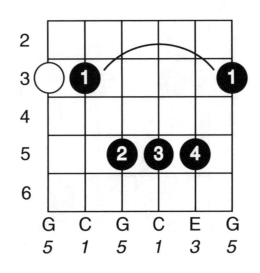

G   C   G   C   E   G
5   *1*   *5*   *1*   *3*   *5*

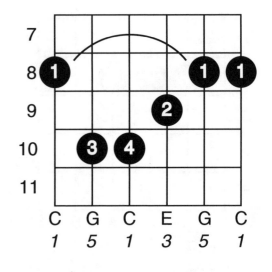

C   G   C   E   G   C
1   *5*   *1*   *3*   *5*   *1*

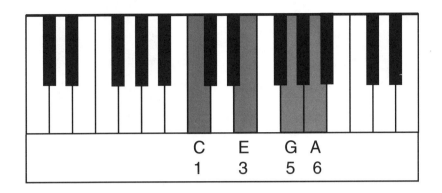

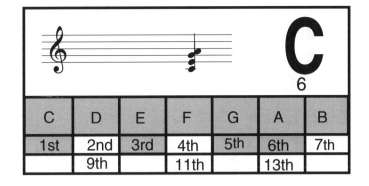

C	D	E	F	G	A	B
1st	2nd	3rd	4th	5th	6th	7th
	9th		11th		13th	

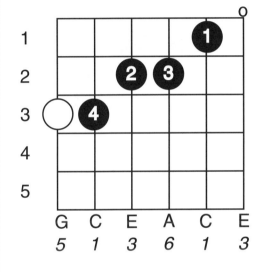

G   C   E   A   C   E
5   *1*   *3*   *6*   *1*   *3*

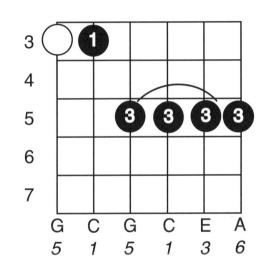

G   C   G   C   E   A
5   *1*   *5*   *1*   *3*   *6*

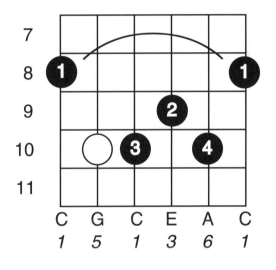

C   G   C   E   A   C
1   *5*   *1*   *3*   *6*   *1*

97

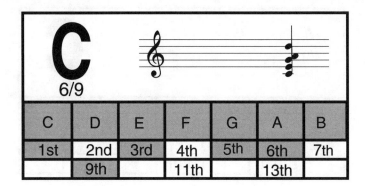

C
6/9

C	D	E	F	G	A	B
1st	2nd	3rd	4th	5th	6th	7th
	9th		11th		13th	

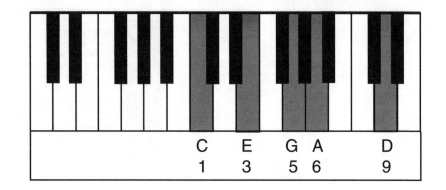

C	E	G	A	D
1	3	5	6	9

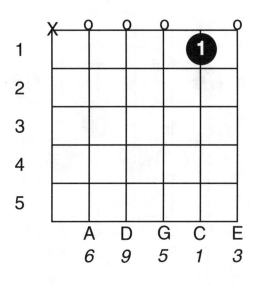

A	D	G	C	E
6	*9*	*5*	*1*	*3*

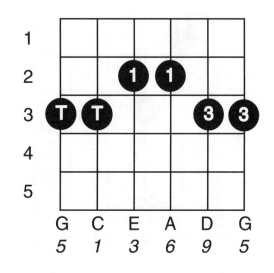

G	C	E	A	D	G
5	*1*	*3*	*6*	*9*	*5*

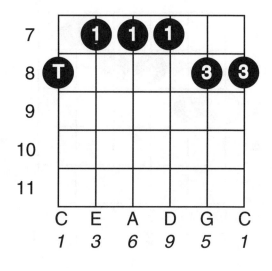

C	E	A	D	G	C
1	*3*	*6*	*9*	*5*	*1*

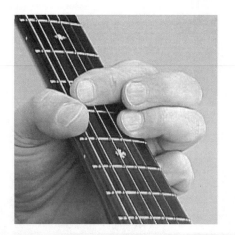

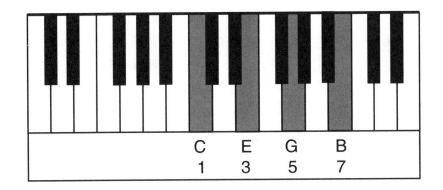

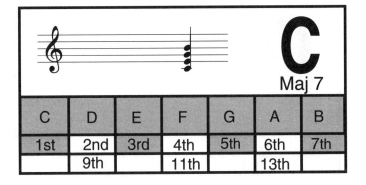

C
Maj 7

C	D	E	F	G	A	B
1st	2nd	3rd	4th	5th	6th	7th
	9th		11th		13th	

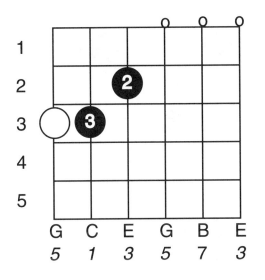

G C E G B E
5 *1* *3* *5* *7* *3*

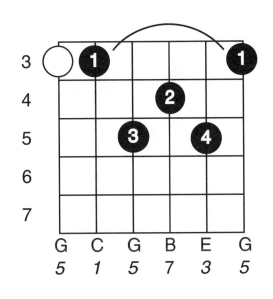

G C G B E G
5 *1* *5* *7* *3* *5*

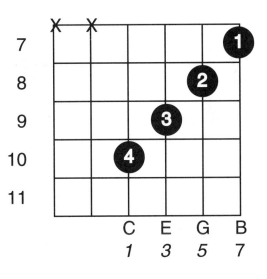

C E G B
1 *3* *5* *7*

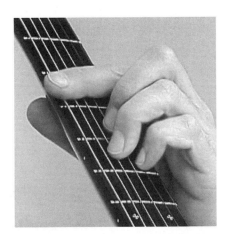

99

C

mMaj7

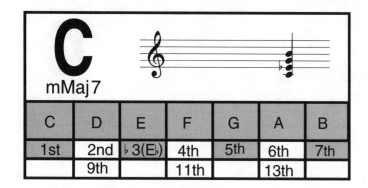

C	D	E	F	G	A	B
1st	2nd	♭3(E♭)	4th	5th	6th	7th
	9th		11th		13th	

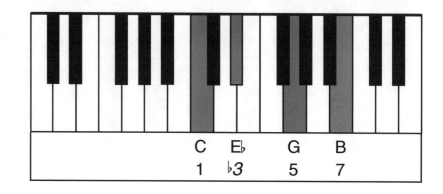

		C	E♭		G		B	
		1	♭3		5		7	

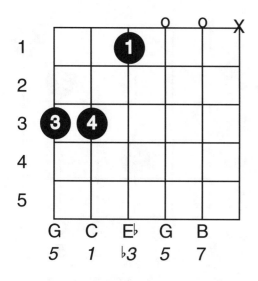

G	C	E♭	G	B
5	*1*	*♭3*	*5*	*7*

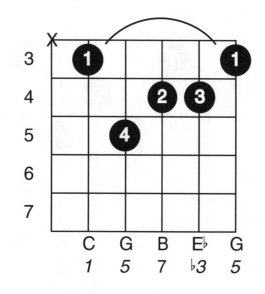

C	G	B	E♭	G
1	*5*	*7*	*♭3*	*5*

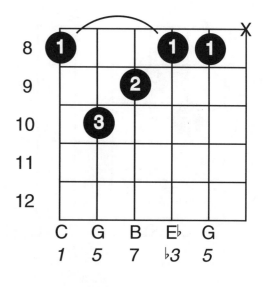

C	G	B	E♭	G
1	*5*	*7*	*♭3*	*5*

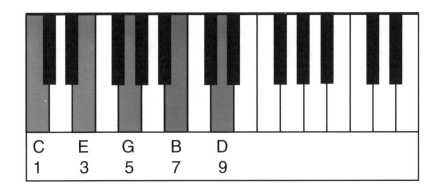

C	E	G	B	D
1	3	5	7	9

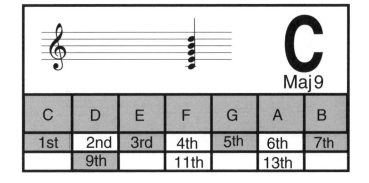

C Maj9

C	D	E	F	G	A	B
1st	2nd	3rd	4th	5th	6th	7th
	9th		11th		13th	

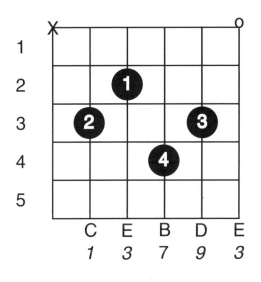

C	E	B	D	E
1	3	7	9	3

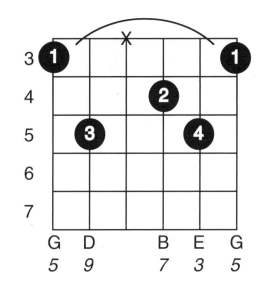

G	D		B	E	G
5	9		7	3	5

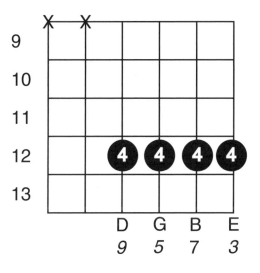

D	G	B	E
9	5	7	3

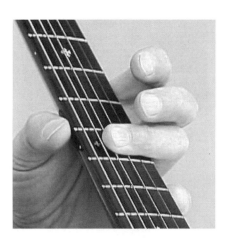

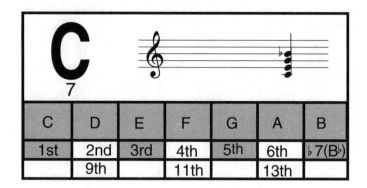

C	D	E	F	G	A	B
1st	2nd	3rd	4th	5th	6th	♭7(B♭)
	9th		11th		13th	

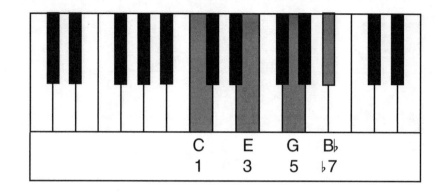

C E G B♭
1 3 5 ♭7

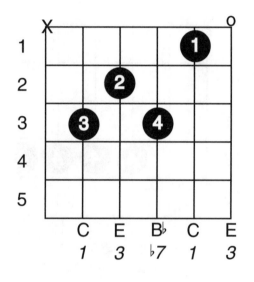

C E B♭ C E
1 3 ♭7 1 3

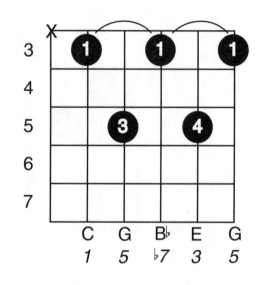

C G B♭ E G
1 5 ♭7 3 5

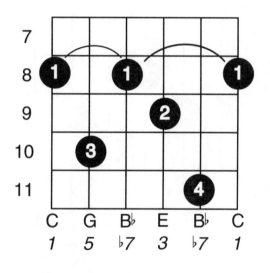

C G B♭ E B♭ C
1 5 ♭7 3 ♭7 1

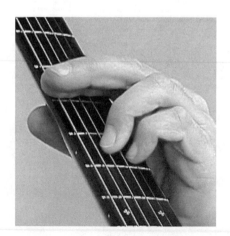

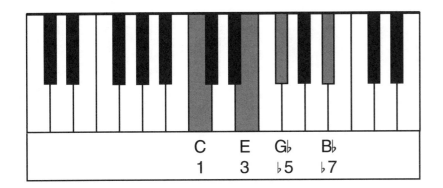

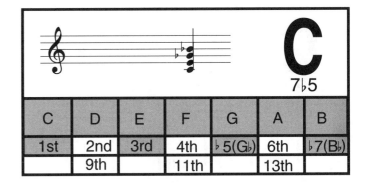

C 7♭5

C	D	E	F	G	A	B
1st	2nd	3rd	4th	♭5(G♭)	6th	♭7(B♭)
	9th		11th		13th	

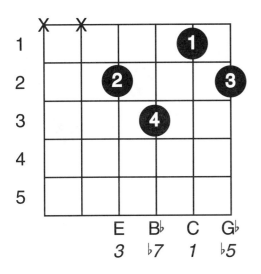

E   B♭   C   G♭
3   *♭7*   *1*   *♭5*

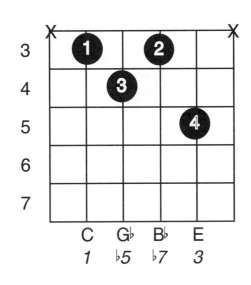

C   G♭   B♭   E
1   *♭5*   *♭7*   *3*

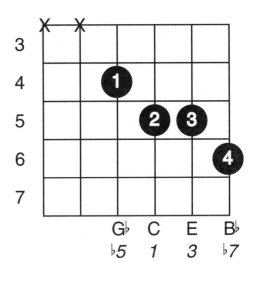

G♭   C   E   B♭
♭5   *1*   *3*   *♭7*

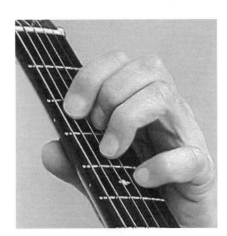

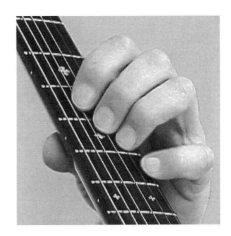

103

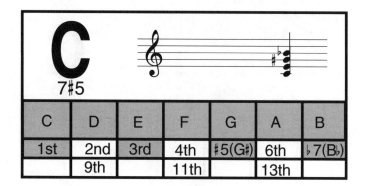

C	D	E	F	G	A	B
1st	2nd	3rd	4th	#5(G#)	6th	♭7(B♭)
	9th		11th		13th	

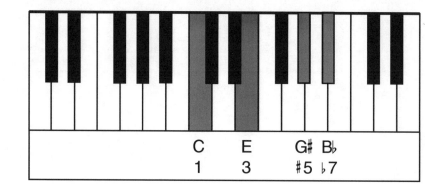

C E G# B♭
1 3 #5 ♭7

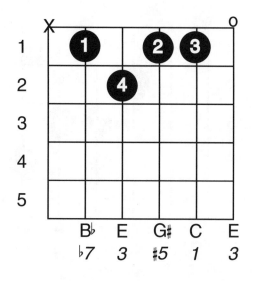

B♭ E G# C E
♭7 3 #5 1 3

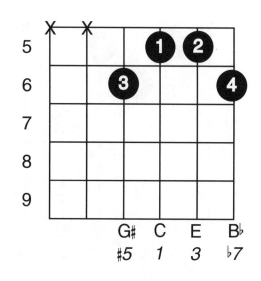

G# C E B♭
#5 1 3 ♭7

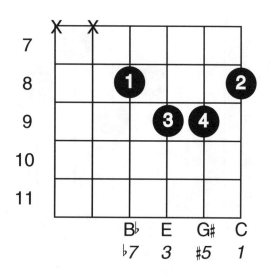

B♭ E G# C
♭7 3 #5 1

104

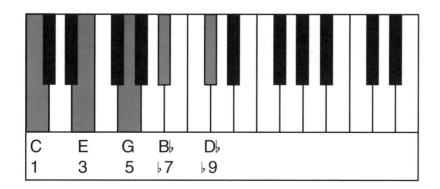

C | E | G | B♭ | D♭
1 | 3 | 5 | ♭7 | ♭9

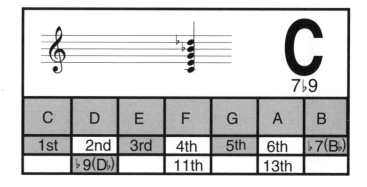

C
7♭9

C	D	E	F	G	A	B
1st	2nd	3rd	4th	5th	6th	♭7(B♭)
	♭9(D♭)		11th		13th	

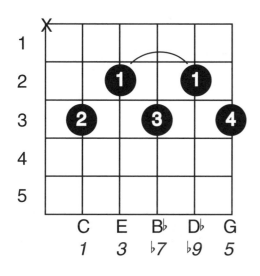

C | E | B♭ | D♭ | G
1 | 3 | ♭7 | ♭9 | 5

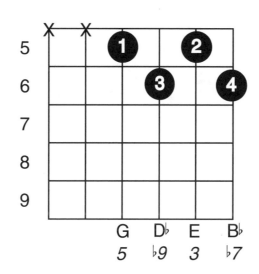

G | D♭ | E | B♭
5 | ♭9 | 3 | ♭7

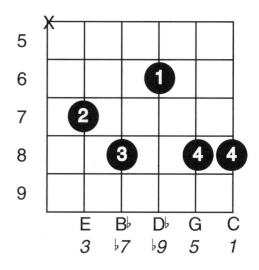

E | B♭ | D♭ | G | C
3 | ♭7 | ♭9 | 5 | 1

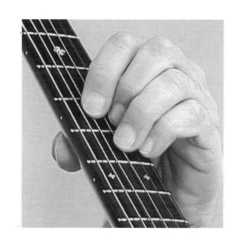

C
7#9

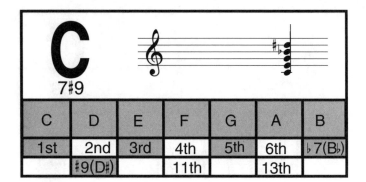

C	D	E	F	G	A	B
1st	2nd	3rd	4th	5th	6th	♭7(B♭)
	#9(D#)		11th		13th	

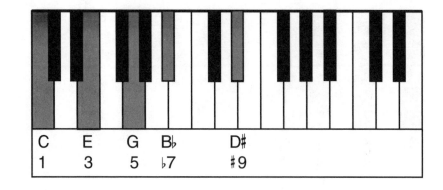

C   E   G   B♭   D#
1   3   5   ♭7   #9

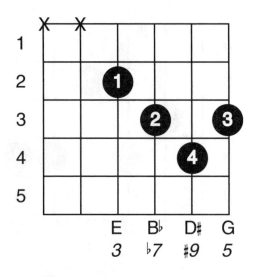

E B♭ D# G
3 ♭7 #9 5

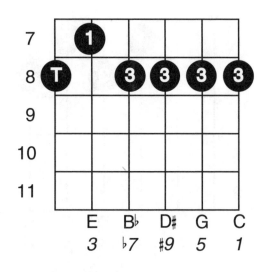

E B♭ D# G C
3 ♭7 #9 5 1

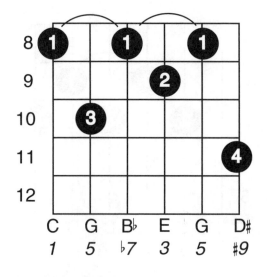

C G B♭ E G D#
1 5 ♭7 3 5 #9

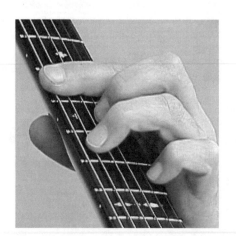

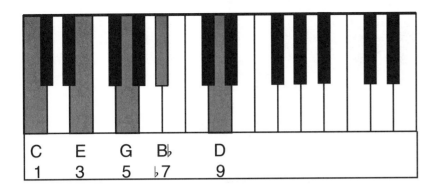

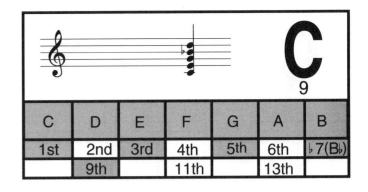

C	D	E	F	G	A	B
1st	2nd	3rd	4th	5th	6th	♭7(B♭)
	9th		11th		13th	

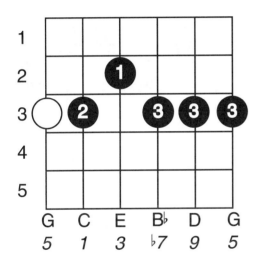

G C E B♭ D G
5 1 3 ♭7 9 5

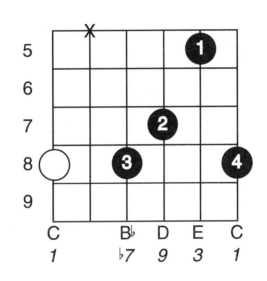

C B♭ D E C
1 ♭7 9 3 1

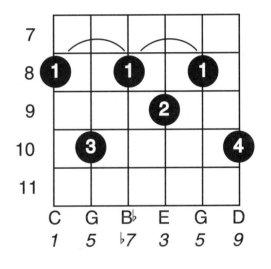

C G B♭ E G D
1 5 ♭7 3 5 9

C
9♭5

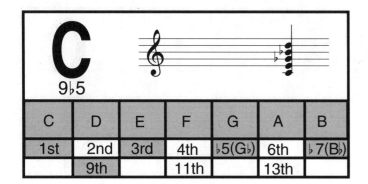

C	D	E	F	G	A	B
1st	2nd	3rd	4th	♭5(G♭)	6th	♭7(B♭)
	9th		11th		13th	

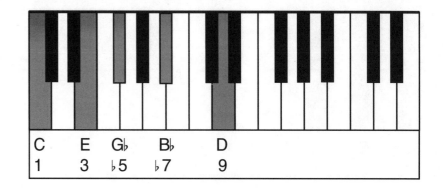

C	E	G♭	B♭	D
1	3	♭5	♭7	9

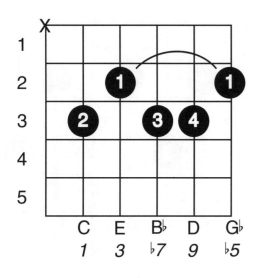

C E B♭ D G♭
1 3 ♭7 9 ♭5

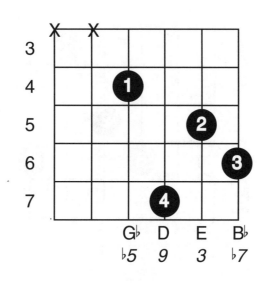

G♭ D E B♭
♭5 9 3 ♭7

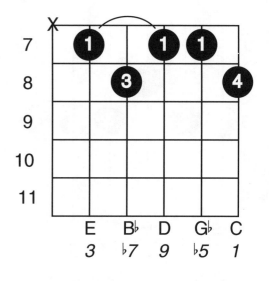

E B♭ D G♭ C
3 ♭7 9 ♭5 1

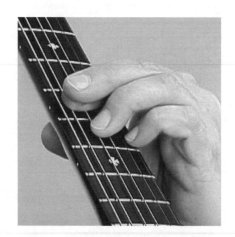

108

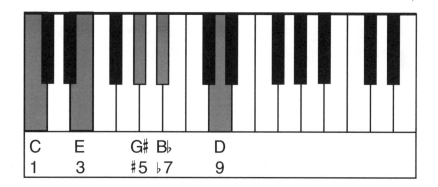

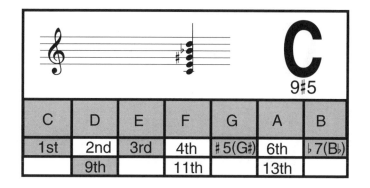

C 9#5

C	D	E	F	G	A	B
1st	2nd	3rd	4th	#5(G#)	6th	♭7(B♭)
	9th		11th		13th	

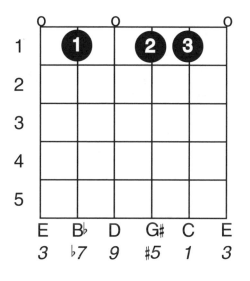

E B♭ D G# C E
3 ♭7 9 #5 1 3

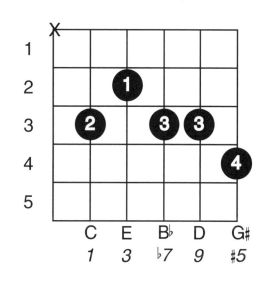

C E B♭ D G#
1 3 ♭7 9 #5

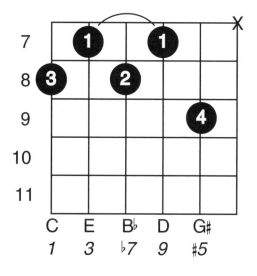

C E B♭ D G#
1 3 ♭7 9 #5

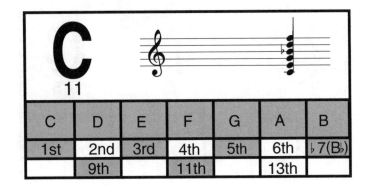

C
11

C	D	E	F	G	A	B
1st	2nd	3rd	4th	5th	6th	♭7(B♭)
	9th		11th		13th	

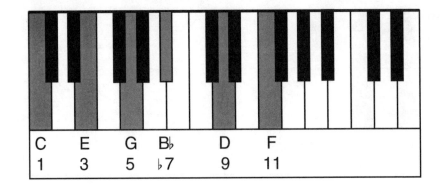

C	E	G	B♭	D	F
1	3	5	♭7	9	11

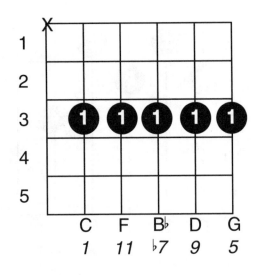

C	F	B♭	D	G
1	11	♭7	9	5

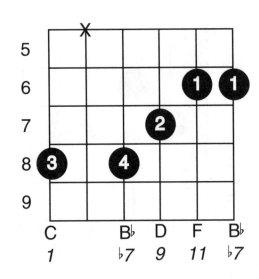

C		B♭	D	F	B♭
1		♭7	9	11	♭7

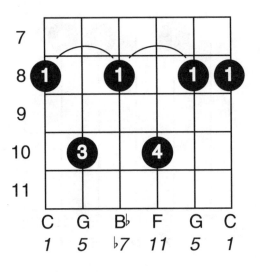

C	G	B♭	F	G	C
1	5	♭7	11	5	1

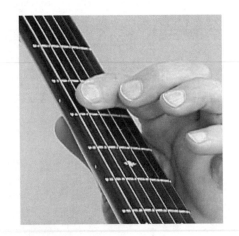

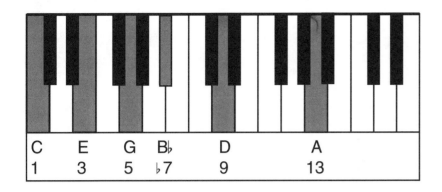

C E G B♭ D A
1 3 5 ♭7 9 13

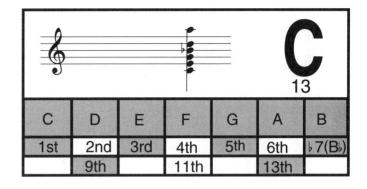

C
13

C	D	E	F	G	A	B
1st	2nd	3rd	4th	5th	6th	♭7(B♭)
	9th		11th		13th	

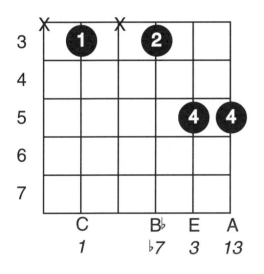

3
4
5
6
7

C   B♭ E A
1   ♭7 3 13

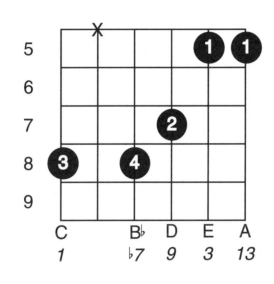

5
6
7
8
9

C   B♭ D E A
1   ♭7 9 3 13

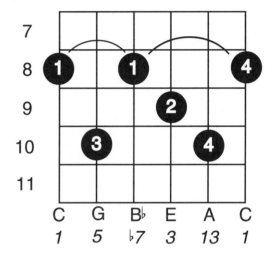

7
8
9
10
11

C G B♭ E A C
1 5 ♭7 3 13 1

111

C

13♭5♭9

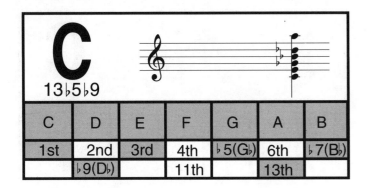

C	D	E	F	G	A	B
1st	2nd	3rd	4th	♭5(G♭)	6th	♭7(B♭)
	♭9(D♭)		11th		13th	

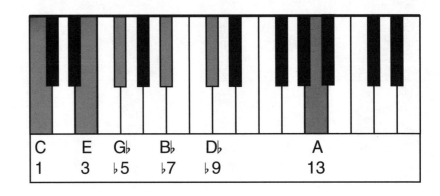

C	E	G♭	B♭	D♭		A	
1	3	♭5	♭7	♭9		13	

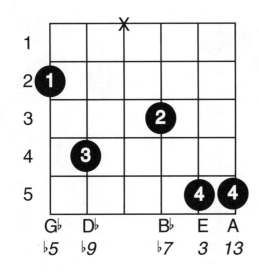

		G♭	D♭		B♭	E	A
		♭5	♭9		♭7	3	13

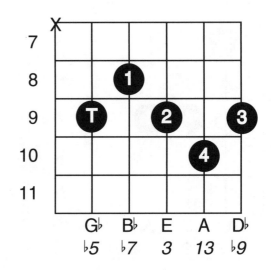

	G♭	B♭	E	A	D♭
	♭5	♭7	3	13	♭9

112

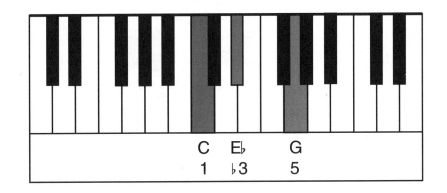

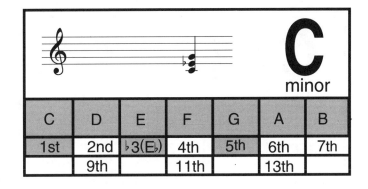

C	D	E	F	G	A	B
1st	2nd	♭3(E♭)	4th	5th	6th	7th
	9th		11th		13th	

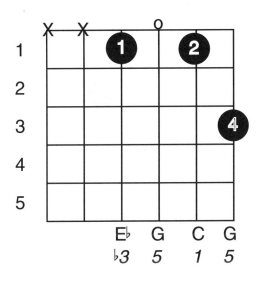

E♭ G   C   G
♭3 5   1   5

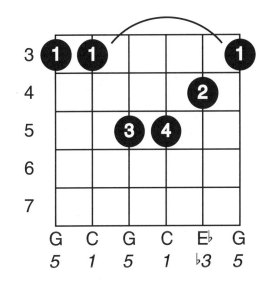

G   C   G   C   E♭ G
5   1   5   1   ♭3 5

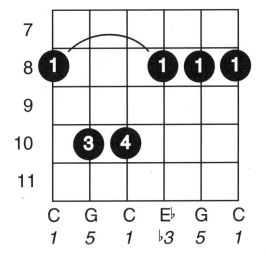

C   G   C   E♭ G   C
1   5   1   ♭3 5   1

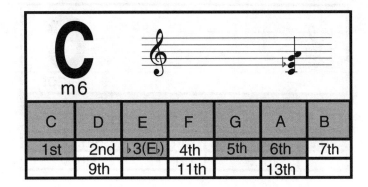

C
m6

C	D	E	F	G	A	B
1st	2nd	♭3(E♭)	4th	5th	6th	7th
	9th		11th		13th	

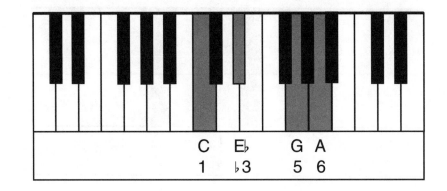

C E♭   G A
1 ♭3   5 6

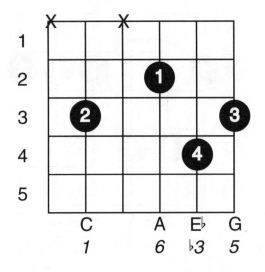

```
        x       x
1
2               1
3       2               3
4               4
5
        C       A  E♭  G
        1       6  ♭3  5
```

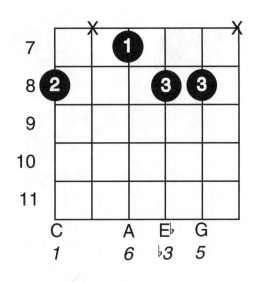

```
        x   1       x
7
8   2           3   3
9
10
11
    C       A   E♭  G
    1       6   ♭3  5
```

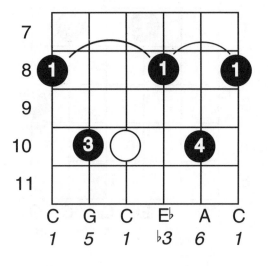

```
7
8   1           1       1
9
10      3   ○       4
11
    C   G   C   E♭  A   C
    1   5   1   ♭3  6   1
```

114

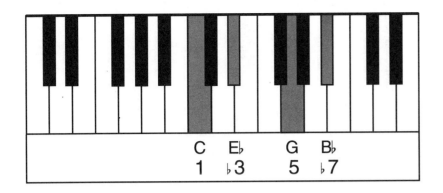

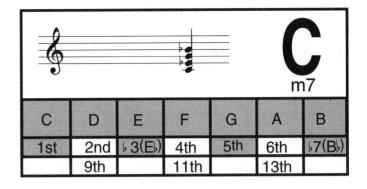

C	D	E	F	G	A	B
1st	2nd	♭3(E♭)	4th	5th	6th	♭7(B♭)
	9th		11th		13th	

C E♭ G B♭
1 ♭3 5 ♭7

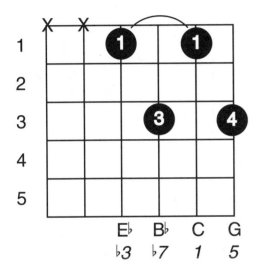

E♭   B♭   C   G
♭3   ♭7   1   5

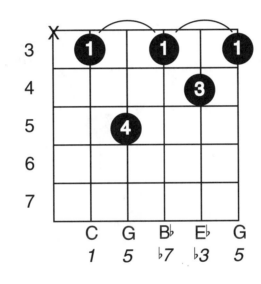

C   G   B♭   E♭   G
1   5   ♭7   ♭3   5

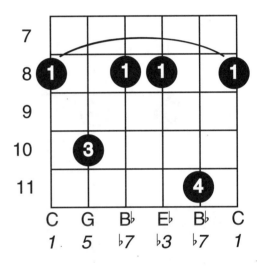

C   G   B♭   E♭   B♭   C
1   5   ♭7   ♭3   ♭7   1

C

m7♭5

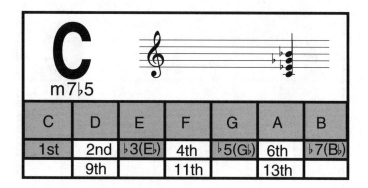

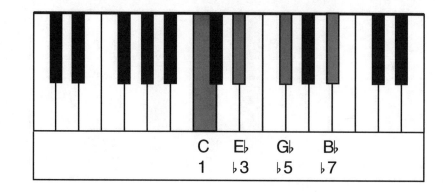

C	D	E	F	G	A	B
1st	2nd	♭3(E♭)	4th	♭5(G♭)	6th	♭7(B♭)
	9th		11th		13th	

C E♭ G♭ B♭
1 ♭3 ♭5 ♭7

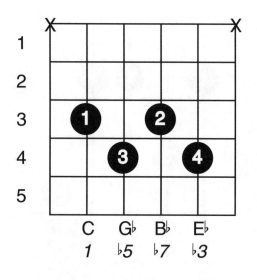

C G♭ B♭ E♭
1 *♭5* *♭7* *♭3*

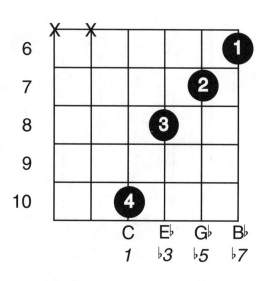

C E♭ G♭ B♭
1 *♭3* *♭5* *♭7*

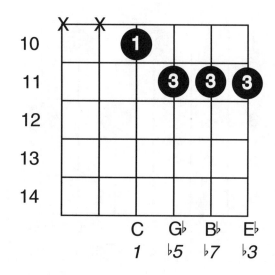

C G♭ B♭ E♭
1 *♭5* *♭7* *♭3*

116

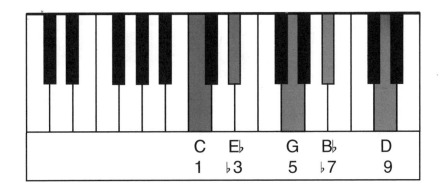

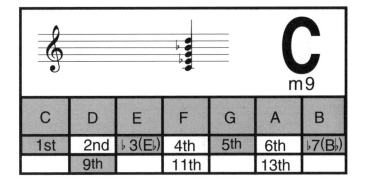

C m9

C	D	E	F	G	A	B
1st	2nd	♭3 (E♭)	4th	5th	6th	♭7 (B♭)
	9th		11th		13th	

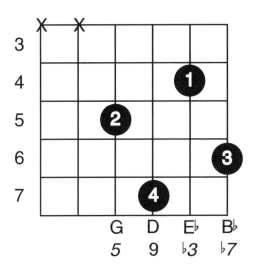

G 5 D 9 E♭ ♭3 B♭ ♭7

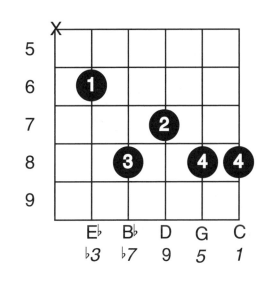

E♭ ♭3 B♭ ♭7 D 9 G 5 C 1

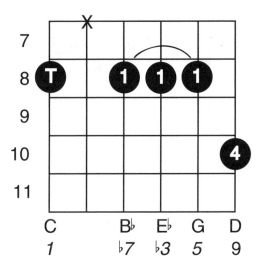

C 1 B♭ ♭7 E♭ ♭3 G 5 D 9

C
dim 7

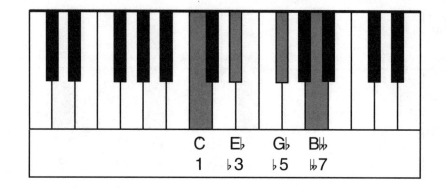

C	D	E	F	G	A	B
1st	2nd	♭3(E♭)	4th	♭5(G♭)	6th	♭♭7(B♭♭)
	9th		11th		13th	

C   E♭   G♭   B♭♭
1   ♭3   ♭5   ♭♭7

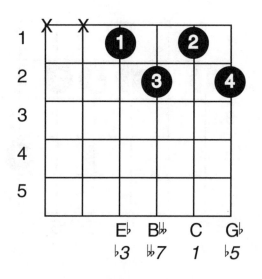

E♭   B♭♭   C   G♭
♭3   ♭♭7   1   ♭5

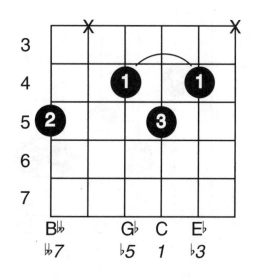

B♭♭   G♭   C   E♭
♭♭7   ♭5   1   ♭3

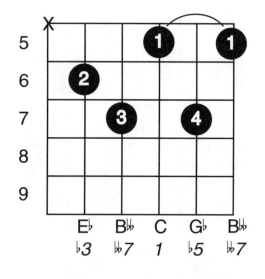

E♭   B♭♭   C   G♭   B♭♭
♭3   ♭♭7   1   ♭5   ♭♭7

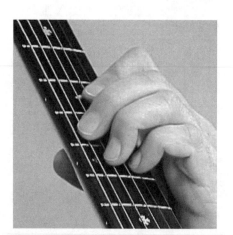

118

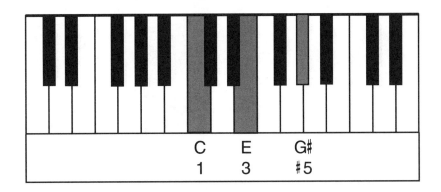

C 1
E 3
G# #5

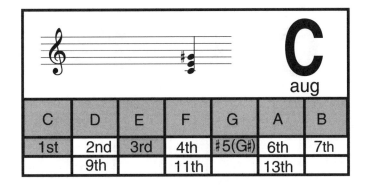

C	D	E	F	G	A	B
1st	2nd	3rd	4th	#5(G#)	6th	7th
	9th		11th		13th	

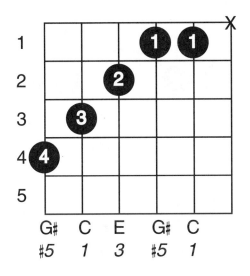

G# #5 | C 1 | E 3 | G# #5 | C 1

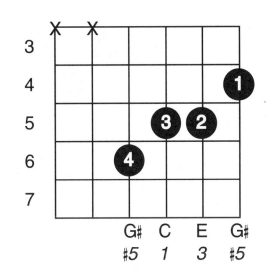

G# #5 | C 1 | E 3 | G# #5

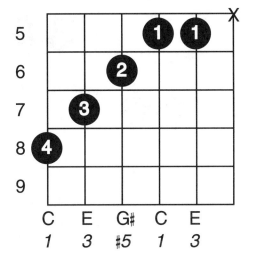

C 1 | E 3 | G# #5 | C 1 | E 3

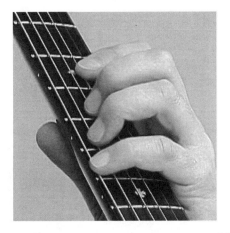

119

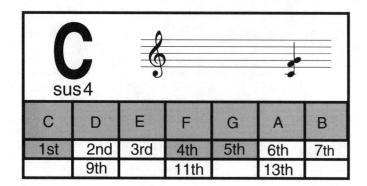

C	D	E	F	G	A	B
1st	2nd	3rd	4th	5th	6th	7th
	9th		11th		13th	

C sus 4

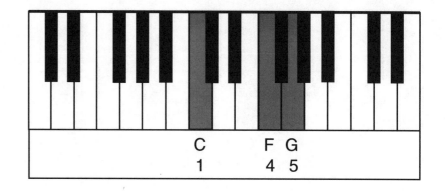

C   F G
1   4 5

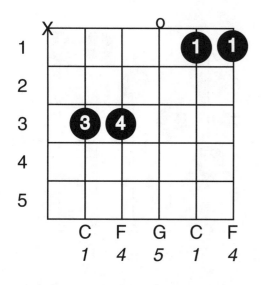

C   F   G   C   F
1   *4*   *5*   *1*   *4*

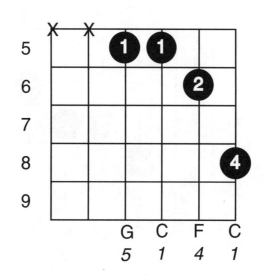

G   C   F   C
5   *1*   *4*   *1*

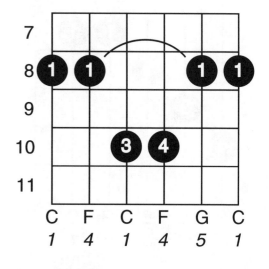

C   F   C   F   G   C
1   *4*   *1*   *4*   *5*   *1*

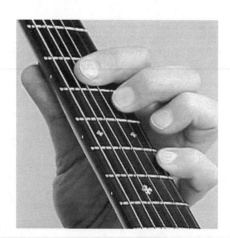

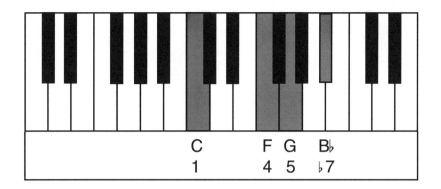

C 1   F 4   G 5   B♭ ♭7

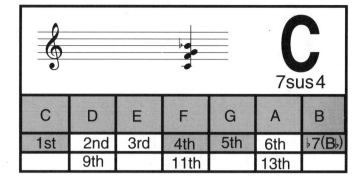

C 7sus4

C	D	E	F	G	A	B
1st	2nd	3rd	4th	5th	6th	♭7(B♭)
	9th		11th		13th	

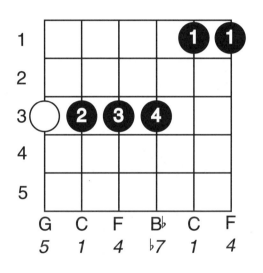

G	C	F	B♭	C	F
5	1	4	♭7	1	4

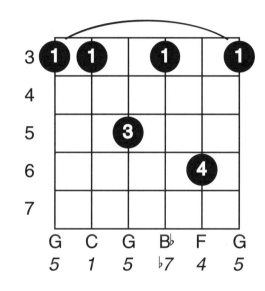

G	C	G	B♭	F	G
5	1	5	♭7	4	5

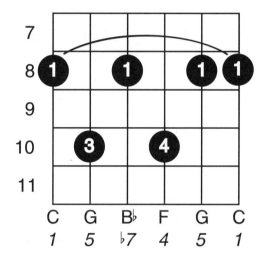

C	G	B♭	F	G	C
1	5	♭7	4	5	1

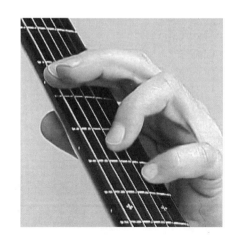

121

C#
Major

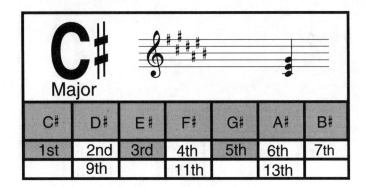

C#	D#	E#	F#	G#	A#	B#
1st	2nd	3rd	4th	5th	6th	7th
	9th		11th		13th	

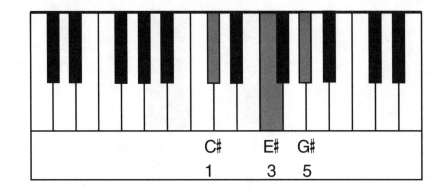

C# E# G#
1   3   5

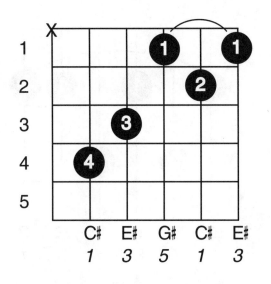

C# E# G# C# E#
1   3   5   1   3

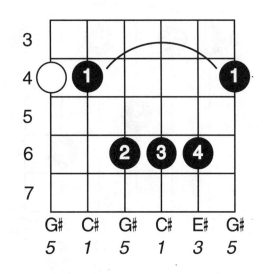

G# C# G# C# E# G#
5   1   5   1   3   5

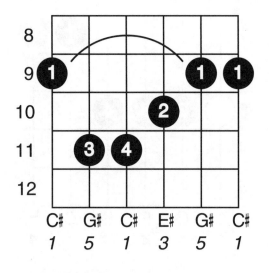

C# G# C# E# G# C#
1   5   1   3   5   1

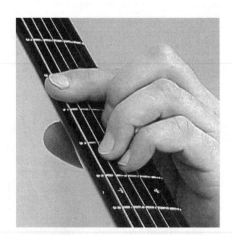

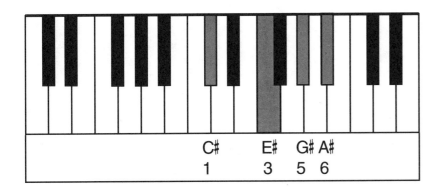

C# 1 E# 3 G# 5 A# 6

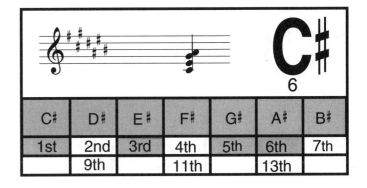

C#
6

C#	D#	E#	F#	G#	A#	B#
1st	2nd	3rd	4th	5th	6th	7th
	9th		11th		13th	

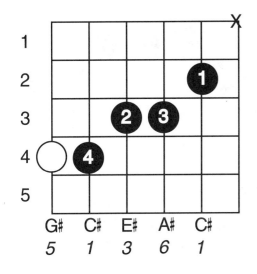

G#	C#	E#	A#	C#
5	*1*	*3*	*6*	*1*

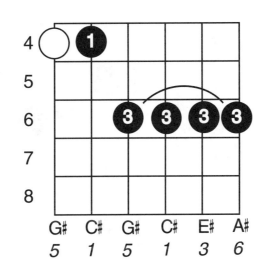

G#	C#	G#	C#	E#	A#
5	*1*	*5*	*1*	*3*	*6*

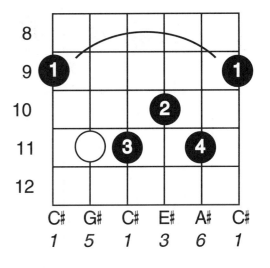

C#	G#	C#	E#	A#	C#
1	*5*	*1*	*3*	*6*	*1*

123

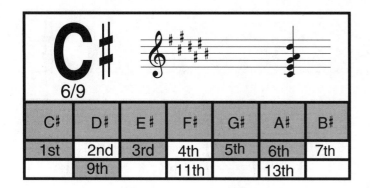

C# 6/9

C#	D#	E#	F#	G#	A#	B#
1st	2nd	3rd	4th	5th	6th	7th
	9th		11th		13th	

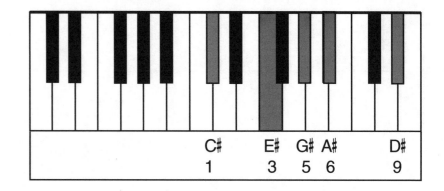

							C#		E#	G#	A#		D#
							1		3	5	6		9

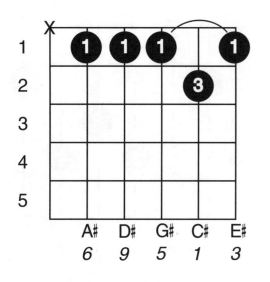

A#	D#	G#	C#	E#
6	*9*	*5*	*1*	*3*

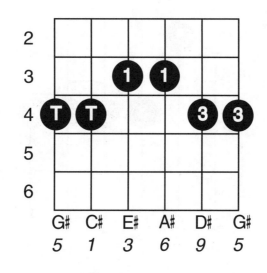

G#	C#	E#	A#	D#	G#
5	*1*	*3*	*6*	*9*	*5*

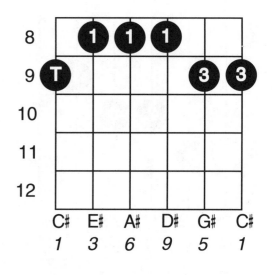

C#	E#	A#	D#	G#	C#
1	*3*	*6*	*9*	*5*	*1*

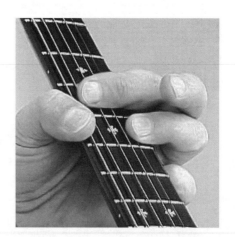

124

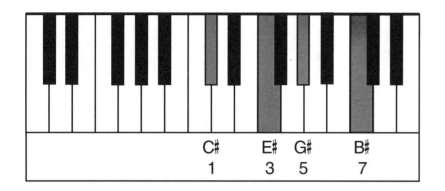

C# 1   E# 3   G# 5   B# 7

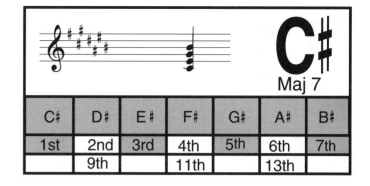

C# Maj 7

C#	D#	E#	F#	G#	A#	B#
1st	2nd	3rd	4th	5th	6th	7th
	9th		11th		13th	

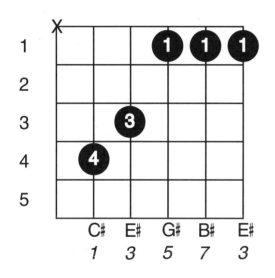

1
2
3
4
5

C# E# G# B# E#
1   3   5   7   3

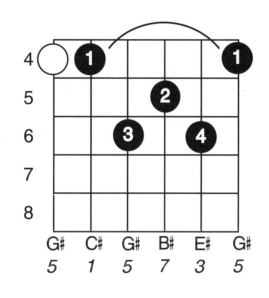

4
5
6
7
8

G# C# G# B# E# G#
5   1   5   7   3   5

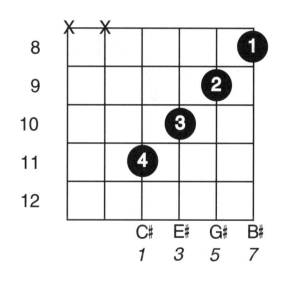

8
9
10
11
12

C# E# G# B#
1   3   5   7

125

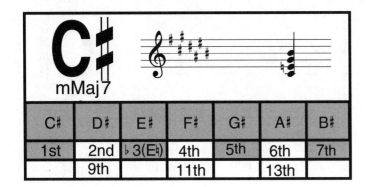

C♯
mMaj7

C#	D#	E#	F#	G#	A#	B#
1st	2nd	♭3(E♮)	4th	5th	6th	7th
	9th		11th		13th	

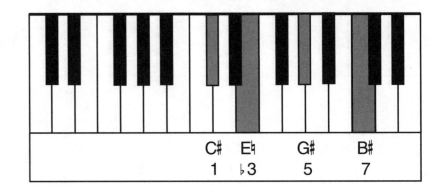

C# E♮ G# B#
1   ♭3   5   7

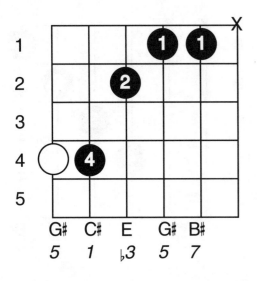

1	
2	
3	
4	
5	

G# C# E G# B#
5   1   ♭3   5   7

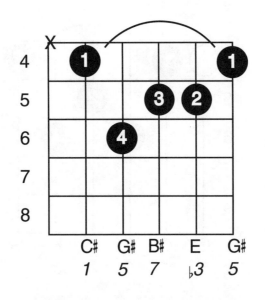

4	
5	
6	
7	
8	

C# G# B# E G#
1   5   7   ♭3   5

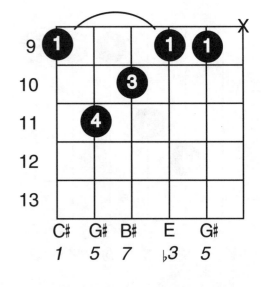

9	
10	
11	
12	
13	

C# G# B# E G#
1   5   7   ♭3   5

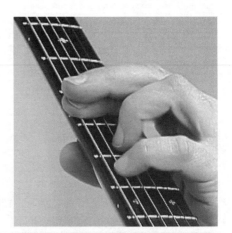

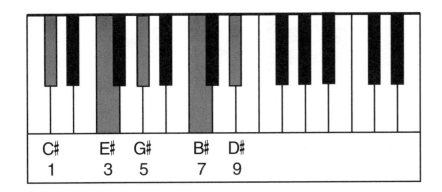

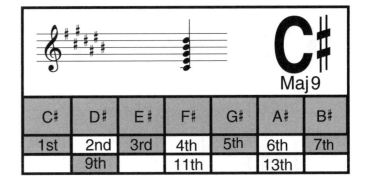

C#
Maj9

C#	D#	E#	F#	G#	A#	B#
1st	2nd	3rd	4th	5th	6th	7th
	9th		11th		13th	

Piano keys:
C# (1) E# (3) G# (5) B# (7) D# (9)

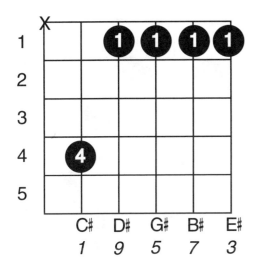

C# D# G# B# E#
1 *9* *5* *7* *3*

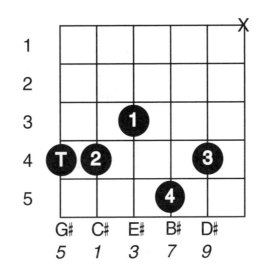

G# C# E# B# D#
5 *1* *3* *7* *9*

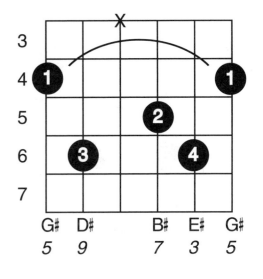

G# D# B# E# G#
5 *9* *7* *3* *5*

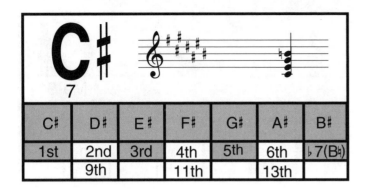

C#7

C#	D#	E#	F#	G#	A#	B#
1st	2nd	3rd	4th	5th	6th	♭7(B♮)
	9th		11th		13th	

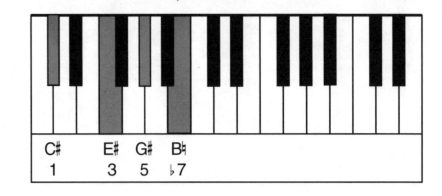

C#	E#	G#	B♮
1	3	5	♭7

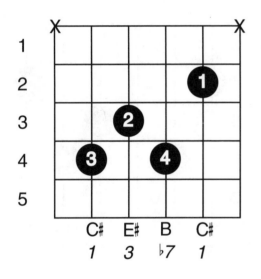

C#	E#	B	C#
1	*3*	*♭7*	*1*

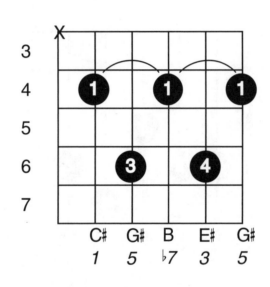

C#	G#	B	E#	G#
1	*5*	*♭7*	*3*	*5*

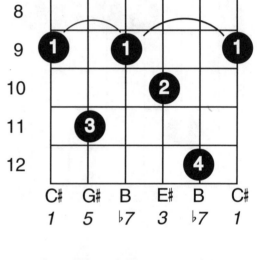

C#	G#	B	E#	B	C#
1	*5*	*♭7*	*3*	*♭7*	*1*

128

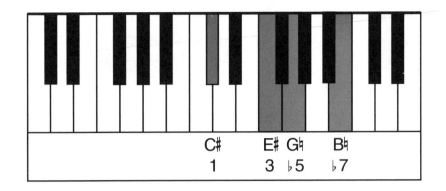

C# 7♭5

C# E# G♮ B♭
1   3 ♭5 ♭7

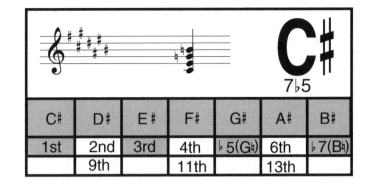

C#	D#	E #	F#	G#	A#	B#
1st	2nd	3rd	4th	♭5(G♮)	6th	♭7(B♮)
	9th		11th		13th	

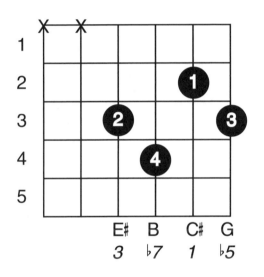

E# B   C# G
3 ♭7   1 ♭5

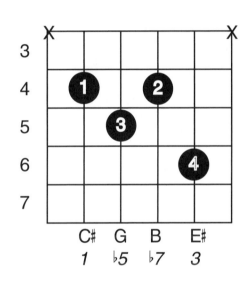

C# G   B   E#
1 ♭5 ♭7   3

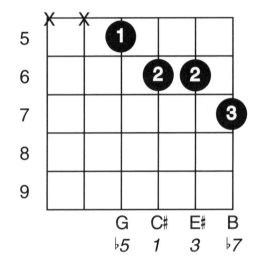

G   C# E# B
♭5   1   3 ♭7

129

C#

7#5

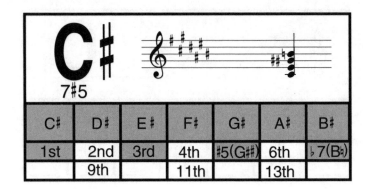

C#	D#	E#	F#	G#	A#	B#
1st	2nd	3rd	4th	#5(G##)	6th	♭7(B♮)
	9th		11th		13th	

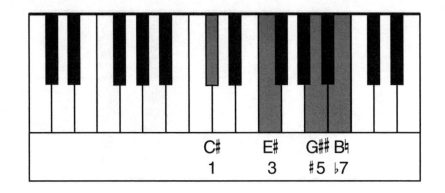

C#   E#   G## B♮
1   3   #5 ♭7

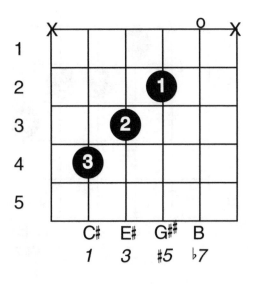

C#   E#   G##   B
1   *3*   *#5*   *♭7*

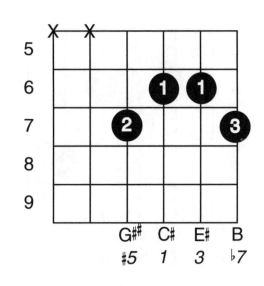

G## C# E#   B
#5 *1* *3* *♭7*

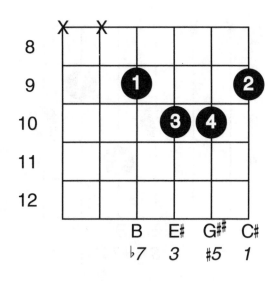

B   E# G## C#
♭7 *3* *#5* *1*

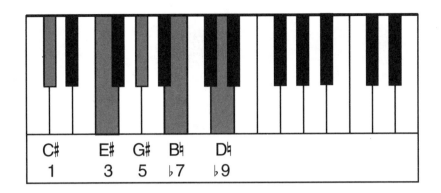

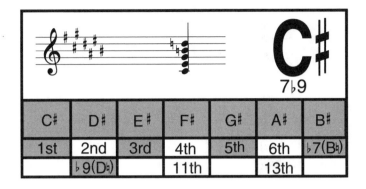

C#	D#	E#	F#	G#	A#	B#
1st	2nd	3rd	4th	5th	6th	♭7(B♭)
	♭9(D♮)		11th		13th	

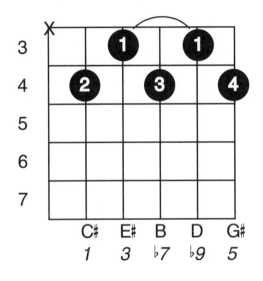

C# E# B D G#
1 *3* *♭7* *♭9* *5*

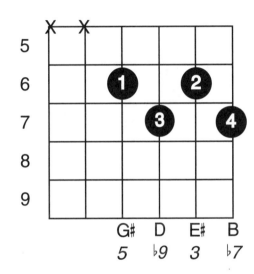

G# D E# B
5 *♭9* *3* *♭7*

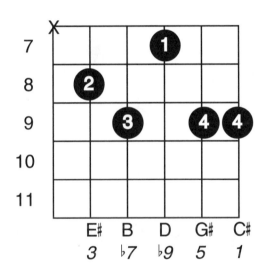

E# B D G# C#
3 *♭7* *♭9* *5* *1*

C♯
7♯9

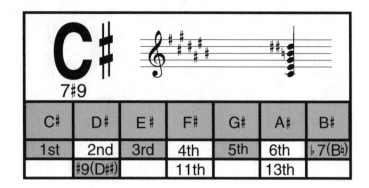

C♯	D♯	E♯	F♯	G♯	A♯	B♯
1st	2nd	3rd	4th	5th	6th	♭7(B♮)
	♯9(D♯♯)		11th		13th	

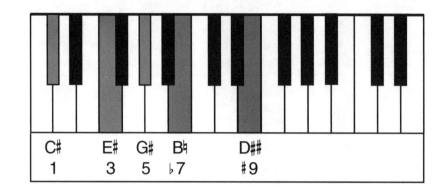

C♯   E♯   G♯   B♮   D♯♯
1   3   5   ♭7   ♯9

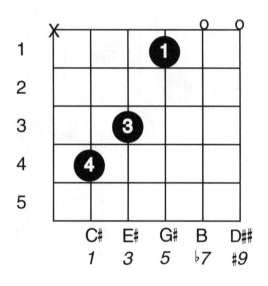

C♯   E♯   G♯   B   D♯♯
1   *3*   *5*   *♭7*   *♯9*

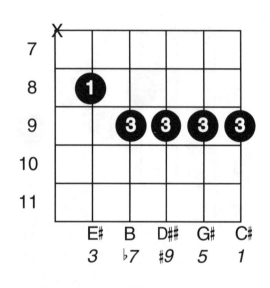

E♯   B   D♯♯   G♯   C♯
3   *♭7*   *♯9*   *5*   *1*

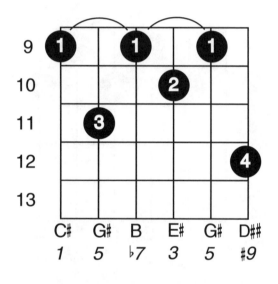

C♯   G♯   B   E♯   G♯   D♯♯
1   *5*   *♭7*   *3*   *5*   *♯9*

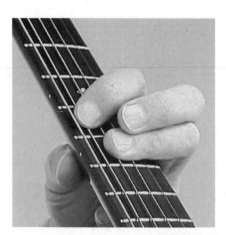

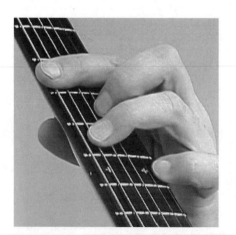

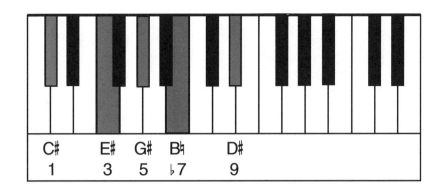

C# 1 · E# 3 · G# 5 · B♮ ♭7 · D# 9

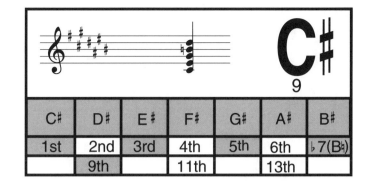

C#9

C#	D#	E#	F#	G#	A#	B#
1st	2nd	3rd	4th	5th	6th	♭7(B♮)
	9th		11th		13th	

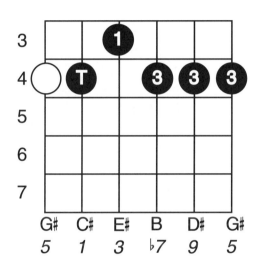

G# / C# / E# / B / D# / G#
5 / 1 / 3 / ♭7 / 9 / 5

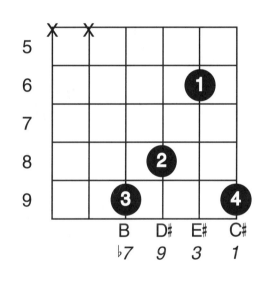

B / D# / E# / C#
♭7 / 9 / 3 / 1

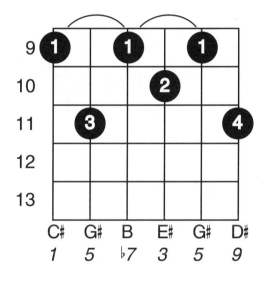

C# / G# / B / E# / G# / D#
1 / 5 / ♭7 / 3 / 5 / 9

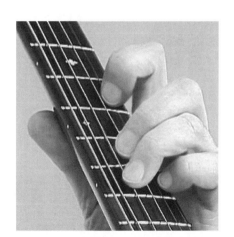

133

C♯
9♭5

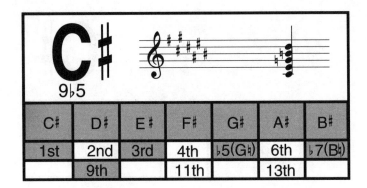

C♯	D♯	E♯	F♯	G♯	A♯	B♯
1st	2nd	3rd	4th	♭5(G♮)	6th	♭7(B♮)
	9th		11th		13th	

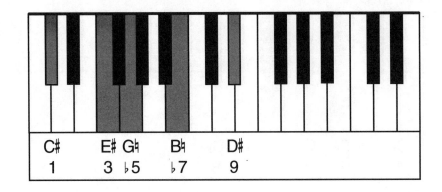

C♯   E♯ G♮   B♮   D♯
1   3 ♭5   ♭7   9

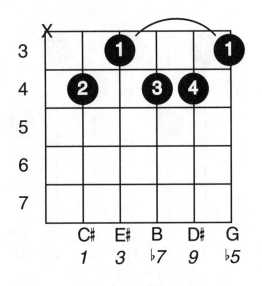

C♯   E♯   B   D♯   G
1   *3*   *♭7*   *9*   *♭5*

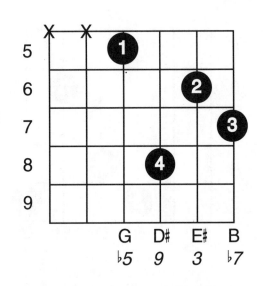

G   D♯   E♯   B
♭5   *9*   *3*   *♭7*

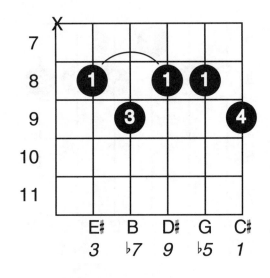

E♯   B   D♯   G   C♯
3   *♭7*   *9*   *♭5*   *1*

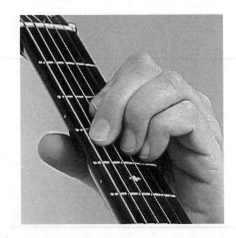

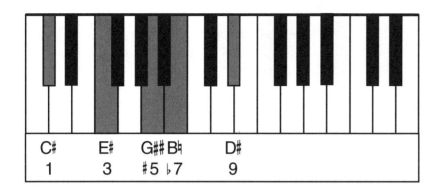

C# 1 · E# 3 · G## #5 · B♮ ♭7 · D# 9

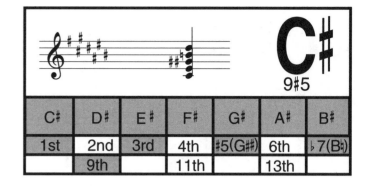

C#
9#5

C#	D#	E#	F#	G#	A#	B#
1st	2nd	3rd	4th	#5(G##)	6th	♭7(B♮)
	9th		11th		13th	

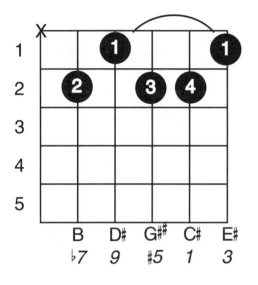

B	D#	G##	C#	E#
♭7	9	#5	1	3

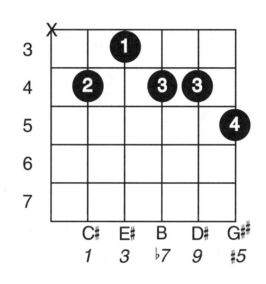

C#	E#	B	D#	G##
1	3	♭7	9	#5

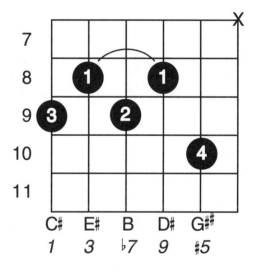

C#	E#	B	D#	G##
1	3	♭7	9	#5

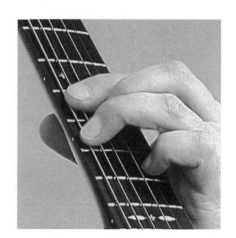

C# 11

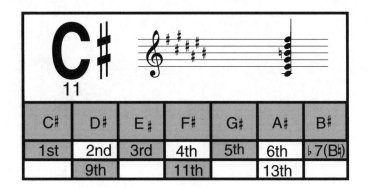

C#	D#	E#	F#	G#	A#	B#
1st	2nd	3rd	4th	5th	6th	♭7(B♮)
	9th		11th		13th	

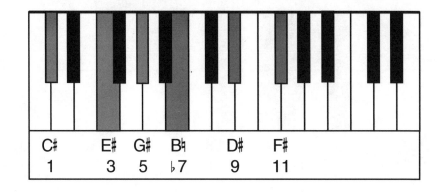

C#		E#	G#	B♮		D#	F#
1		3	5	♭7		9	11

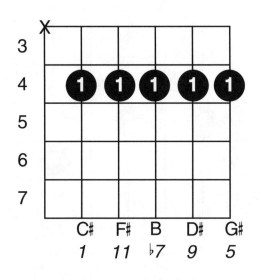

C#	F#	B	D#	G#
1	11	♭7	9	5

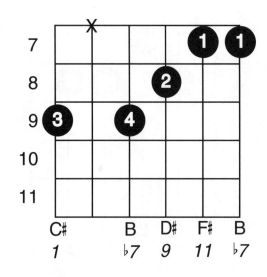

C#		B	D#	F#	B
1		♭7	9	11	♭7

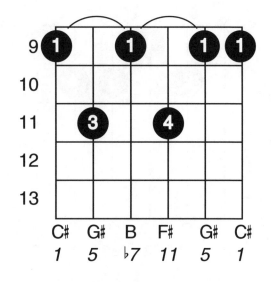

C#	G#	B	F#	G#	C#
1	5	♭7	11	5	1

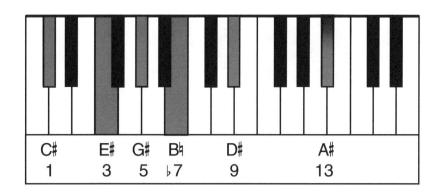

C# 1 E# 3 G# 5 B♭ ♭7 D# 9 A# 13

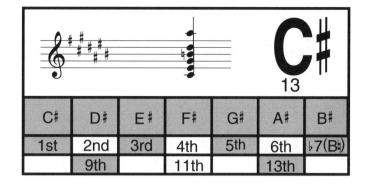

C#13

C#	D#	E#	F#	G#	A#	B#
1st	2nd	3rd	4th	5th	6th	♭7(B♭)
	9th		11th		13th	

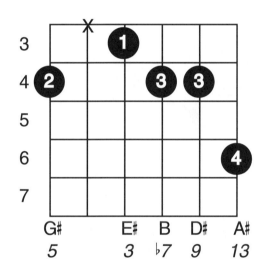

G#		E#	B	D#	A#
5		3	♭7	9	13

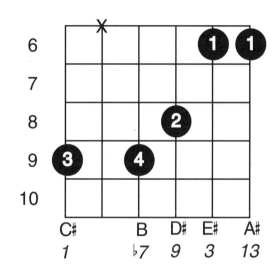

C#		B	D#	E#	A#
1		♭7	9	3	13

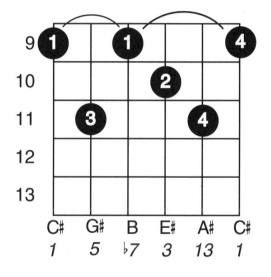

C#	G#	B	E#	A#	C#
1	5	♭7	3	13	1

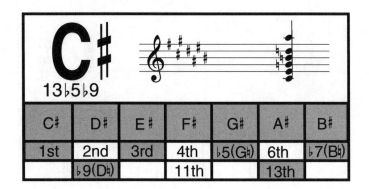

C# 13♭5♭9

C#	D#	E#	F#	G#	A#	B#
1st	2nd	3rd	4th	♭5(G♮)	6th	♭7(B♮)
	♭9(D♮)		11th		13th	

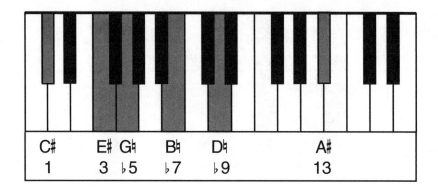

C#		E#	G♮	B♮	D♮		A#	
1		3	♭5	♭7	♭9		13	

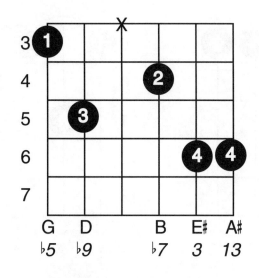

	G	D		B	E#	A#
	♭5	♭9		♭7	3	13

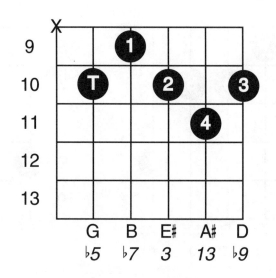

	G	B	E#	A#	D
	♭5	♭7	3	13	♭9

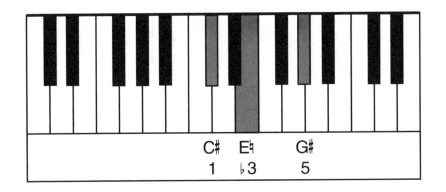

C#, E♮, G#
1 ♭3 5

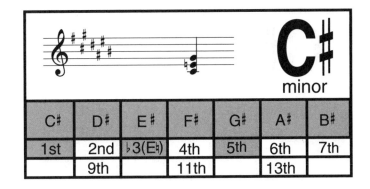

C#
minor

C#	D#	E#	F#	G#	A#	B#
1st	2nd	♭3(E♮)	4th	5th	6th	7th
	9th		11th		13th	

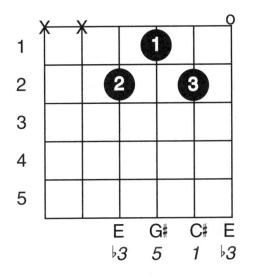

```
x  x              o
1         1
2     2       3
3
4
5
```
E   G#   C#   E
♭3   5   1   ♭3

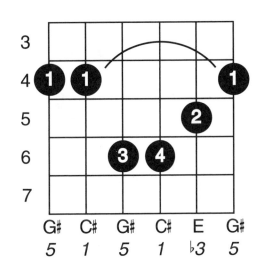

```
3
4  1  1          1
5              2
6        3  4
7
```
G#   C#   G#   C#   E   G#
5   1   5   1   ♭3   5

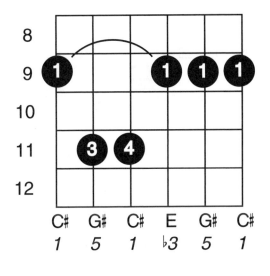

```
8
9  1        1  1  1
10
11    3  4
12
```
C#   G#   C#   E   G#   C#
1   5   1   ♭3   5   1

C♯
m6

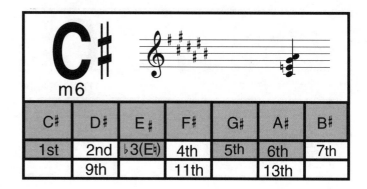

C♯	D♯	E♯	F♯	G♯	A♯	B♯
1st	2nd	♭3(E♮)	4th	5th	6th	7th
	9th		11th		13th	

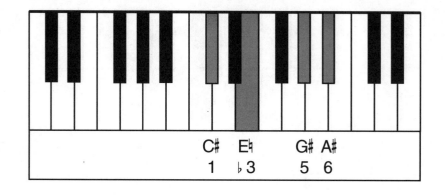

C♯ E♮ G♯ A♯
1   ♭3 5   6

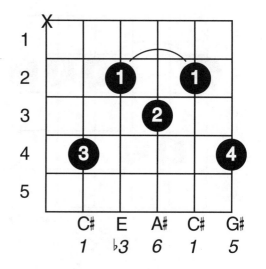

C♯   E   A♯   C♯   G♯
1   ♭3   6   1   5

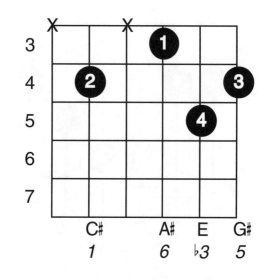

C♯   A♯   E   G♯
1   6   ♭3   5

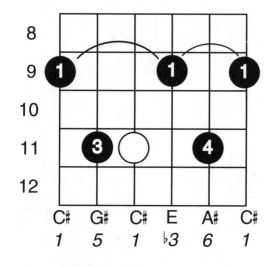

C♯   G♯   C♯   E   A♯   C♯
1   5   1   ♭3   6   1

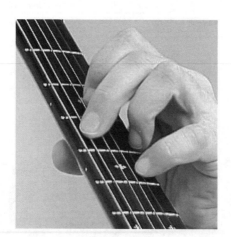

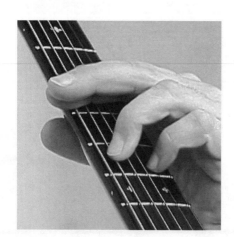

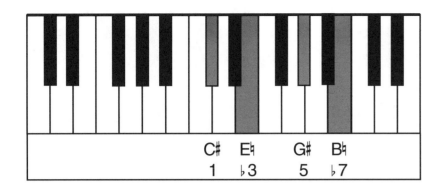

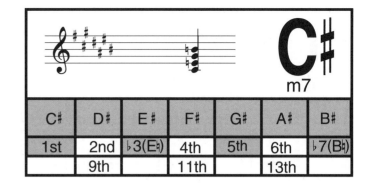

C#m7

C#	D#	E#	F#	G#	A#	B#
1st	2nd	♭3(E♮)	4th	5th	6th	♭7(B♮)
	9th		11th		13th	

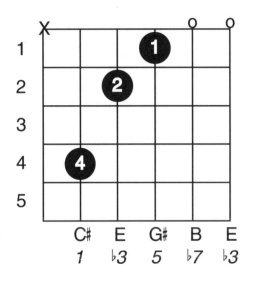

C#	E	G#	B	E
1	*♭3*	*5*	*♭7*	*♭3*

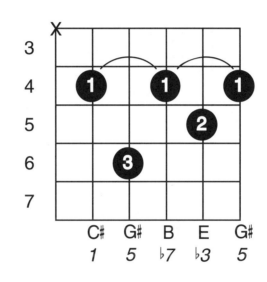

C#	G#	B	E	G#
1	*5*	*♭7*	*♭3*	*5*

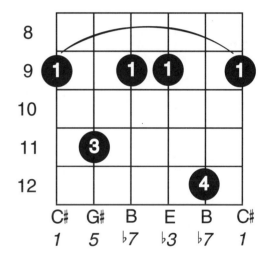

C#	G#	B	E	B	C#
1	*5*	*♭7*	*♭3*	*♭7*	*1*

141

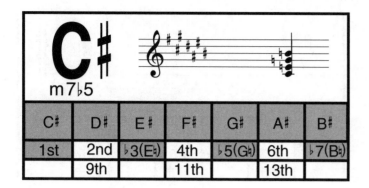

C#
m7♭5

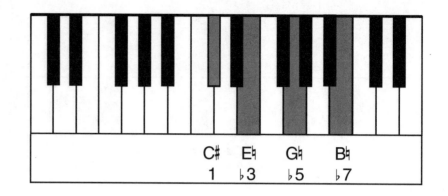

C#	D#	E#	F#	G#	A#	B#
1st	2nd	♭3(E♮)	4th	♭5(G♮)	6th	♭7(B♮)
	9th		11th		13th	

	C#	E♮	G♮	B♮
	1	♭3	♭5	♭7

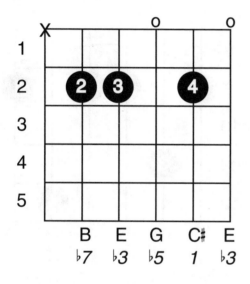

	B	E	G	C#	E
	♭7	♭3	♭5	1	♭3

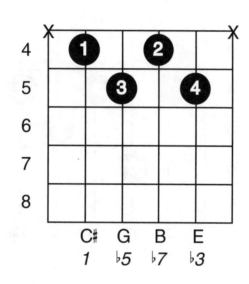

	C#	G	B	E
	1	♭5	♭7	♭3

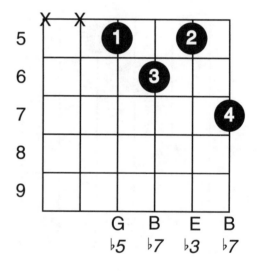

	G	B	E	B
	♭5	♭7	♭3	♭7

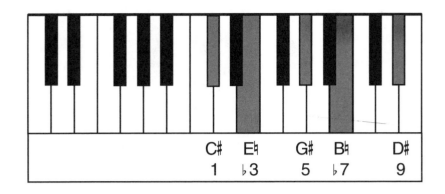

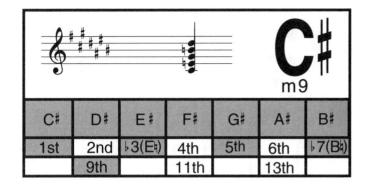

C#	D#	E#	F#	G#	A#	B#
1st	2nd	♭3(E♮)	4th	5th	6th	♭7(B♮)
	9th		11th		13th	

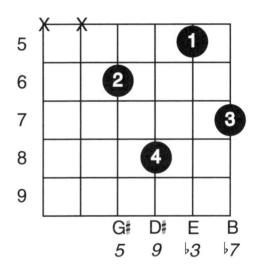

G# D# E B
5 *9* *♭3* *♭7*

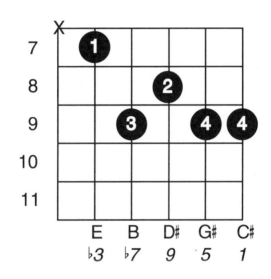

E B D# G# C#
♭3 *♭7* *9* *5* *1*

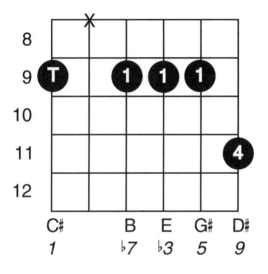

C# B E G# D#
1 *♭7* *♭3* *5* *9*

143

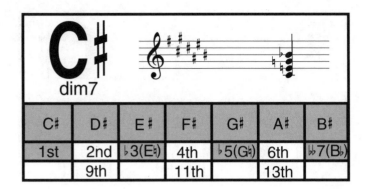

C♯
dim7

C♯	D♯	E♯	F♯	G♯	A♯	B♯
1st	2nd	♭3(E♮)	4th	♭5(G♮)	6th	♭♭7(B♭)
	9th		11th		13th	

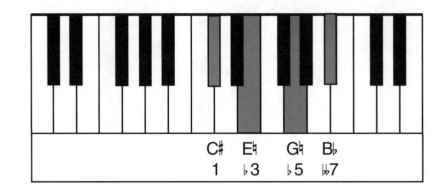

C♯   E♮   G♮   B♭
1   ♭3   ♭5   ♭♭7

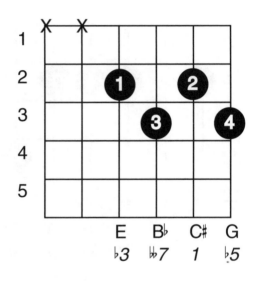

E   B♭   C♯   G
♭3   ♭♭7   1   ♭5

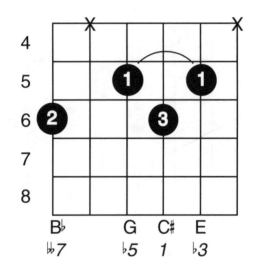

B♭   G   C♯   E
♭♭7   ♭5   1   ♭3

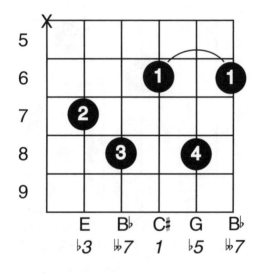

E   B♭   C♯   G   B♭
♭3   ♭♭7   1   ♭5   ♭♭7

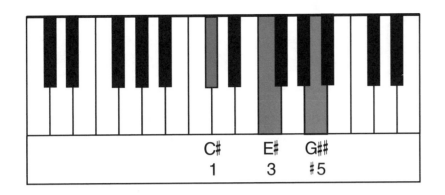

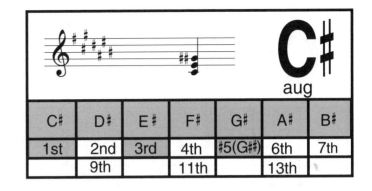

C#
aug

C#	D#	E#	F#	G#	A#	B#
1st	2nd	3rd	4th	#5(G##)	6th	7th
	9th		11th		13th	

C# E# G##
1   3   #5

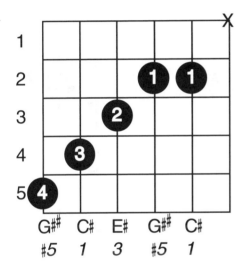

```
1

2          1    1

3        2

4      3

5    4
```
G## C# E# G## C#
#5   1   3   #5   1

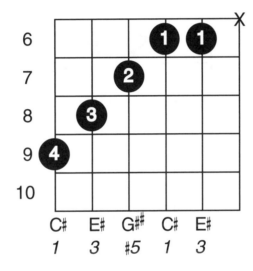

```
6              1    1

7           2

8         3

9    4

10
```
C# E# G## C# E#
1   3   #5   1   3

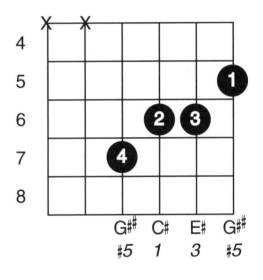

```
4

5                    1

6            2    3

7        4

8
```
G## C# E# G##
#5   1   3   #5

C#
sus4

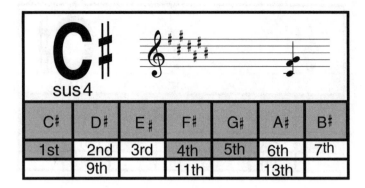

C#	D#	E#	F#	G#	A#	B#
1st	2nd	3rd	4th	5th	6th	7th
	9th		11th		13th	

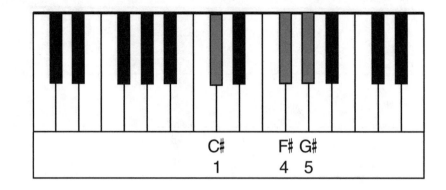

C# F# G#
1   4 5

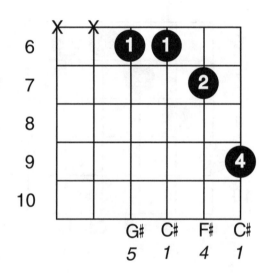

C# F# G# C#
1 4 5 1

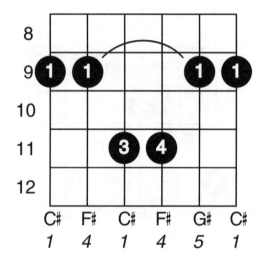

G# C# F# C#
5 1 4 1

G# C# F# C#
5 1 4 1

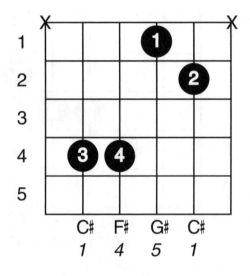

C# F# C# F# G# C#
1 4 1 4 5 1

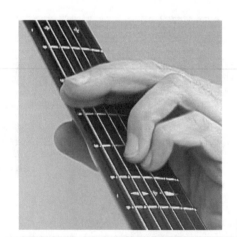

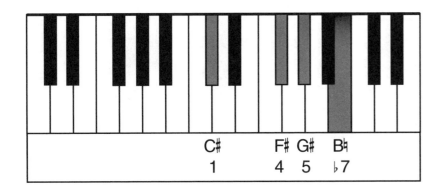

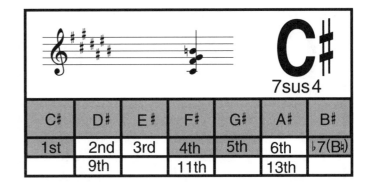

C#
7sus4

C#	D#	E#	F#	G#	A#	B#
1st	2nd	3rd	4th	5th	6th	♭7(B♮)
	9th		11th		13th	

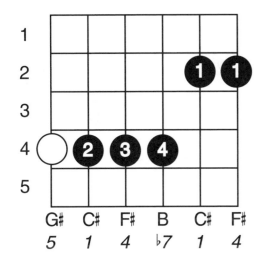

G#	C#	F#	B	C#	F#
5	*1*	*4*	*♭7*	*1*	*4*

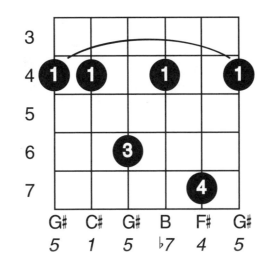

G#	C#	G#	B	F#	G#
5	*1*	*5*	*♭7*	*4*	*5*

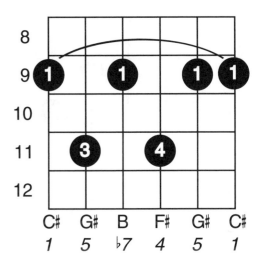

C#	G#	B	F#	G#	C#
1	*5*	*♭7*	*4*	*5*	*1*

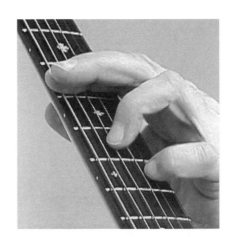

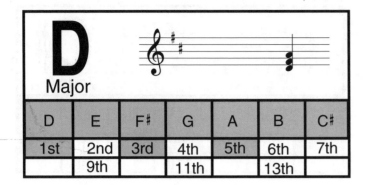

D
Major

D	E	F#	G	A	B	C#
1st	2nd	3rd	4th	5th	6th	7th
	9th		11th		13th	

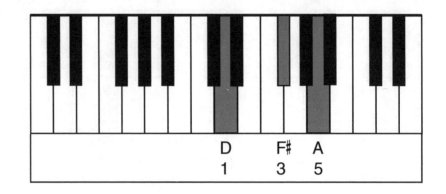

D   F#   A
1   3   5

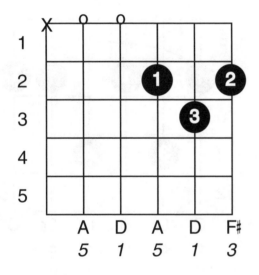

A D A D F#
5 1 5 1 3

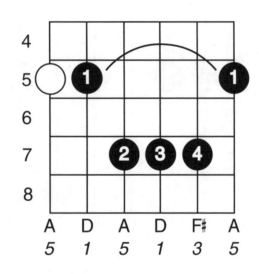

A D A D F# A
5 1 5 1 3 5

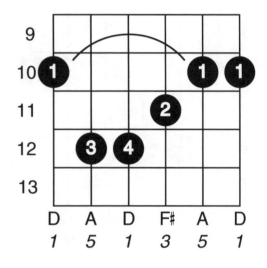

D A D F# A D
1 5 1 3 5 1

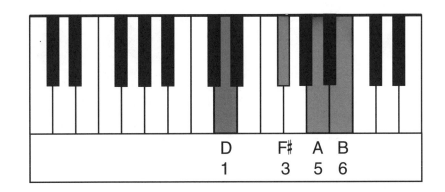

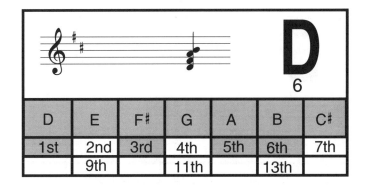

D

6

D	E	F#	G	A	B	C#
1st	2nd	3rd	4th	5th	6th	7th
	9th		11th		13th	

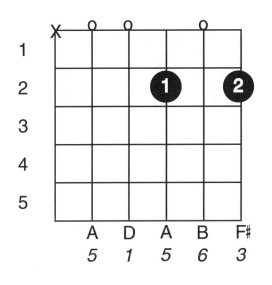

A   D   A   B   F#
5   1   5   6   3

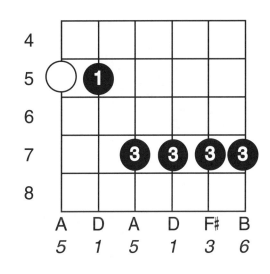

A   D   A   D   F#   B
5   1   5   1   3   6

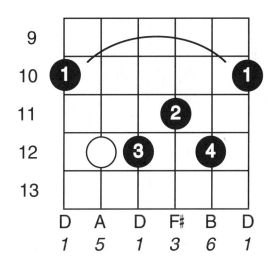

D   A   D   F#   B   D
1   5   1   3   6   1

149

D
6/9

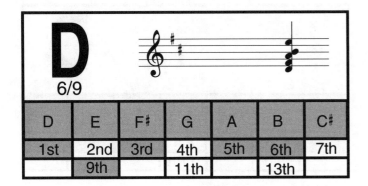

D	E	F#	G	A	B	C#
1st	2nd	3rd	4th	5th	6th	7th
	9th		11th		13th	

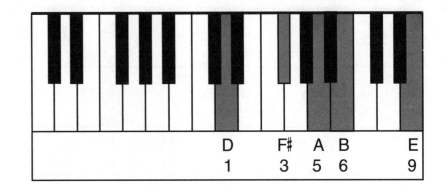

				D		F#	A	B			E
				1		3	5	6			9

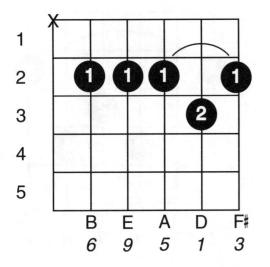

B	E	A	D	F#
6	*9*	*5*	*1*	*3*

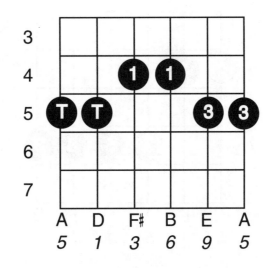

A	D	F#	B	E	A
5	*1*	*3*	*6*	*9*	*5*

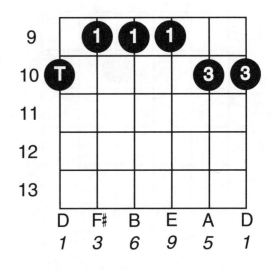

D	F#	B	E	A	D
1	*3*	*6*	*9*	*5*	*1*

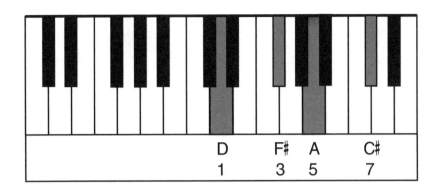

D
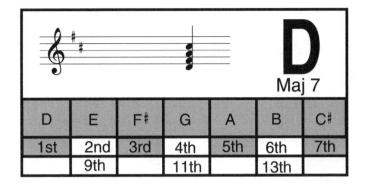

Maj 7

D	E	F#	G	A	B	C#
1st	2nd	3rd	4th	5th	6th	7th
	9th		11th		13th	

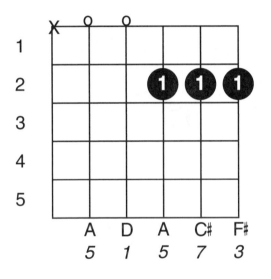

A　D　A　C#　F#
5　1　5　7　3

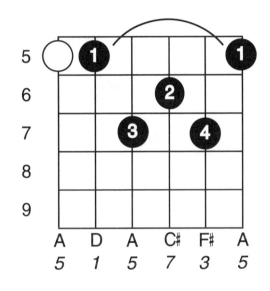

A　D　A　C#　F#　A
5　1　5　7　3　5

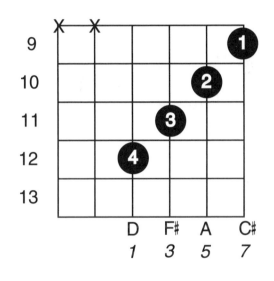

D　F#　A　C#
1　3　5　7

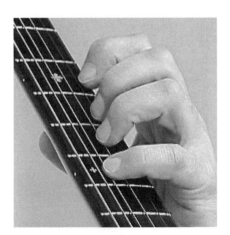

151

D

mMaj7

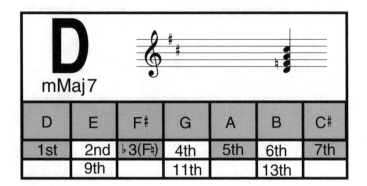

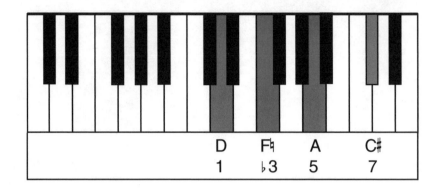

D	E	F#	G	A	B	C#
1st	2nd	♭3(F♮)	4th	5th	6th	7th
	9th		11th		13th	

Piano keyboard:

D	F♮	A	C#
1	♭3	5	7

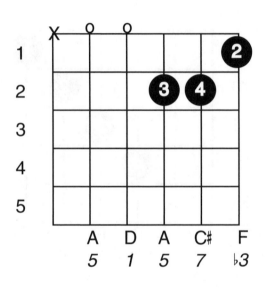

A	D	A	C#	F
5	1	5	7	♭3

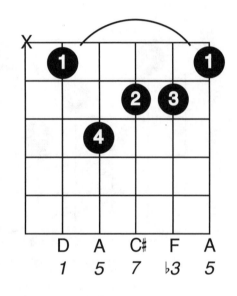

D	A	C#	F	A
1	5	7	♭3	5

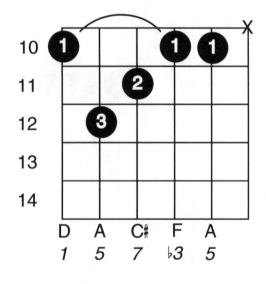

D	A	C#	F	A
1	5	7	♭3	5

152

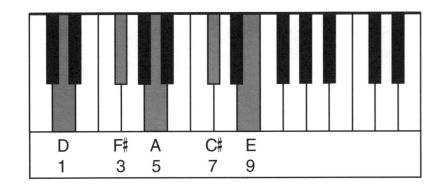

D
F# A
C# E
1 3 5 7 9

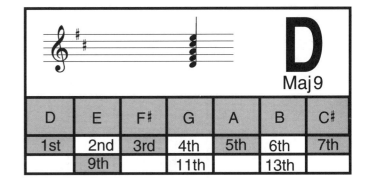

D Maj9

D	E	F#	G	A	B	C#
1st	2nd	3rd	4th	5th	6th	7th
	9th		11th		13th	

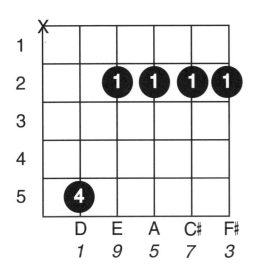

D E A C# F#
1 9 5 7 3

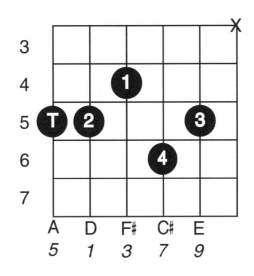

A D F# C# E
5 1 3 7 9

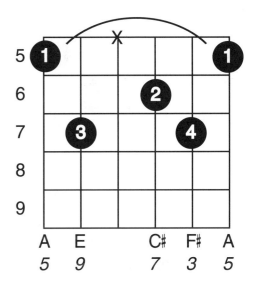

A E C# F# A
5 9 7 3 5

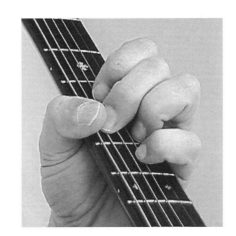

153

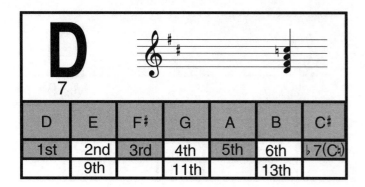

D	E	F♯	G	A	B	C♯
1st	2nd	3rd	4th	5th	6th	♭7(C♮)
	9th		11th		13th	

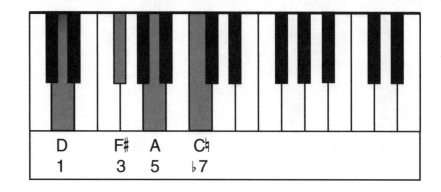

D   F♯   A   C♮
1   3   5   ♭7

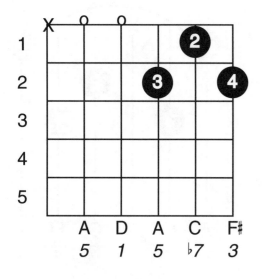

A   D   A   C   F♯
5   *1*   *5*   *♭7*   *3*

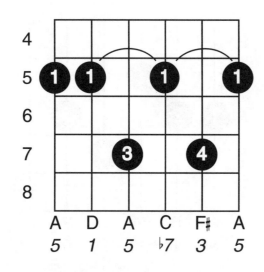

A   D   A   C   F♯   A
5   *1*   *5*   *♭7*   *3*   *5*

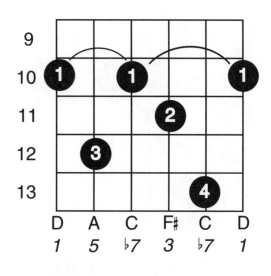

D   A   C   F♯   C   D
1   *5*   *♭7*   *3*   *♭7*   *1*

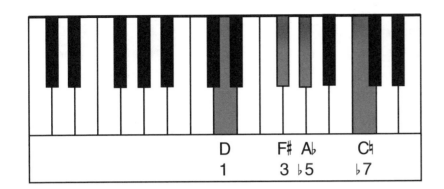

D 1   F# Ab   Ch
       3 b5   b7

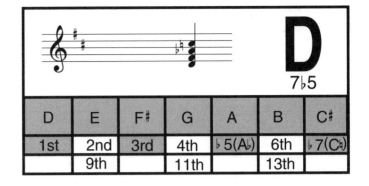

$7\flat5$

D	E	F#	G	A	B	C#
1st	2nd	3rd	4th	♭5(A♭)	6th	♭7(C♮)
	9th		11th		13th	

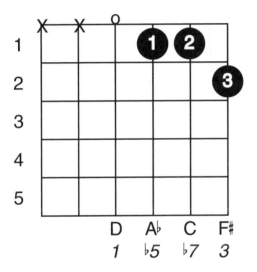

D   A♭ C   F#
1   ♭5 ♭7 3

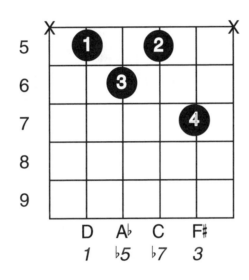

D   A♭ C   F#
1   ♭5 ♭7 3

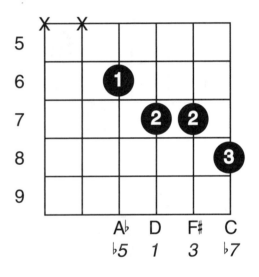

A♭ D   F# C
♭5 1   3   ♭7

155

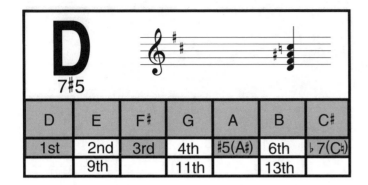

D
7♯5

D	E	F♯	G	A	B	C♯
1st	2nd	3rd	4th	♯5(A♯)	6th	♭7(C♮)
	9th		11th		13th	

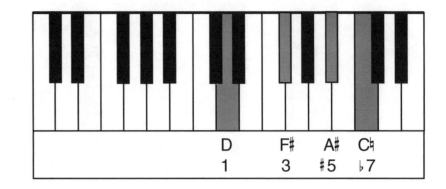

D	F♯	A♯	C♮
1	3	♯5	♭7

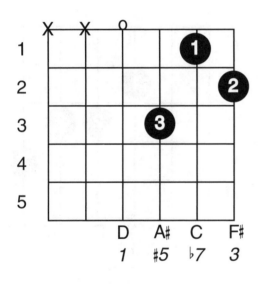

D	A♯	C	F♯
1	♯5	♭7	3

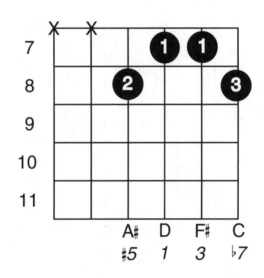

A♯	D	F♯	C
♯5	1	3	♭7

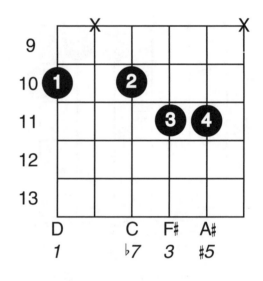

D	C	F♯	A♯
1	♭7	3	♯5

156

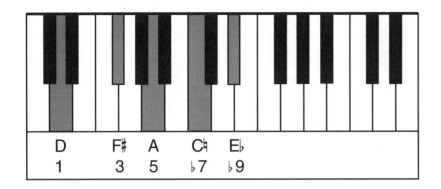

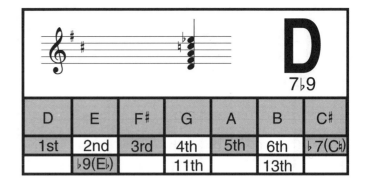

D	E	F#	G	A	B	C#
1st	2nd	3rd	4th	5th	6th	♭7(C♮)
	♭9(E♭)		11th		13th	

D 7♭9

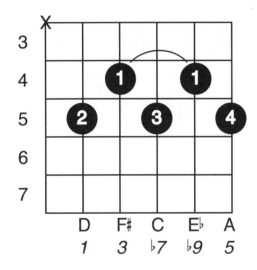

D   F#   C   E♭   A
1   3   ♭7   ♭9   5

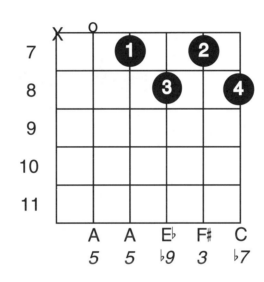

A   A   E♭   F#   C
5   5   ♭9   3   ♭7

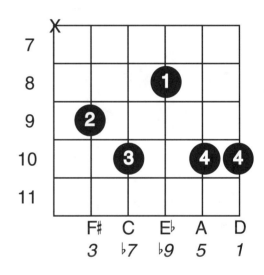

F#   C   E♭   A   D
3   ♭7   ♭9   5   1

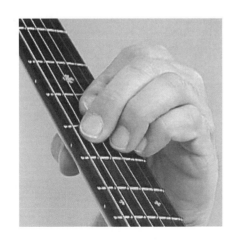

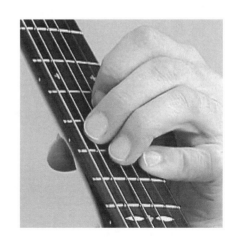

D

7#9

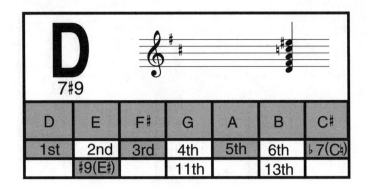

D	E	F#	G	A	B	C#
1st	2nd	3rd	4th	5th	6th	♭7(C♮)
	#9(E#)		11th		13th	

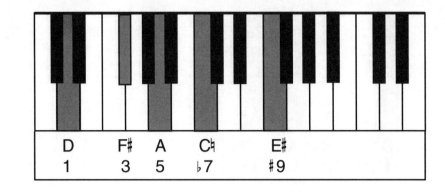

D	F#	A	C♮	E#
1	3	5	♭7	#9

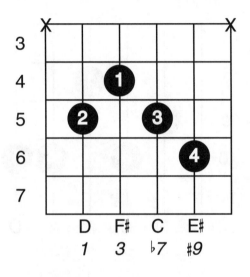

D	F#	C	E#
1	3	♭7	#9

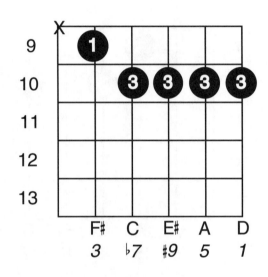

F#	C	E#	A	D
3	♭7	#9	5	1

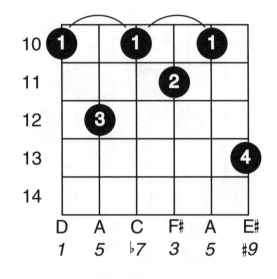

D	A	C	F#	A	E#
1	5	♭7	3	5	#9

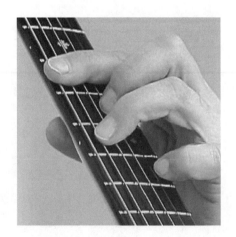

158

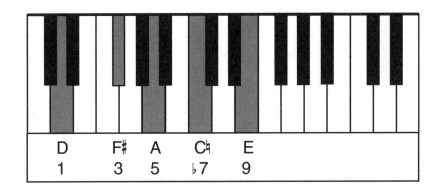

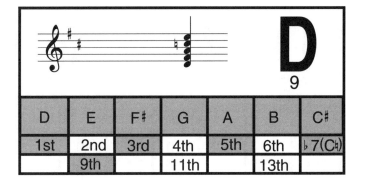

D	E	F#	G	A	B	C#
1st	2nd	3rd	4th	5th	6th	♭7(C♮)
	9th		11th		13th	

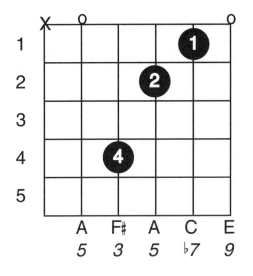

A F# A C E
5 3 5 ♭7 9

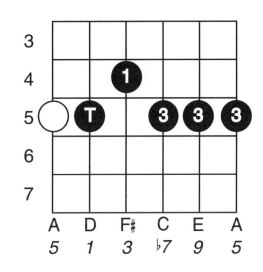

A D F# C E A
5 1 3 ♭7 9 5

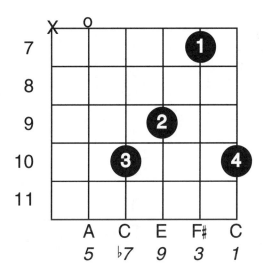

A C E F# C
5 ♭7 9 3 1

159

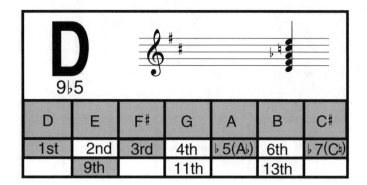

D
9♭5

D	E	F♯	G	A	B	C♯
1st	2nd	3rd	4th	♭5(A♭)	6th	♭7(C♮)
	9th		11th		13th	

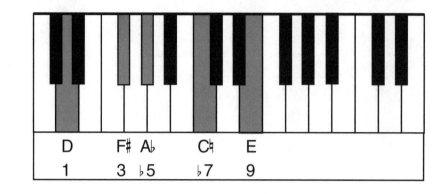

D		F♯	A♭		C♮	E	
1		3	♭5		♭7	9	

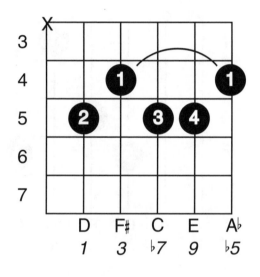

D	F♯	C	E	A♭
1	*3*	*♭7*	*9*	*♭5*

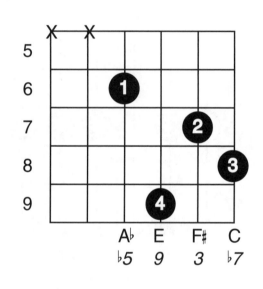

A♭	E	F♯	C
♭5	*9*	*3*	*♭7*

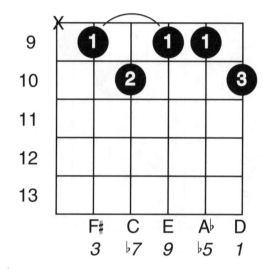

F♯	C	E	A♭	D
3	*♭7*	*9*	*♭5*	*1*

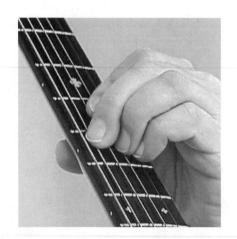

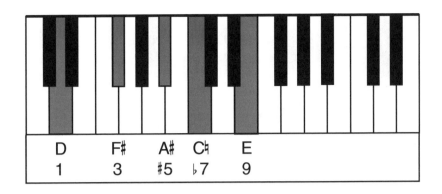

D F# A# C♮ E
1 3 #5 ♭7 9

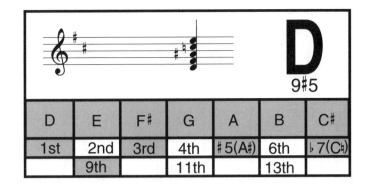

D

9#5

D	E	F#	G	A	B	C#
1st	2nd	3rd	4th	#5(A#)	6th	♭7(C♮)
	9th		11th		13th	

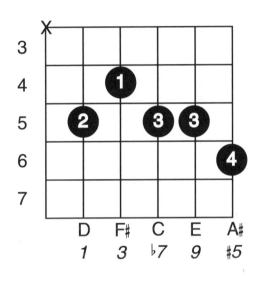

D F# C E A#
1 3 ♭7 9 #5

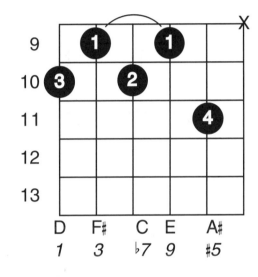

D F# C E A#
1 3 ♭7 9 #5

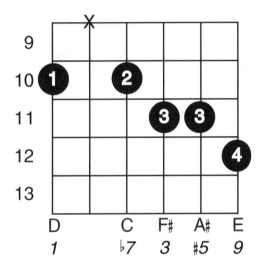

D C F# A# E
1 ♭7 3 #5 9

D 11

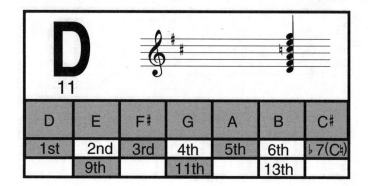

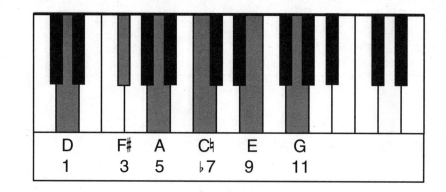

D	E	F#	G	A	B	C#
1st	2nd	3rd	4th	5th	6th	♭7(C♮)
	9th		11th		13th	

Piano keyboard notes:

D	F#	A	C♮	E	G
1	3	5	♭7	9	11

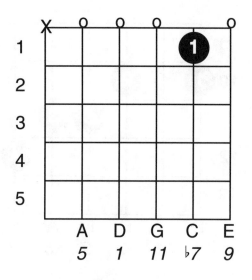

A	D	G	C	E
5	1	11	♭7	9

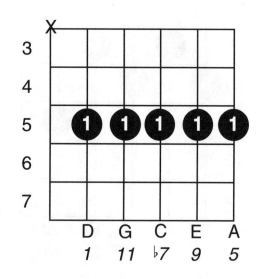

D	G	C	E	A
1	11	♭7	9	5

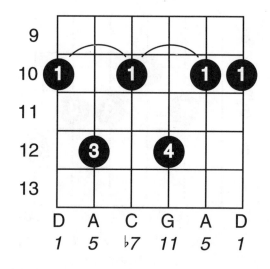

D	A	C	G	A	D
1	5	♭7	11	5	1

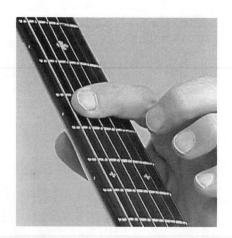

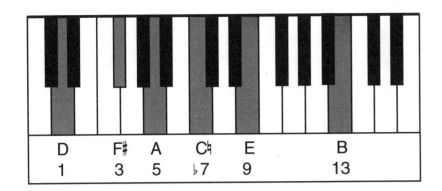

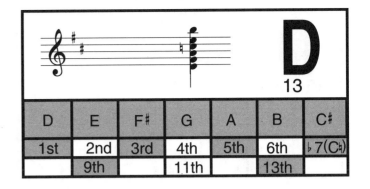

D	E	F#	G	A	B	C#
1st	2nd	3rd	4th	5th	6th	♭7(C♮)
	9th		11th		13th	

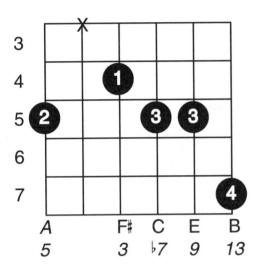

A 5

F# 3

C ♭7

E 9

B 13

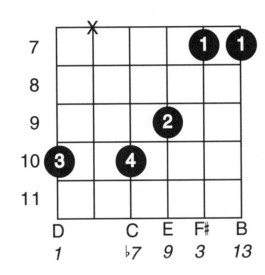

D 1

C ♭7

E 9

F# 3

B 13

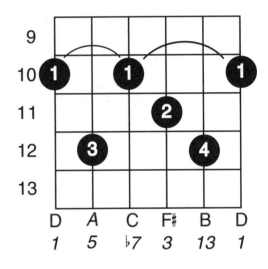

D 1

A 5

C ♭7

F# 3

B 13

D 1

163

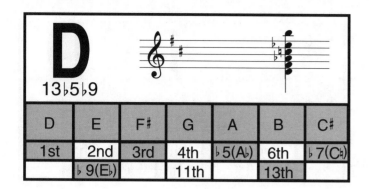

D

13♭5♭9

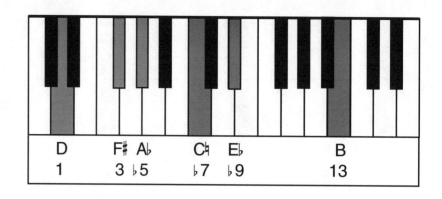

D	E	F#	G	A	B	C#
1st	2nd	3rd	4th	♭5(A♭)	6th	♭7(C♮)
	♭9(E♭)		11th		13th	

D	F#	A♭	C♮	E♭	B
1	3	♭5	♭7	♭9	13

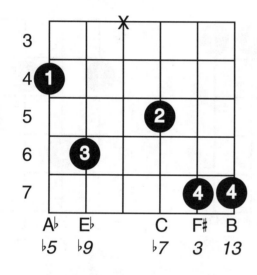

A♭	E♭		C	F#	B
♭5	♭9		♭7	3	13

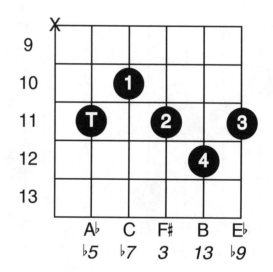

A♭	C	F#	B	E♭
♭5	♭7	3	13	♭9

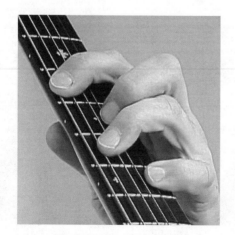

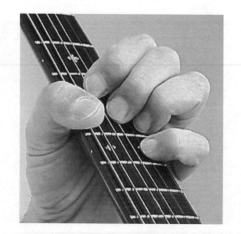

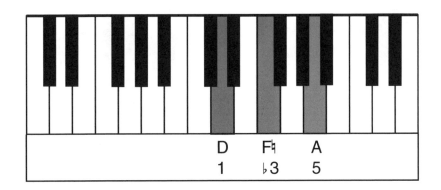

D minor

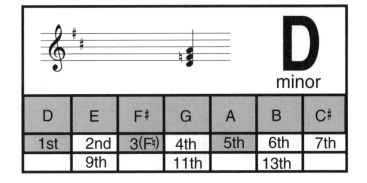

D	E	F#	G	A	B	C#
1st	2nd	3(F♮)	4th	5th	6th	7th
	9th		11th		13th	

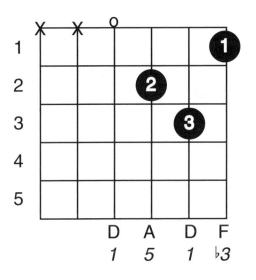

D	A	D	F
1	*5*	*1*	*♭3*

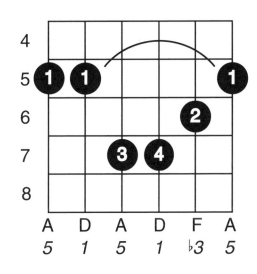

A	D	A	D	F	A
5	*1*	*5*	*1*	*♭3*	*5*

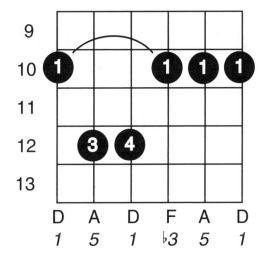

D	A	D	F	A	D
1	*5*	*1*	*♭3*	*5*	*1*

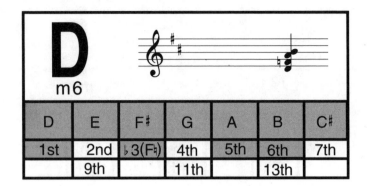

D
m6

D	E	F#	G	A	B	C#
1st	2nd	♭3(F♮)	4th	5th	6th	7th
	9th		11th		13th	

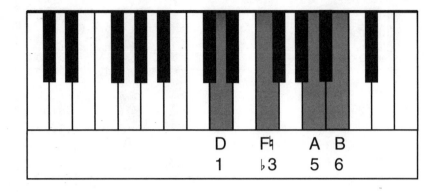

D F♮ A B
1 ♭3 5 6

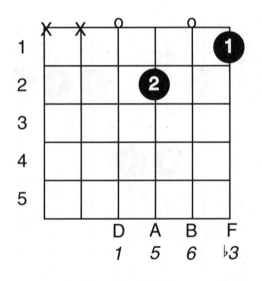

D A B F
1 5 6 ♭3

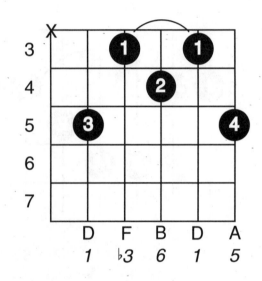

D F B D A
1 ♭3 6 1 5

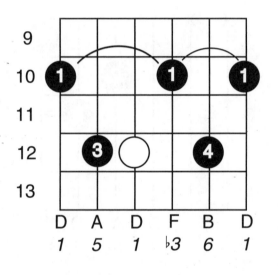

D A D F B D
1 5 1 ♭3 6 1

166

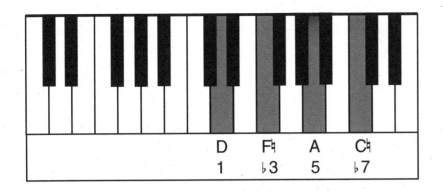

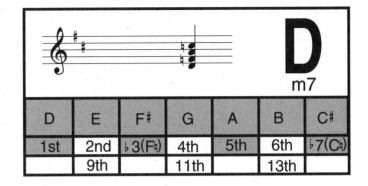

D
m7

D	E	F#	G	A	B	C#
1st	2nd	♭3(F♮)	4th	5th	6th	♭7(C♮)
	9th		11th		13th	

(keyboard labels)
D   F♮   A   C♮
1   ♭3   5   ♭7

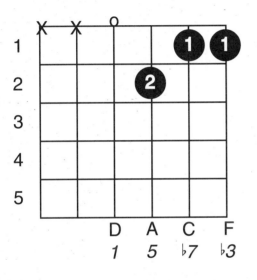

D   A   C   F
1   5   ♭7   ♭3

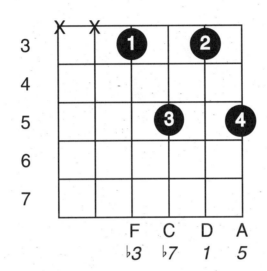

F   C   D   A
♭3   ♭7   1   5

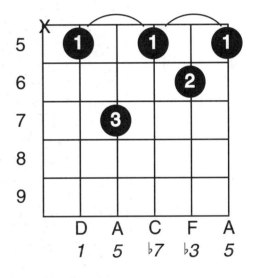

D   A   C   F   A
1   5   ♭7   ♭3   5

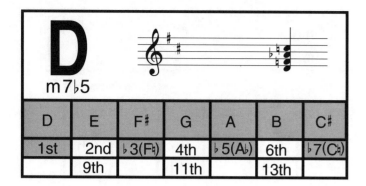

D
m7♭5

D	E	F#	G	A	B	C#
1st	2nd	♭3(F♮)	4th	♭5(A♭)	6th	♭7(C♮)
	9th		11th		13th	

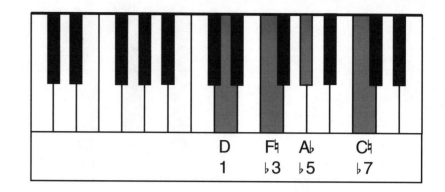

				D	F♮	A♭	C♮
				1	♭3	♭5	♭7

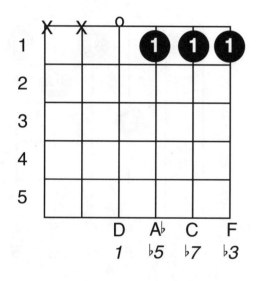

D	A♭	C	F
1	♭5	♭7	♭3

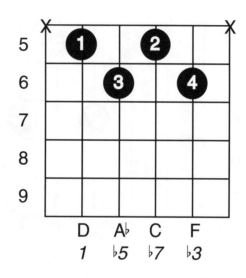

D	A♭	C	F
1	♭5	♭7	♭3

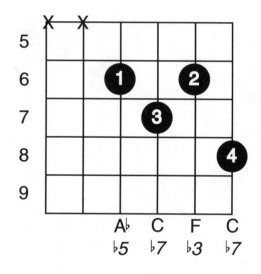

A♭	C	F	C
♭5	♭7	♭3	♭7

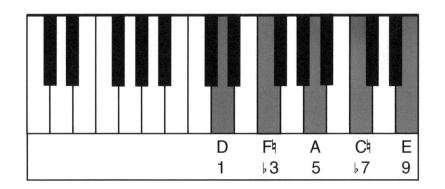

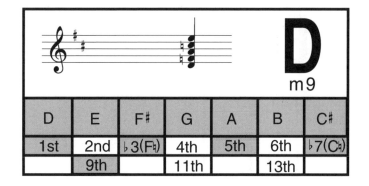

D m9

D	E	F#	G	A	B	C#
1st	2nd	♭3(F♮)	4th	5th	6th	♭7(C♮)
	9th		11th		13th	

Keyboard labels: D 1, F♮ ♭3, A 5, C♮ ♭7, E 9

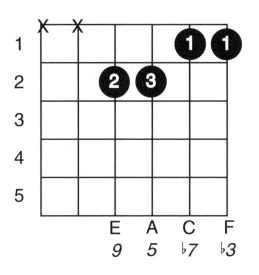

E 9 · A 5 · C ♭7 · F ♭3

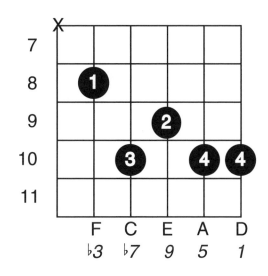

F ♭3 · C ♭7 · E 9 · A 5 · D 1

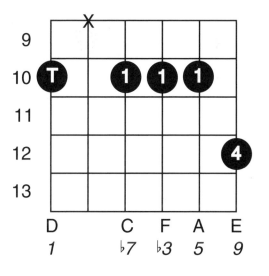

D 1 · C ♭7 · F ♭3 · A 5 · E 9

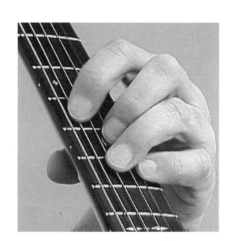

D

dim7

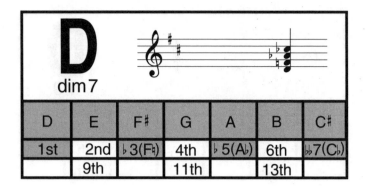

D	E	F#	G	A	B	C#
1st	2nd	♭3(F♮)	4th	♭5(A♭)	6th	♭♭7(C♭)
	9th		11th		13th	

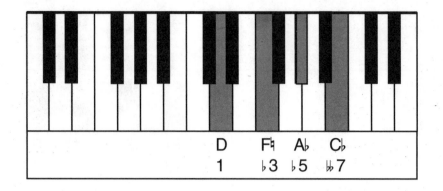

D   F♮   A♭   C♭
1   ♭3   ♭5   ♭♭7

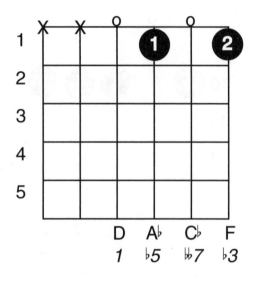

D   A♭   C♭   F
1   *♭5*   *♭♭7*   *♭3*

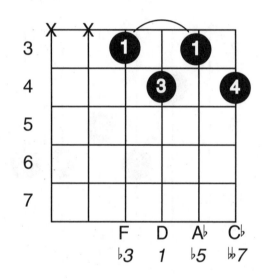

F   D   A♭   C♭
♭3   *1*   *♭5*   *♭♭7*

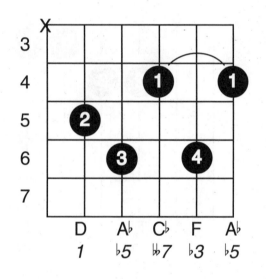

D   A♭   C♭   F   A♭
1   *♭5*   *♭♭7*   *♭3*   *♭5*

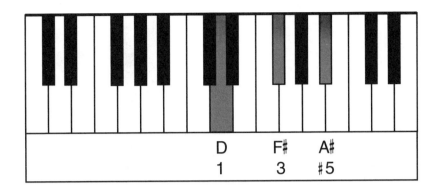

D 1
F# 3
A# #5

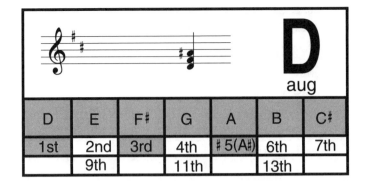

D
aug

D	E	F#	G	A	B	C#
1st	2nd	3rd	4th	#5(A#)	6th	7th
	9th		11th		13th	

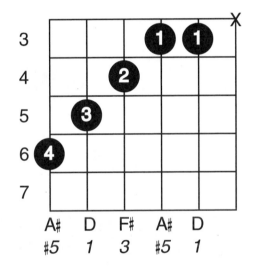

A#	D	F#	A#	D
#5	1	3	#5	1

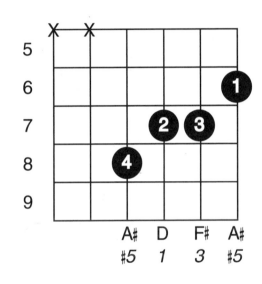

A#	D	F#	A#
#5	1	3	#5

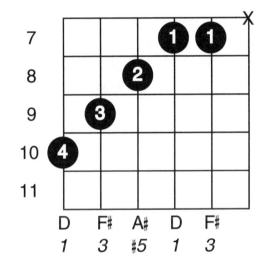

D	F#	A#	D	F#
1	3	#5	1	3

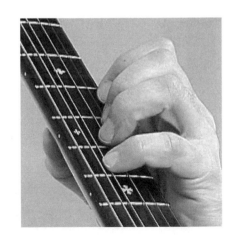

171

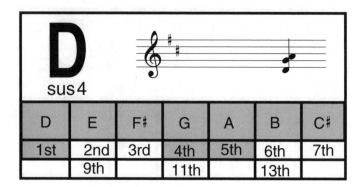

D
sus4

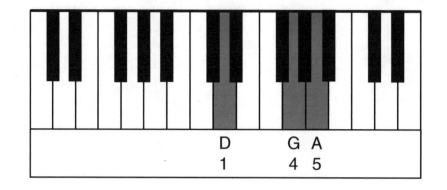

D	E	F#	G	A	B	C#
1st	2nd	3rd	4th	5th	6th	7th
	9th		11th		13th	

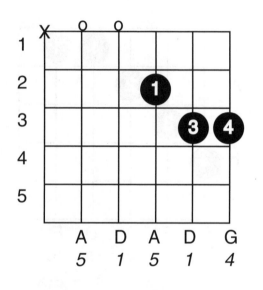

A	D	A	D	G
5	*1*	*5*	*1*	*4*

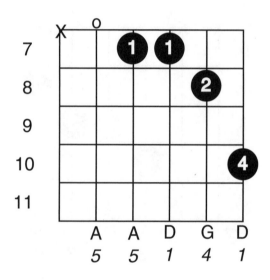

A	A	D	G	D
5	*5*	*1*	*4*	*1*

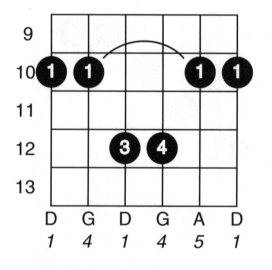

D	G	D	G	A	D
1	*4*	*1*	*4*	*5*	*1*

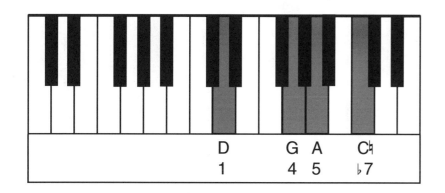

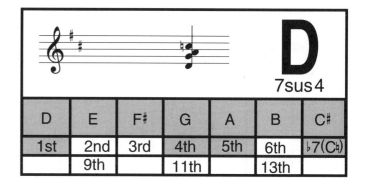

D 7sus4

D	E	F#	G	A	B	C#
1st	2nd	3rd	4th	5th	6th	♭7(C♮)
	9th		11th		13th	

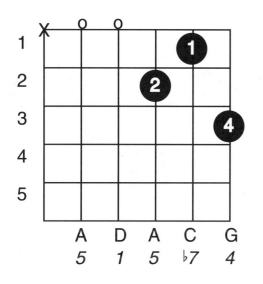

A	D	A	C	G
5	1	5	♭7	4

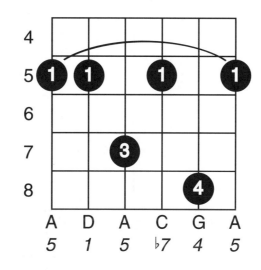

A	D	A	C	G	A
5	1	5	♭7	4	5

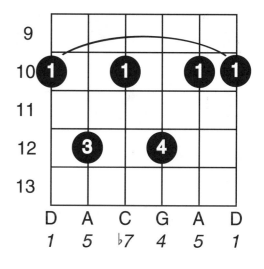

D	A	C	G	A	D
1	5	♭7	4	5	1

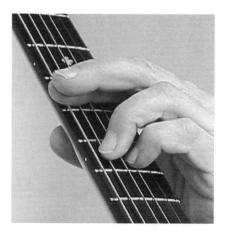

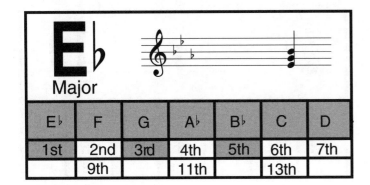

E♭ Major

E♭	F	G	A♭	B♭	C	D
1st	2nd	3rd	4th	5th	6th	7th
	9th		11th		13th	

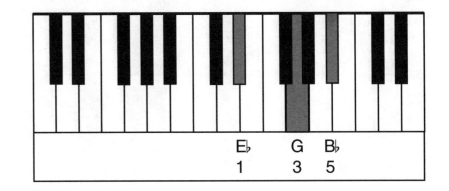

E♭ G B♭
1   3 5

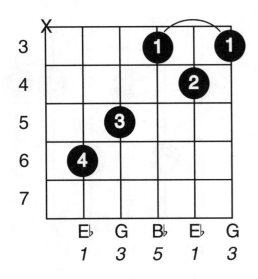

```
    X
3 ────────1───────1
4 ──────────2──────
5 ──────3──────────
6 ──4──────────────
7 ─────────────────
   E♭  G  B♭  E♭  G
   1   3  5   1   3
```

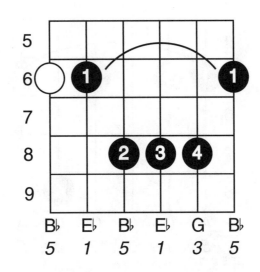

```
5 ──────────────────
6 ○──1──────────1──
7 ───────────────────
8 ────────2──3──4──
9 ───────────────────
   B♭  E♭  B♭  E♭  G  B♭
   5   1   5   1   3  5
```

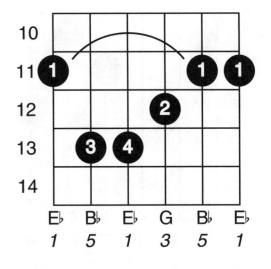

```
10 ────────────────────
11 ─1──────────1──1
12 ──────────2────────
13 ────3──4──────────
14 ────────────────────
   E♭  B♭  E♭  G  B♭  E♭
   1   5   1   3  5   1
```

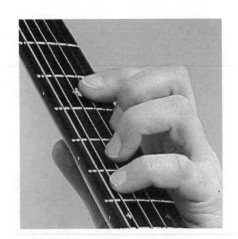

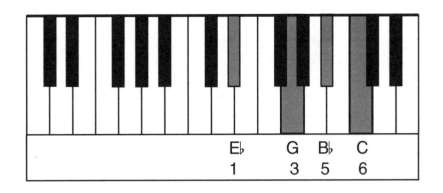

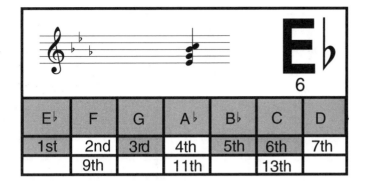

E♭	F	G	A♭	B♭	C	D
1st	2nd	3rd	4th	5th	6th	7th
	9th		11th		13th	

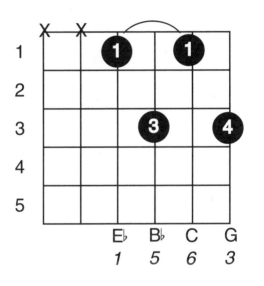

	E♭	B♭	C	G
	1	5	6	3

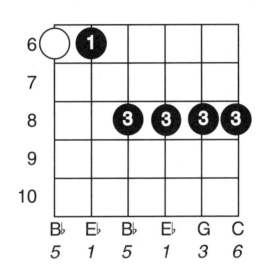

B♭	E♭	B♭	E♭	G	C
5	1	5	1	3	6

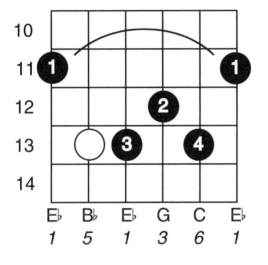

E♭	B♭	E♭	G	C	E♭
1	5	1	3	6	1

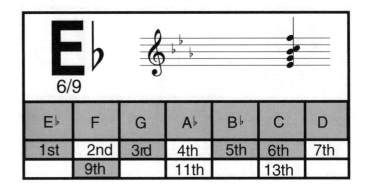

E♭
6/9

E♭	F	G	A♭	B♭	C	D
1st	2nd	3rd	4th	5th	6th	7th
	9th		11th		13th	

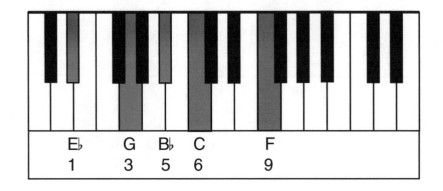

E♭ 1   G 3   B♭ 5   C 6   F 9

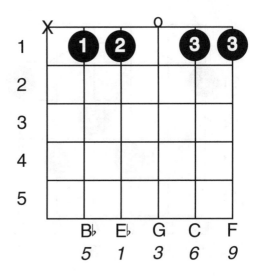

B♭	E♭	G	C	F
5	1	3	6	9

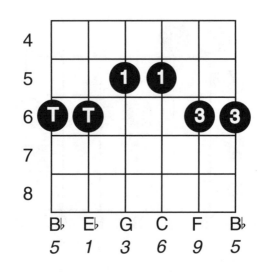

B♭	E♭	G	C	F	B♭
5	1	3	6	9	5

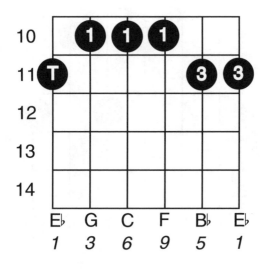

E♭	G	C	F	B♭	E♭
1	3	6	9	5	1

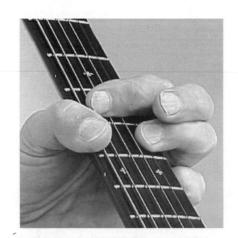

176

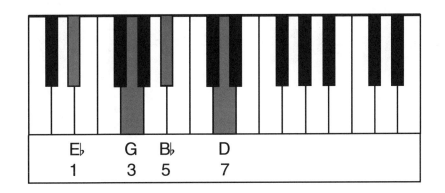

E♭	G	B♭	D
1	3	5	7

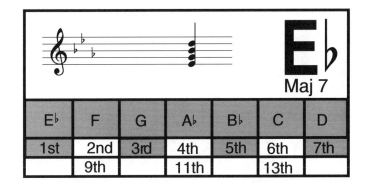

E♭	F	G	A♭	B♭	C	D
1st	2nd	3rd	4th	5th	6th	7th
	9th		11th		13th	

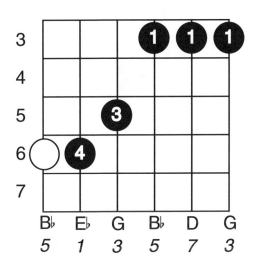

B♭	E♭	G	B♭	D	G
5	1	3	5	7	3

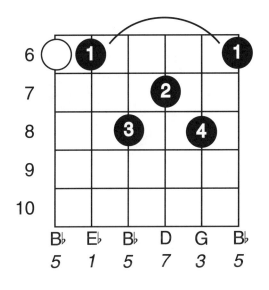

B♭	E♭	B♭	D	G	B♭
5	1	5	7	3	5

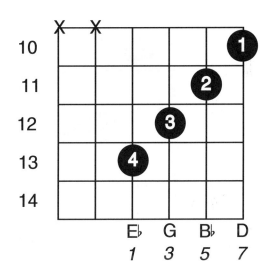

E♭	G	B♭	D
1	3	5	7

E♭
mMaj7

E♭	F	G	A♭	B♭	C	D
1st	2nd	♭3(G♭)	4th	5th	6th	7th
	9th		11th		13th	

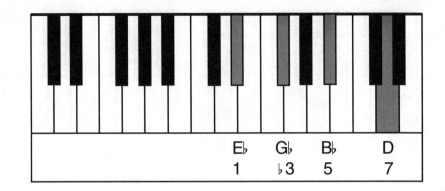

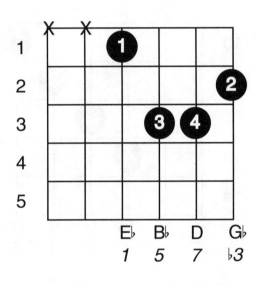

E♭ B♭ D G♭
1   5   7   ♭3

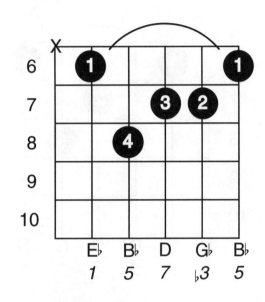

E♭ B♭ D G♭ B♭
1   5   7   ♭3   5

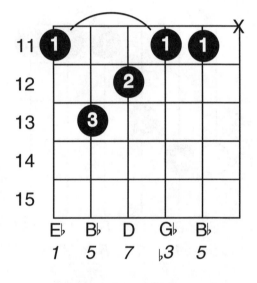

E♭ B♭ D G♭ B♭
1   5   7   ♭3   5

178

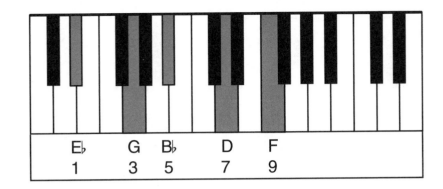

E♭ 1   G 3   B♭ 5   D 7   F 9

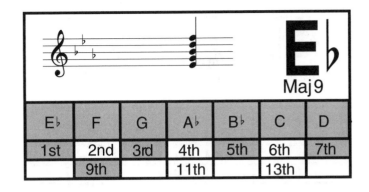

E♭
Maj9

E♭	F	G	A♭	B♭	C	D
1st	2nd	3rd	4th	5th	6th	7th
	9th		11th		13th	

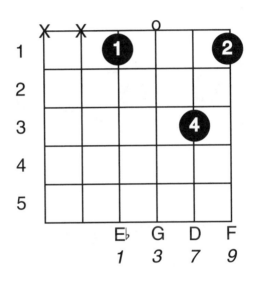

E♭   G   D   F
1   *3*   *7*   *9*

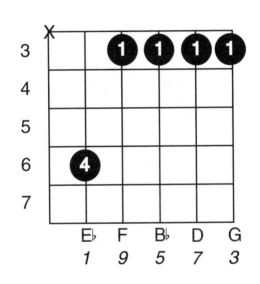

E♭   F   B♭   D   G
1   *9*   *5*   *7*   *3*

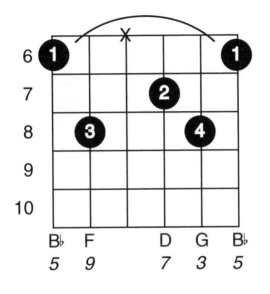

B♭   F   D   G   B♭
5   *9*   *7*   *3*   *5*

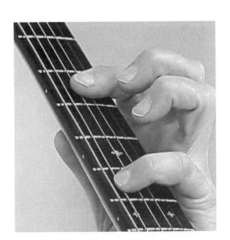

179

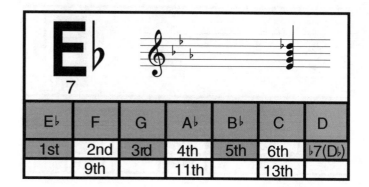

E♭	F	G	A♭	B♭	C	D
1st	2nd	3rd	4th	5th	6th	♭7(D♭)
	9th		11th		13th	

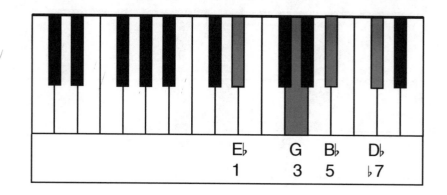

E♭   G   B♭   D♭
1   3   5   ♭7

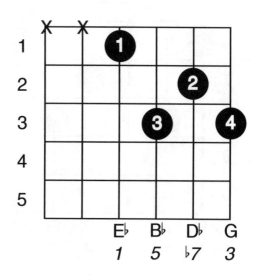

E♭   B♭   D♭   G
1   5   ♭7   3

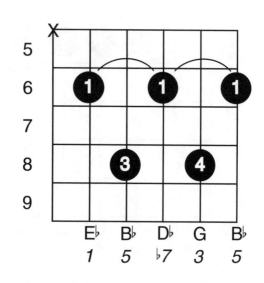

E♭   B♭   D♭   G   B♭
1   5   ♭7   3   5

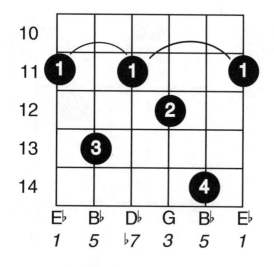

E♭   B♭   D♭   G   B♭   E♭
1   5   ♭7   3   5   1

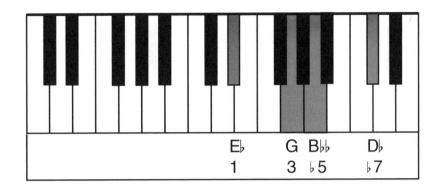

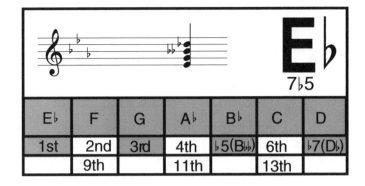

E♭7♭5

E♭	F	G	A♭	B♭	C	D
1st	2nd	3rd	4th	♭5(B♭♭)	6th	♭7(D♭)
	9th		11th		13th	

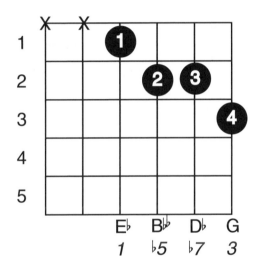

E♭ B♭♭ D♭ G
1 ♭5 ♭7 3

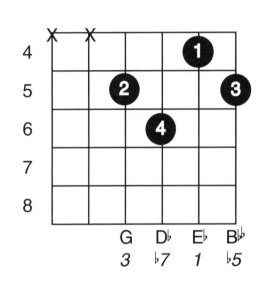

G D♭ E♭ B♭♭
3 ♭7 1 ♭5

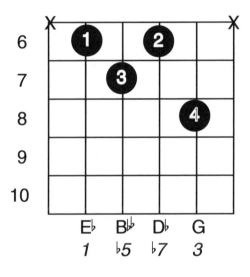

E♭ B♭♭ D♭ G
1 ♭5 ♭7 3

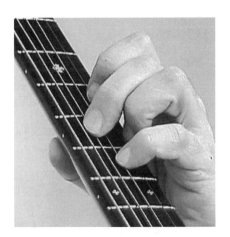

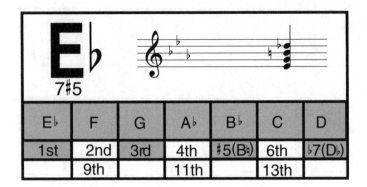

E♭	F	G	A♭	B♭	C	D
1st	2nd	3rd	4th	#5(B♮)	6th	♭7(D♭)
	9th		11th		13th	

E♭7#5

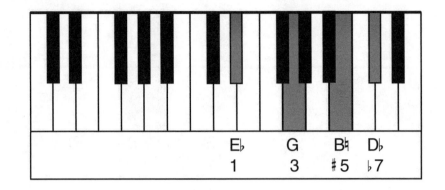

E♭	G	B♮	D♭
1	3	#5	♭7

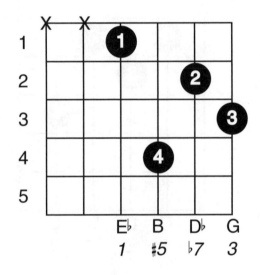

E♭	B	D♭	G
1	#5	♭7	3

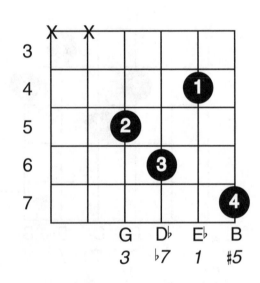

G	D♭	E♭	B
3	♭7	1	#5

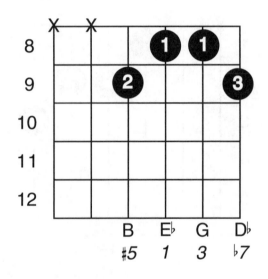

B	E♭	G	D♭
#5	1	3	♭7

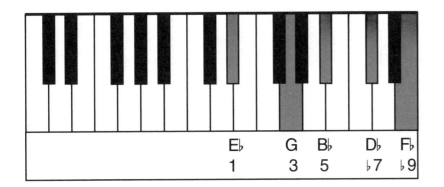

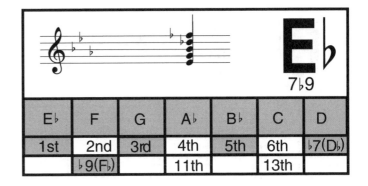

Eb	F	G	Ab	Bb	C	D
1st	2nd	3rd	4th	5th	6th	b7(Db)
	b9(Fb)		11th		13th	

Eb 7b9

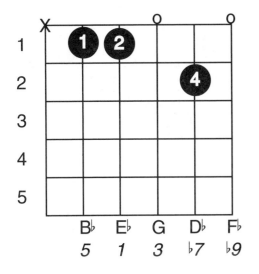

Bb	Eb	G	Db	Fb
5	*1*	*3*	*b7*	*b9*

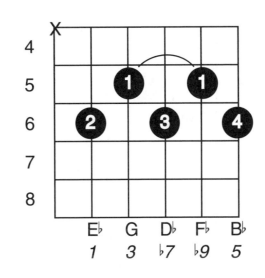

Eb	G	Db	Fb	Bb
1	*3*	*b7*	*b9*	*5*

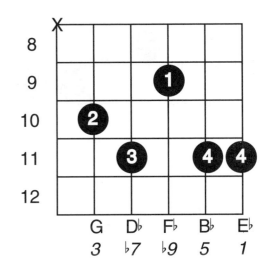

G	Db	Fb	Bb	Eb
3	*b7*	*b9*	*5*	*1*

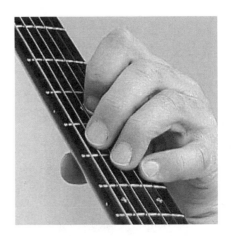

183

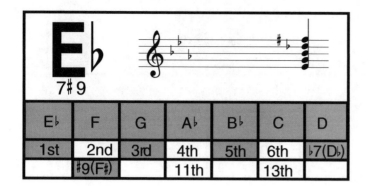

E♭	F	G	A♭	B♭	C	D
1st	2nd	3rd	4th	5th	6th	♭7(D♭)
	#9(F#)		11th		13th	

$E♭$
7#9

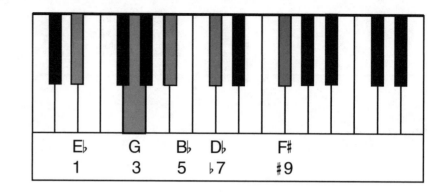

E♭   G   B♭   D♭   F#
1   3   5   ♭7   #9

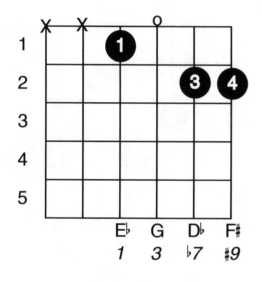

E♭   G   D♭   F#
1   *3*   *♭7*   *#9*

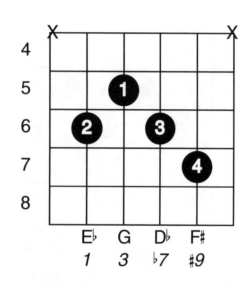

E♭   G   D♭   F#
1   *3*   *♭7*   *#9*

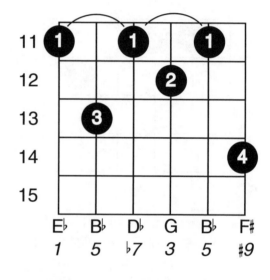

E♭   B♭   D♭   G   B♭   F#
1   *5*   *♭7*   *3*   *5*   *#9*

184

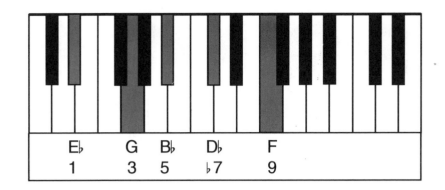

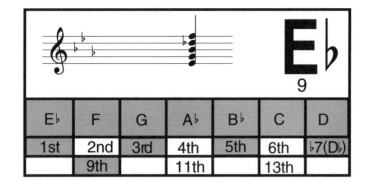

E♭	F	G	A♭	B♭	C	D
1st	2nd	3rd	4th	5th	6th	♭7(D♭)
	9th		11th		13th	

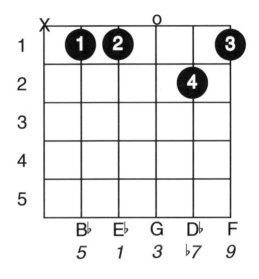

B♭ E♭ G D♭ F
5   1   3   ♭7   9

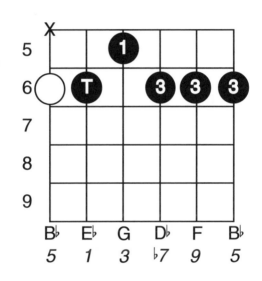

B♭ E♭ G D♭ F B♭
5   1   3   ♭7   9   5

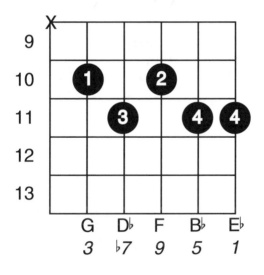

G D♭ F B♭ E♭
3   ♭7   9   5   1

185

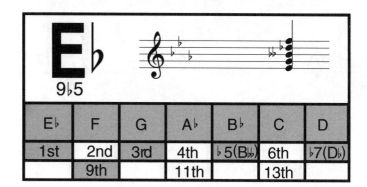

E♭
9♭5

E♭	F	G	A♭	B♭	C	D
1st	2nd	3rd	4th	♭5(B♭♭)	6th	♭7(D♭)
	9th		11th		13th	

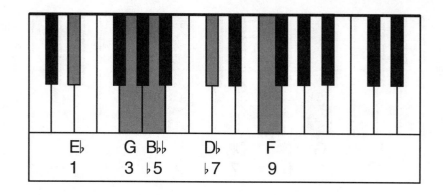

E♭	G	B♭♭	D♭	F
1	3	♭5	♭7	9

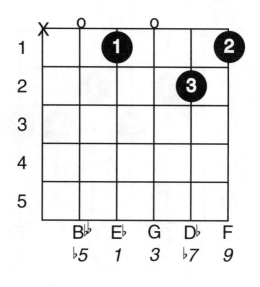

B♭♭	E♭	G	D♭	F
♭5	1	3	♭7	9

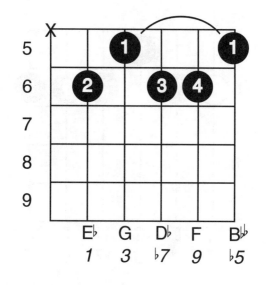

E♭	G	D♭	F	B♭♭
1	3	♭7	9	♭5

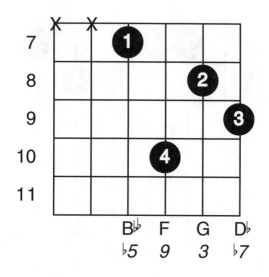

B♭♭	F	G	D♭
♭5	9	3	♭7

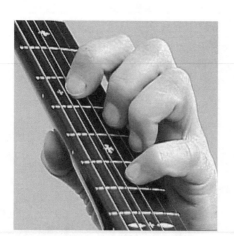

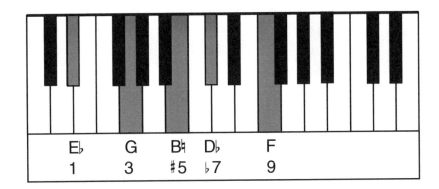

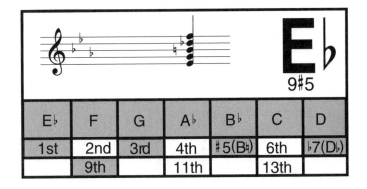

E♭	F	G	A♭	B♭	C	D
1st	2nd	3rd	4th	♯5(B♭)	6th	♭7(D♭)
	9th		11th		13th	

E♭ 9♯5

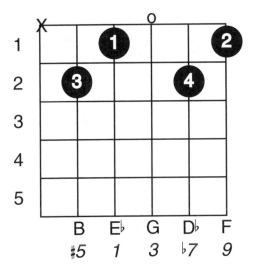

B	E♭	G	D♭	F
♯5	1	3	♭7	9

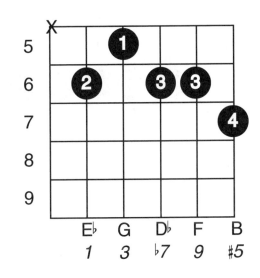

E♭	G	D♭	F	B
1	3	♭7	9	♯5

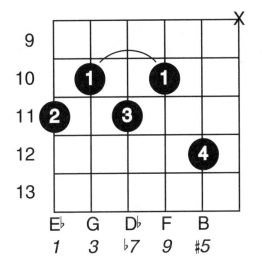

E♭	G	D♭	F	B
1	3	♭7	9	♯5

187

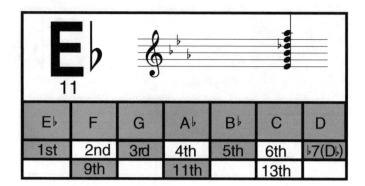

E♭
11

E♭	F	G	A♭	B♭	C	D
1st	2nd	3rd	4th	5th	6th	♭7(D♭)
	9th		11th		13th	

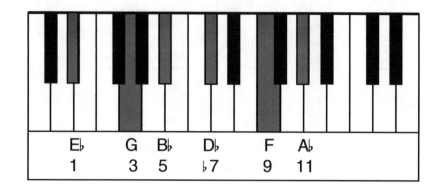

E♭	G	B♭	D♭	F	A♭
1	3	5	♭7	9	11

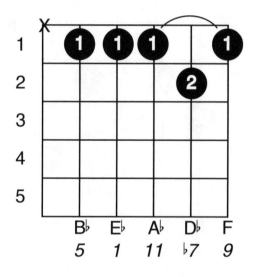

B♭	E♭	A♭	D♭	F
5	1	11	♭7	9

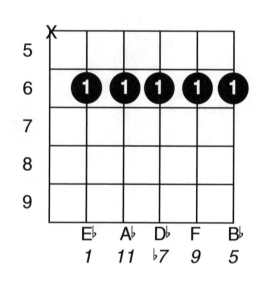

E♭	A♭	D♭	F	B♭
1	11	♭7	9	5

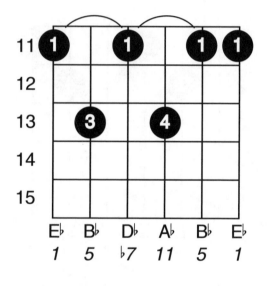

E♭	B♭	D♭	A♭	B♭	E♭
1	5	♭7	11	5	1

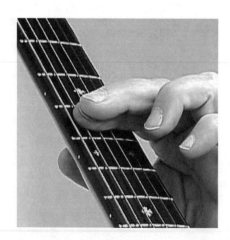

188

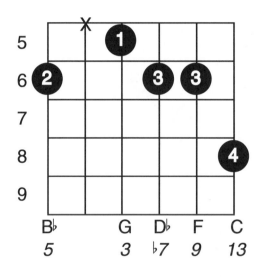

Eb		G	Bb	Db		F			C	
1		3	5	b7		9			13	

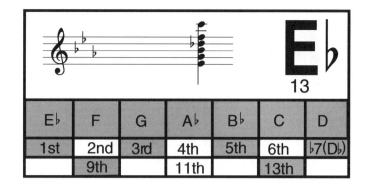

Eb

13

Eb	F	G	Ab	Bb	C	D
1st	2nd	3rd	4th	5th	6th	b7(Db)
	9th		11th		13th	

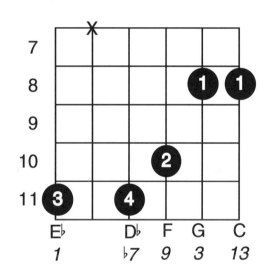

5					
6					
7					
8					
9					

Bb		G	Db	F	C
5		3	b7	9	13

7					
8					
9					
10					
11					

Eb		Db	F	G	C
1		b7	9	3	13

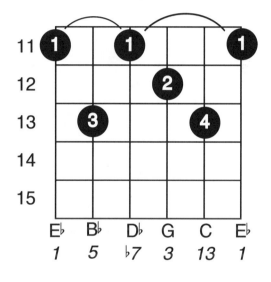

11					
12					
13					
14					
15					

Eb	Bb	Db	G	C	Eb
1	5	b7	3	13	1

189

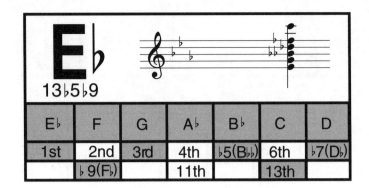

E♭

13♭5♭9

E♭	F	G	A♭	B♭	C	D
1st	2nd	3rd	4th	♭5(B♭♭)	6th	♭7(D♭)
	♭9(F♭)		11th		13th	

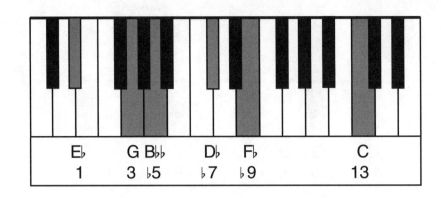

E♭		G	B♭♭		D♭	F♭		C
1		3	♭5		♭7	♭9		13

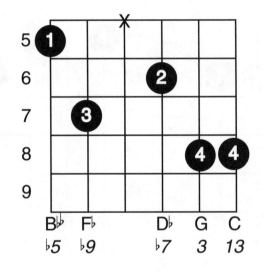

B♭♭	F♭		D♭	G	C
♭5	♭9		♭7	3	13

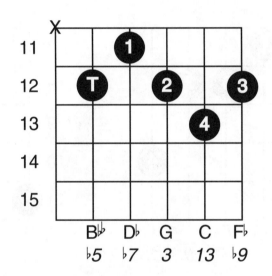

B♭♭	D♭	G	C	F♭
♭5	♭7	3	13	♭9

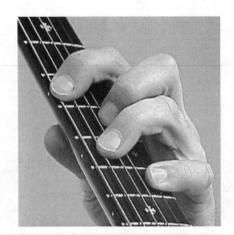

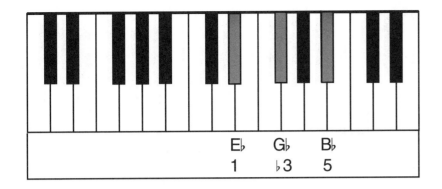

E♭	G♭	B♭
1	♭3	5

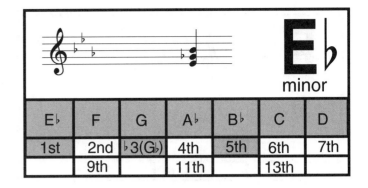

E♭
minor

E♭	F	G	A♭	B♭	C	D
1st	2nd	♭3(G♭)	4th	5th	6th	7th
	9th		11th		13th	

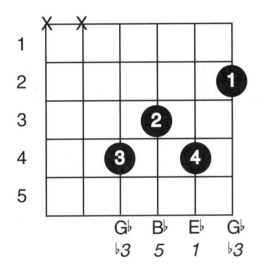

G♭	B♭	E♭	G♭
♭3	5	1	♭3

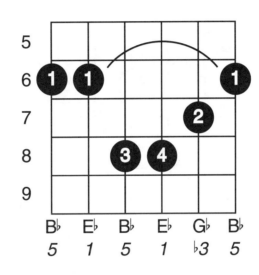

B♭	E♭	B♭	E♭	G♭	B♭
5	1	5	1	♭3	5

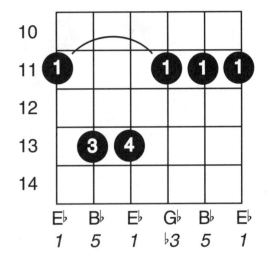

E♭	B♭	E♭	G♭	B♭	E♭
1	5	1	♭3	5	1

191

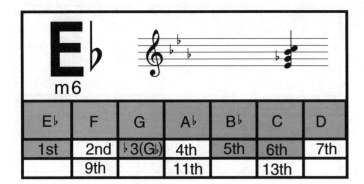

E♭	F	G	A♭	B♭	C	D
1st	2nd	♭3(G♭)	4th	5th	6th	7th
	9th		11th		13th	

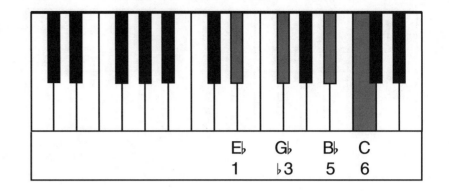

E♭   G♭   B♭   C
1   ♭3   5   6

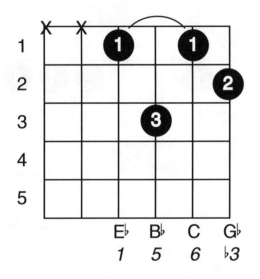

E♭   B♭   C   G♭
1   5   6   ♭3

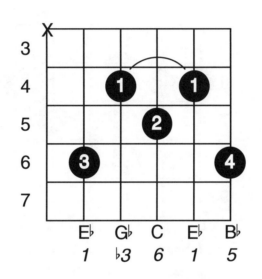

E♭   G♭   C   E♭   B♭
1   ♭3   6   1   5

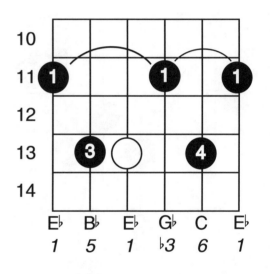

E♭   B♭   E♭   G♭   C   E♭
1   5   1   ♭3   6   1

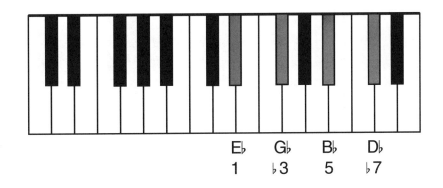

Eb | Gb | Bb | Db
1 | b3 | 5 | b7

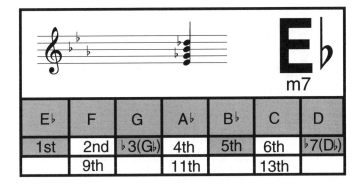

E♭
m7

E♭	F	G	A♭	B♭	C	D
1st	2nd	♭3(G♭)	4th	5th	6th	♭7(D♭)
	9th		11th		13th	

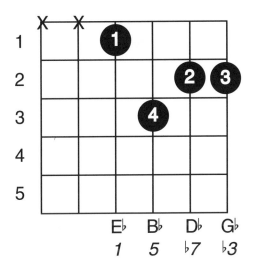

1
2
3
4
5

E♭ B♭ D♭ G♭
1 5 ♭7 ♭3

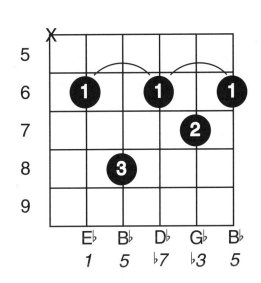

5
6
7
8
9

E♭ B♭ D♭ G♭ B♭
1 5 ♭7 ♭3 5

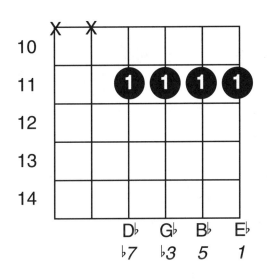

10
11
12
13
14

D♭ G♭ B♭ E♭
♭7 ♭3 5 1

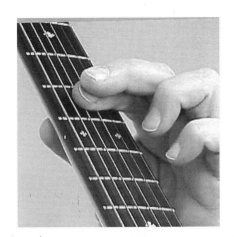

193

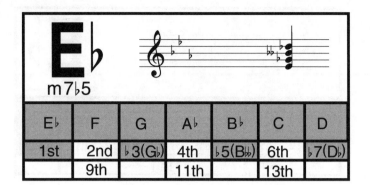

E♭ m7♭5

E♭	F	G	A♭	B♭	C	D
1st	2nd	♭3(G♭)	4th	♭5(B♭♭)	6th	♭7(D♭)
	9th		11th		13th	

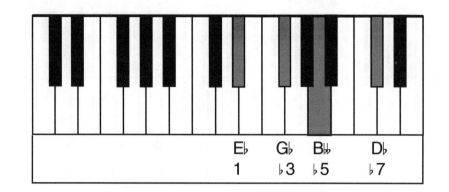

E♭	G♭	B♭♭	D♭
1	♭3	♭5	♭7

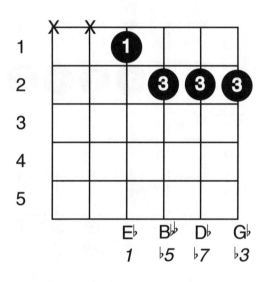

	E♭	B♭♭	D♭	G♭
	1	♭5	♭7	♭3

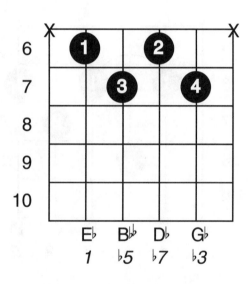

	E♭	B♭♭	D♭	G♭
	1	♭5	♭7	♭3

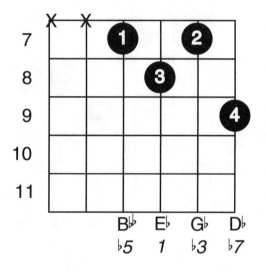

	B♭♭	E♭	G♭	D♭
	♭5	1	♭3	♭7

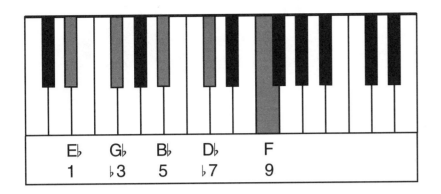

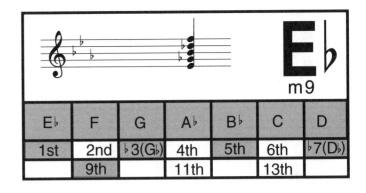

E♭	F	G	A♭	B♭	C	D
1st	2nd	♭3(G♭)	4th	5th	6th	♭7(D♭)
	9th		11th		13th	

E♭ m9

Piano keys: E♭(1), G♭(♭3), B♭(5), D♭(♭7), F(9)

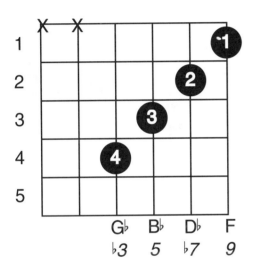

G♭ B♭ D♭ F
♭3   5   ♭7 9

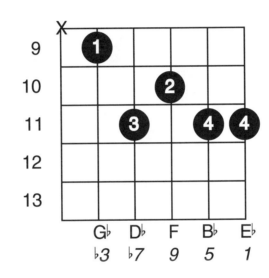

G♭ D♭ F B♭ E♭
♭3   ♭7 9   5   1

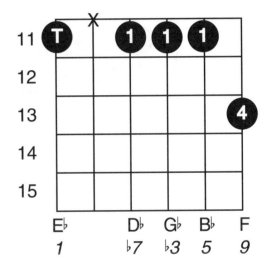

E♭   D♭ G♭ B♭ F
1   ♭7 ♭3 5   9

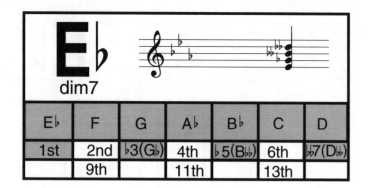

Eb	F	G	Ab	Bb	C	D
1st	2nd	b3(Gb)	4th	b5(Bbb)	6th	bb7(Dbb)
	9th		11th		13th	

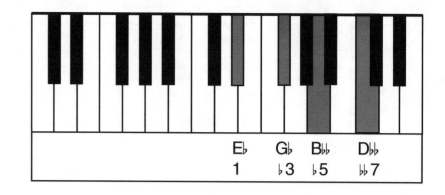

Eb   Gb   Bbb   Dbb
1   b3   b5   bb7

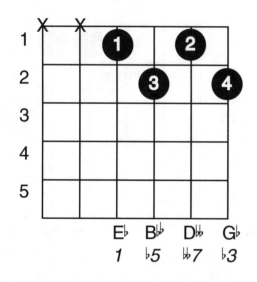

Eb   Bbb   Dbb   Gb
1   b5   bb7   b3

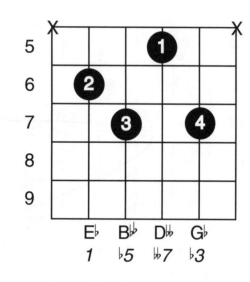

Eb   Bbb   Dbb   Gb
1   b5   bb7   b3

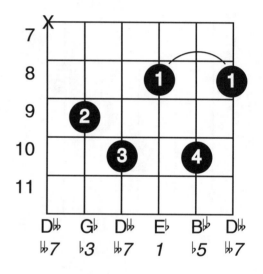

Dbb   Gb   Dbb   Eb   Bbb   Dbb
bb7   b3   bb7   1   b5   bb7

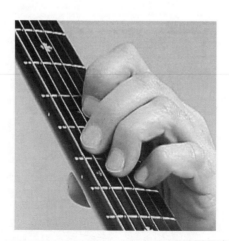

196

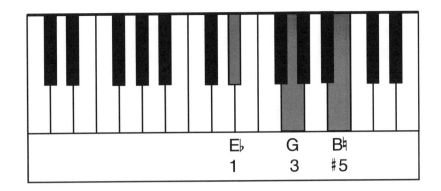

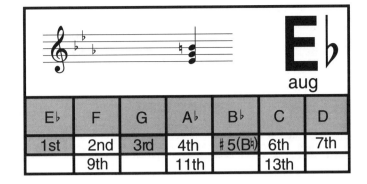

E♭	F	G	A♭	B♭	C	D
1st	2nd	3rd	4th	#5(B♮)	6th	7th
	9th		11th		13th	

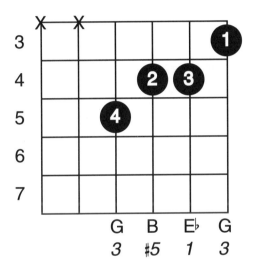

G B E♭ G
3 #5 1 3

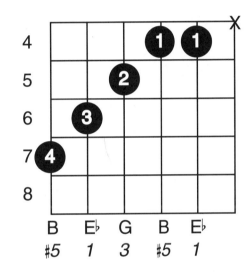

B E♭ G B E♭
#5 1 3 #5 1

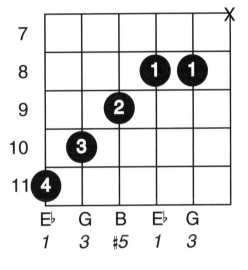

E♭ G B E♭ G
1 3 #5 1 3

197

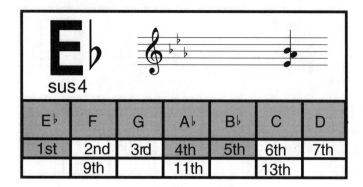

Eb	F	G	Ab	Bb	C	D
1st	2nd	3rd	4th	5th	6th	7th
	9th		11th		13th	

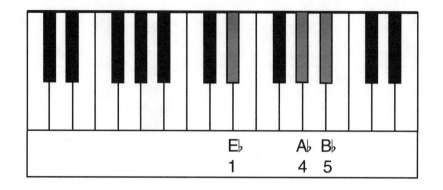

Eb Ab Bb
1 4 5

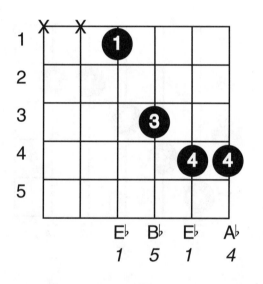

Eb Bb Eb Ab
1 5 1 4

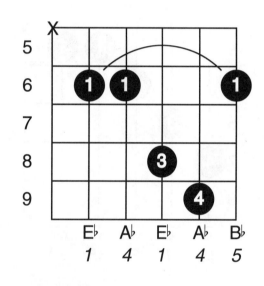

Eb Ab Eb Ab Bb
1 4 1 4 5

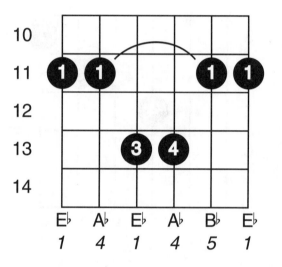

Eb Ab Eb Ab Bb Eb
1 4 1 4 5 1

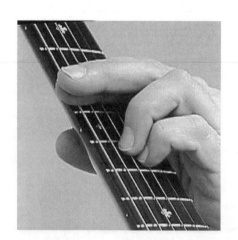

198

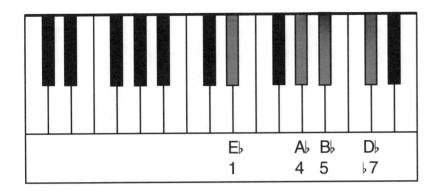

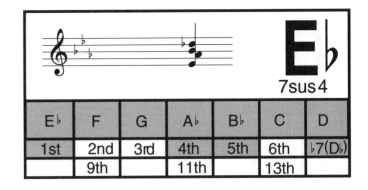

E♭	F	G	A♭	B♭	C	D
1st	2nd	3rd	4th	5th	6th	♭7(D♭)
	9th		11th		13th	

E♭ 7sus4

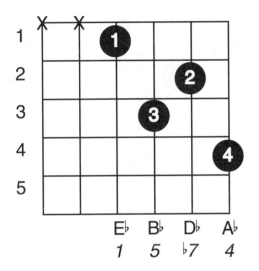

E♭	B♭	D♭	A♭
1	5	♭7	4

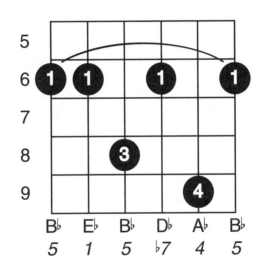

B♭	E♭	B♭	D♭	A♭	B♭
5	1	5	♭7	4	5

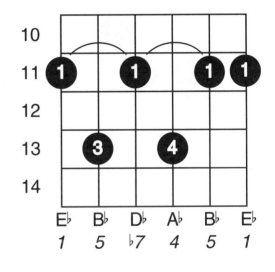

E♭	B♭	D♭	A♭	B♭	E♭
1	5	♭7	4	5	1

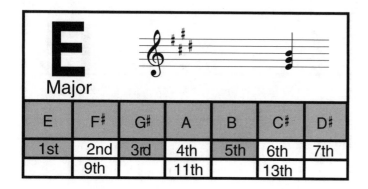

E Major						
E	F#	G#	A	B	C#	D#
1st	2nd	3rd	4th	5th	6th	7th
	9th		11th		13th	

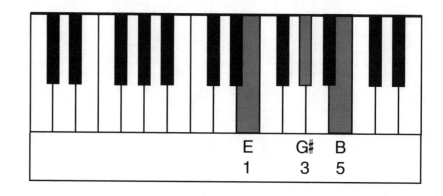

E 1   G# 3   B 5

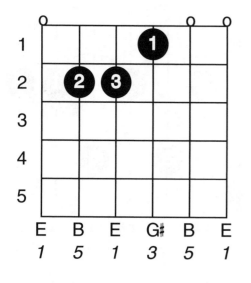

E B E G# B E
1 5 1 3   5 1

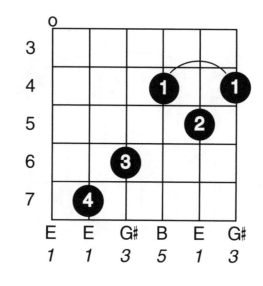

E E G# B E G#
1 1 3   5 1 3

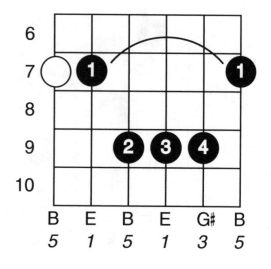

B E B E G# B
5 1 5 1 3   5

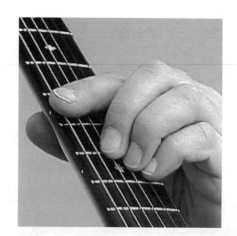

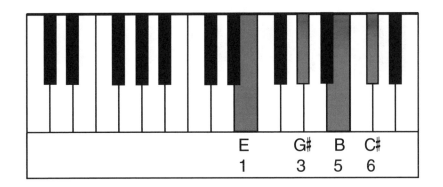

E G# B C#
1 3 5 6

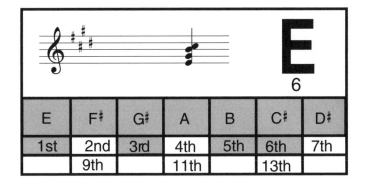

E
6

E	F#	G#	A	B	C#	D#
1st	2nd	3rd	4th	5th	6th	7th
	9th		11th		13th	

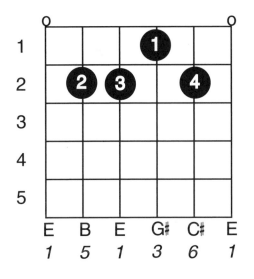

E B E G# C# E
1 5 1 3 6 1

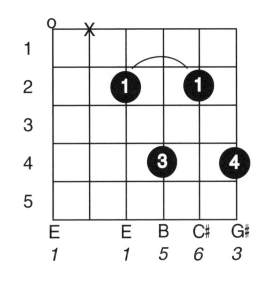

E E B C# G#
1 1 5 6 3

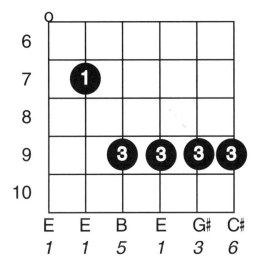

E E B E G# C#
1 1 5 1 3 6

201

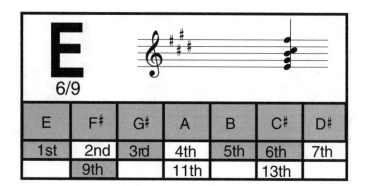

E	F#	G#	A	B	C#	D#
1st	2nd	3rd	4th	5th	6th	7th
	9th		11th		13th	

E 6/9

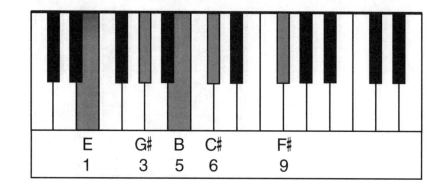

E   G#   B C#   F#
1   3   5 6   9

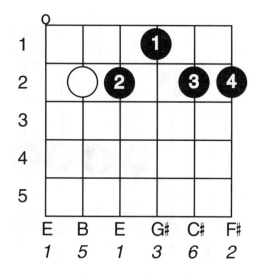

E B E G# C# F#
1 5 1 3 6 2

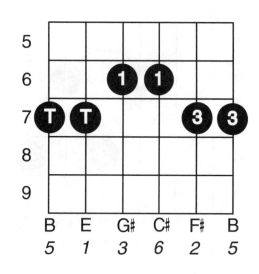

B E G# C# F# B
5 1 3 6 2 5

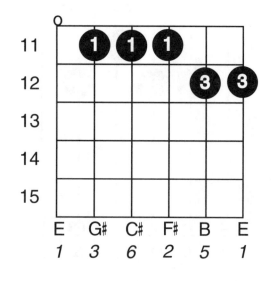

E G# C# F# B E
1 3 6 2 5 1

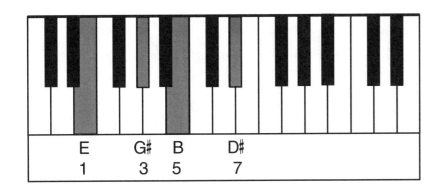

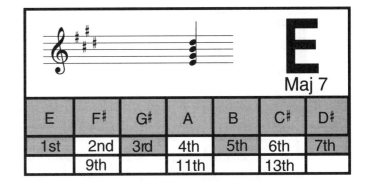

E
Maj 7

E	F#	G#	A	B	C#	D#
1st	2nd	3rd	4th	5th	6th	7th
	9th		11th		13th	

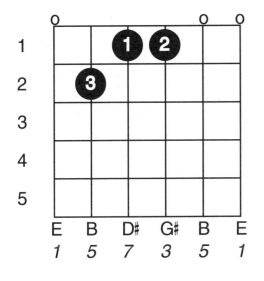

E	B	D#	G#	B	E
1	*5*	*7*	*3*	*5*	*1*

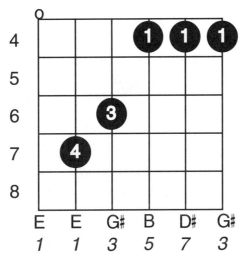

E	E	G#	B	D#	G#
1	*1*	*3*	*5*	*7*	*3*

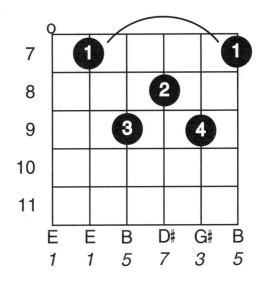

E	E	B	D#	G#	B
1	*1*	*5*	*7*	*3*	*5*

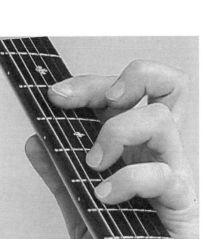

203

E
mMaj7

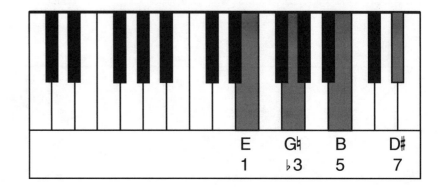

E	F#	G#	A	B	C#	D#
1st	2nd	♭3(G♮)	4th	5th	6th	7th
	9th		11th		13th	

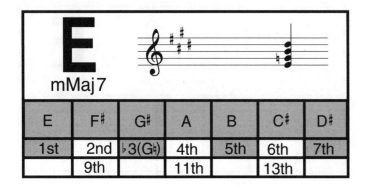

E   G♮   B   D#
1   ♭3   5   7

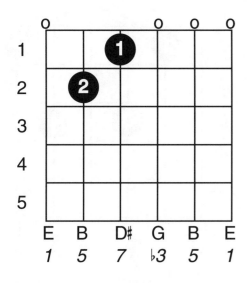

E   B   D#   G   B   E
1   *5*   *7*   *♭3*   *5*   *1*

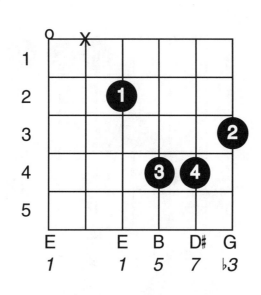

E   E   B   D#   G
1   *1*   *5*   *7*   *♭3*

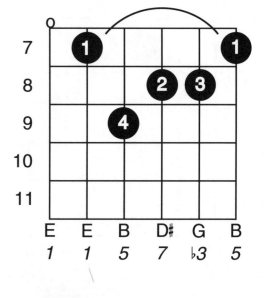

E   E   B   D#   G   B
1   *1*   *5*   *7*   *♭3*   *5*

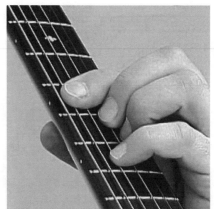

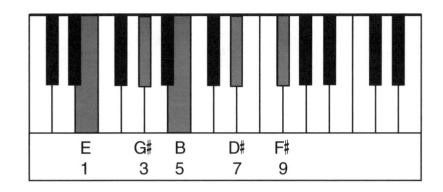

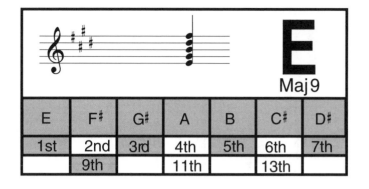

E	F#	G#	A	B	C#	D#
1st	2nd	3rd	4th	5th	6th	7th
	9th		11th		13th	

E Maj9

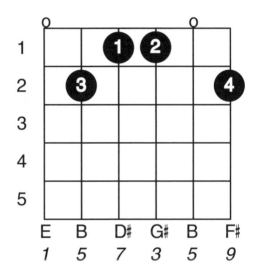

E	B	D#	G#	B	F#
1	*5*	*7*	*3*	*5*	*9*

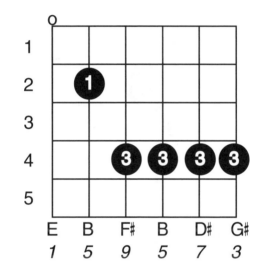

E	B	F#	B	D#	G#
1	*5*	*9*	*5*	*7*	*3*

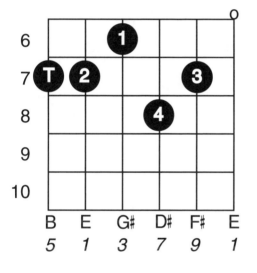

B	E	G#	D#	F#	E
5	*1*	*3*	*7*	*9*	*1*

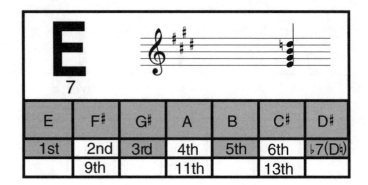

E7

E	F#	G#	A	B	C#	D#
1st	2nd	3rd	4th	5th	6th	♭7(D♮)
	9th		11th		13th	

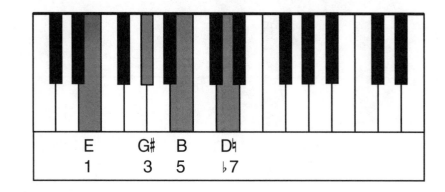

E · G# · B · D♮
1 · 3 · 5 · ♭7

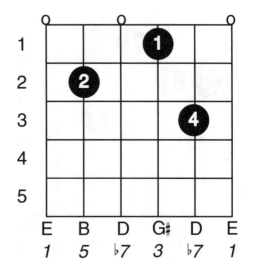

E	B	D	G#	D	E
1	*5*	*♭7*	*3*	*♭7*	*1*

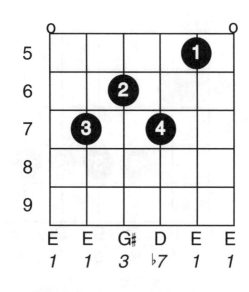

E	E	G#	D	E	E
1	*1*	*3*	*♭7*	*1*	*1*

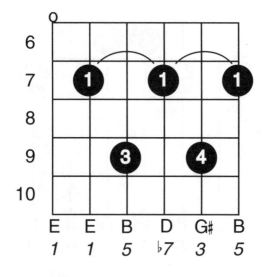

E	E	B	D	G#	B
1	*1*	*5*	*♭7*	*3*	*5*

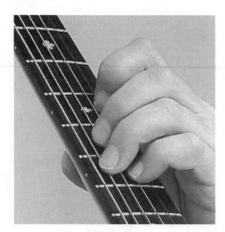

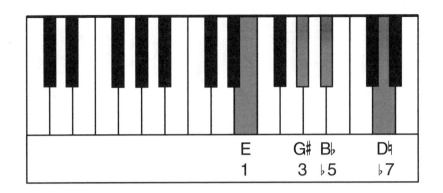

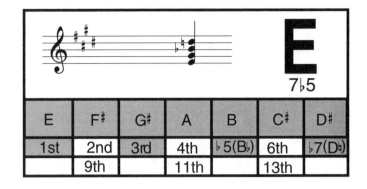

E	F#	G#	A	B	C#	D#
1st	2nd	3rd	4th	♭5(B♭)	6th	♭7(D♮)
	9th		11th		13th	

E 7♭5

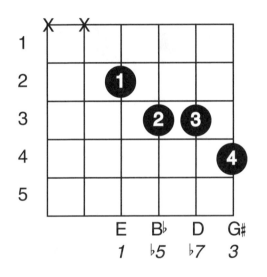

E   B♭   D   G#
1   ♭5   ♭7   3

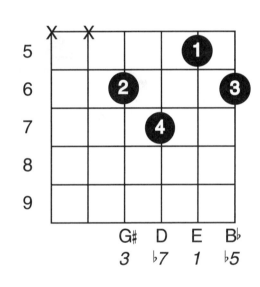

G#   D   E   B♭
3   ♭7   1   ♭5

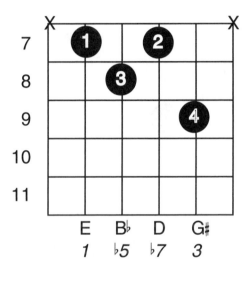

E   B♭   D   G#
1   ♭5   ♭7   3

E

7#5

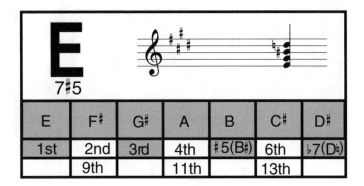

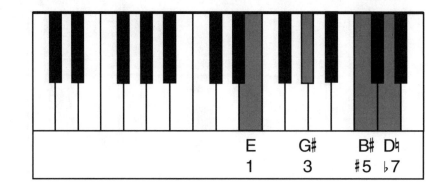

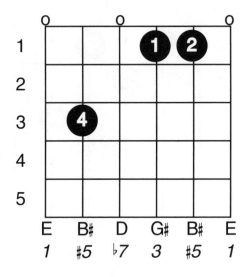

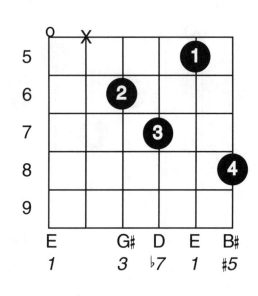

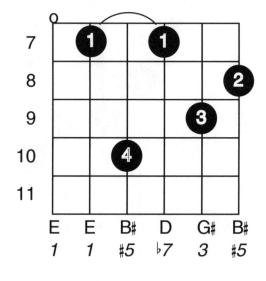

208

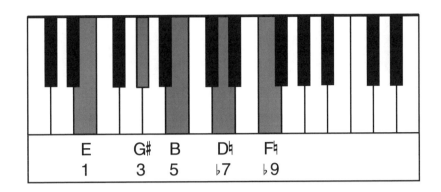

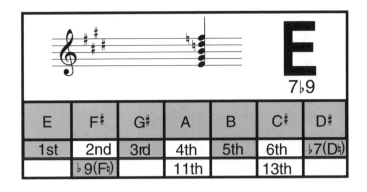

E	F♯	G♯	A	B	C♯	D♯
1st	2nd	3rd	4th	5th	6th	♭7(D♮)
	♭9(F♮)		11th		13th	

E 7♭9

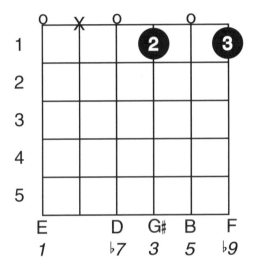

E   D   G♯   B   F
1   *♭7*   *3*   *5*   *♭9*

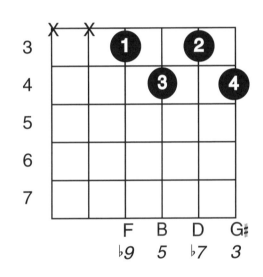

F   B   D   G♯
♭9   *5*   *♭7*   *3*

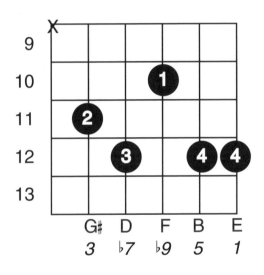

G♯   D   F   B   E
3   *♭7*   *♭9*   *5*   *1*

209

E

7#9

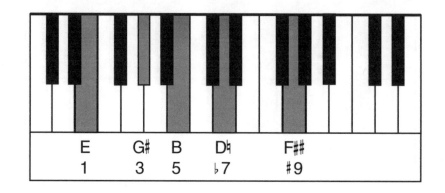

E	F#	G#	A	B	C#	D#
1st	2nd	3rd	4th	5th	6th	♭7(D♮)
	#9(F#)		11th		13th	

E	G#	B	D♮	F##
1	3	5	♭7	#9

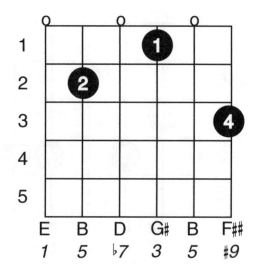

E	B	D	G#	B	F##
1	5	♭7	3	5	#9

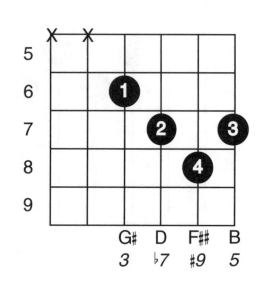

G#	D	F##	B
3	♭7	#9	5

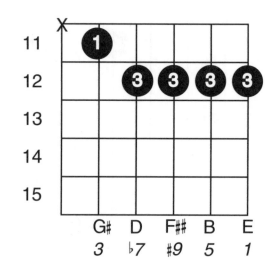

G#	D	F##	B	E
3	♭7	#9	5	1

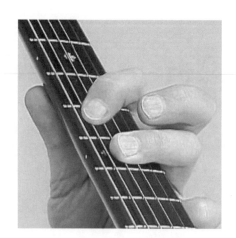

210

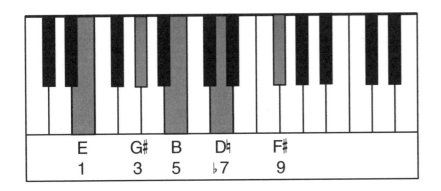

E | G# | B | D♮ | F#
1 | 3 | 5 | ♭7 | 9

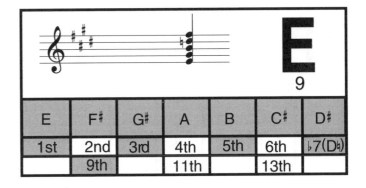

E
9

E	F#	G#	A	B	C#	D#
1st	2nd	3rd	4th	5th	6th	♭7(D♮)
	9th		11th		13th	

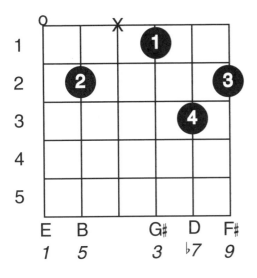

E | B | | G# | D | F#
1 | 5 | | 3 | ♭7 | 9

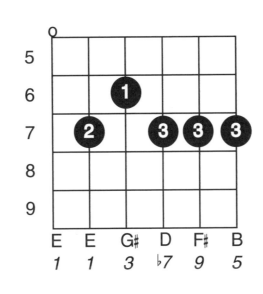

E | E | G# | D | F# | B
1 | 1 | 3 | ♭7 | 9 | 5

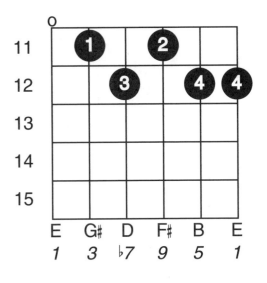

E | G# | D | F# | B | E
1 | 3 | ♭7 | 9 | 5 | 1

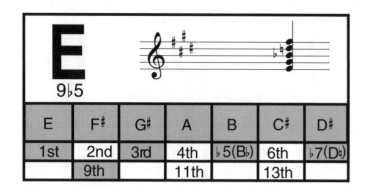

E	F#	G#	A	B	C#	D#
1st	2nd	3rd	4th	♭5(B♭)	6th	♭7(D♮)
	9th		11th		13th	

E 9♭5

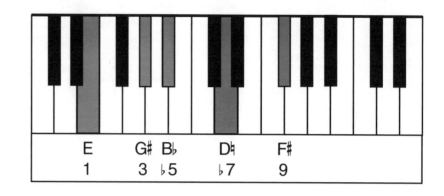

E	G# B♭	D♮	F#
1	3 ♭5	♭7	9

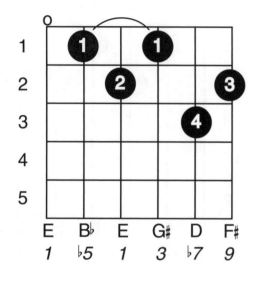

E B♭ E G# D F#
1 ♭5 1 3 ♭7 9

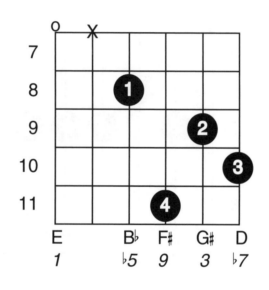

E B♭ F# G# D
1 ♭5 9 3 ♭7

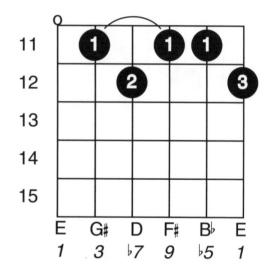

E G# D F# B♭ E
1 3 ♭7 9 ♭5 1

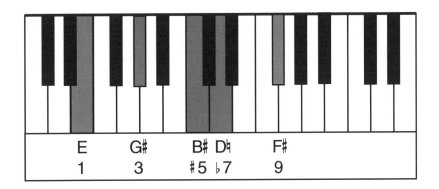

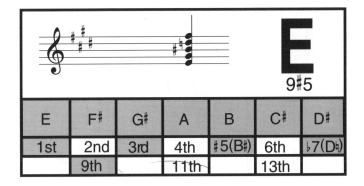

E	F♯	G♯	A	B	C♯	D♯
1st	2nd	3rd	4th	♯5(B♯)	6th	♭7(D♮)
	9th			11th		13th	

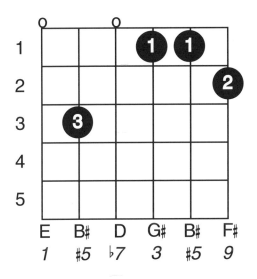

E	B♯	D	G♯	B♯	F♯
1	*♯5*	*♭7*	*3*	*♯5*	*9*

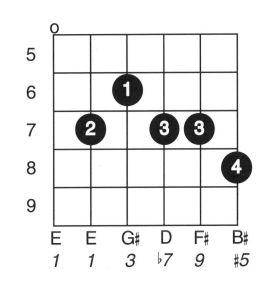

E	E	G♯	D	F♯	B♯
1	*1*	*3*	*♭7*	*9*	*♯5*

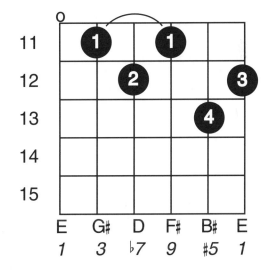

E	G♯	D	F♯	B♯	E
1	*3*	*♭7*	*9*	*♯5*	*1*

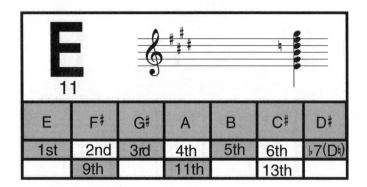

E	F#	G#	A	B	C#	D#
1st	2nd	3rd	4th	5th	6th	♭7(D♮)
	9th		11th		13th	

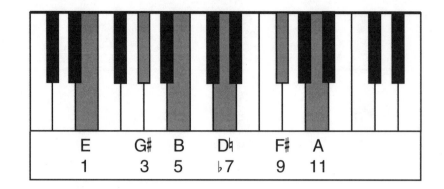

E   G#   B   D♮   F#   A
1   3   5   ♭7   9   11

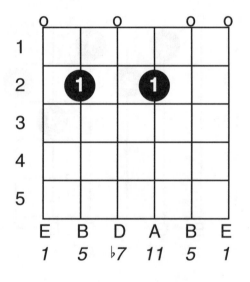

E	B	D	A	B	E
1	*5*	*♭7*	*11*	*5*	*1*

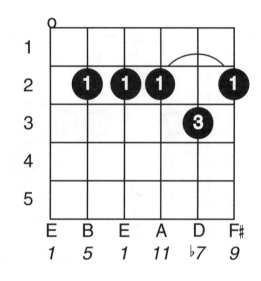

E	B	E	A	D	F#
1	*5*	*1*	*11*	*♭7*	*9*

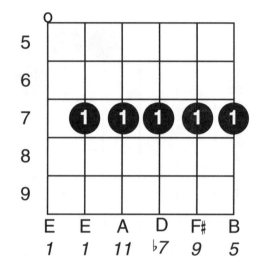

E	E	A	D	F#	B
1	*1*	*11*	*♭7*	*9*	*5*

214

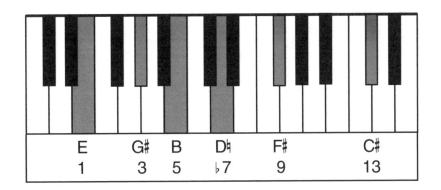

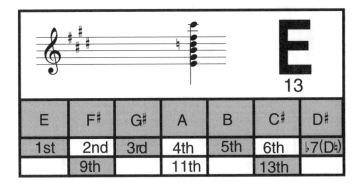

E	F#	G#	A	B	C#	D#
1st	2nd	3rd	4th	5th	6th	♭7(D♮)
	9th		11th		13th	

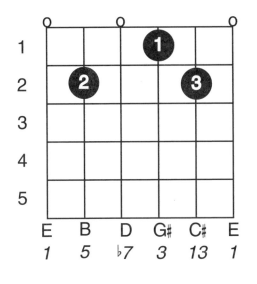

E B D G# C# E
1 5 ♭7 3 13 1

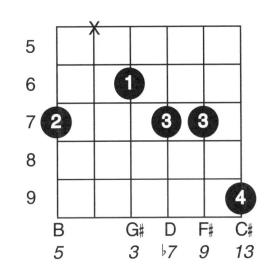

B G# D F# C#
5 3 ♭7 9 13

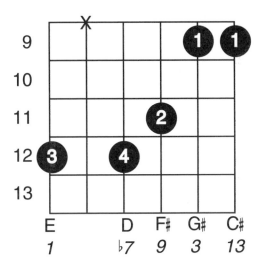

E D F# G# C#
1 ♭7 9 3 13

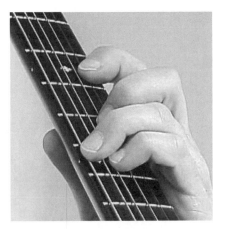

215

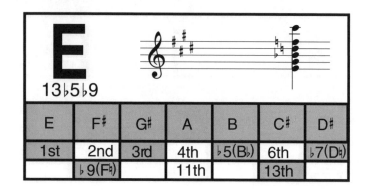

E 13♭5♭9

E	F#	G#	A	B	C#	D#
1st	2nd	3rd	4th	♭5(B♭)	6th	♭7(D♮)
	♭9(F♮)		11th		13th	

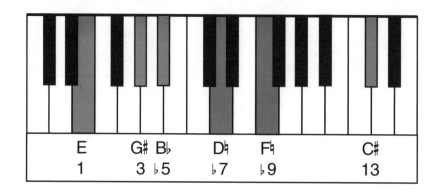

E G# B♭ D♮ F♮ C#
1   3 ♭5 ♭7 ♭9 13

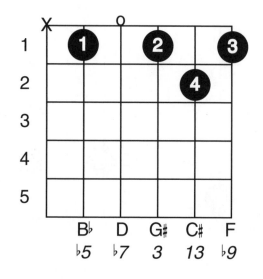

B♭ D G# C# F
♭5 ♭7 3 13 ♭9

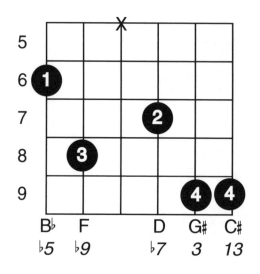

B♭ F D G# C#
♭5 ♭9 ♭7 3 13

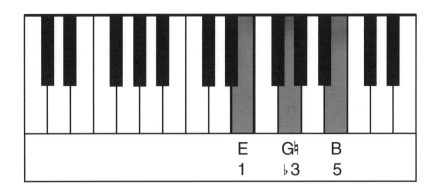

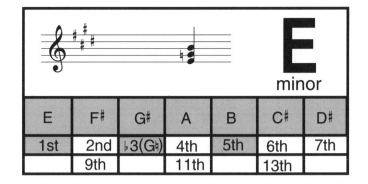

E minor

E	F#	G#	A	B	C#	D#
1st	2nd	♭3(G♮)	4th	5th	6th	7th
	9th		11th		13th	

Keyboard diagram:

E (1), G♮ (♭3), B (5)

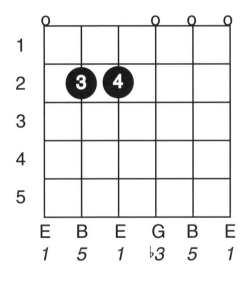

E   B   E   G   B   E
1   5   1   ♭3 5   1

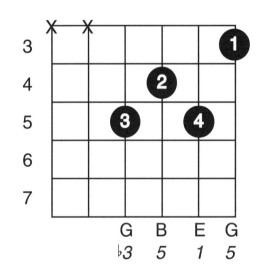

G   B   E   G
♭3 5   1   5

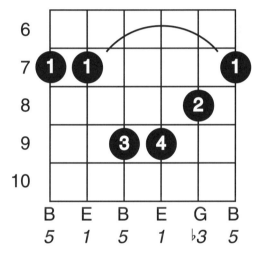

B   E   B   E   G   B
5   1   5   1   ♭3 5

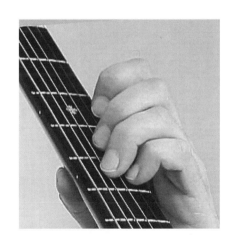

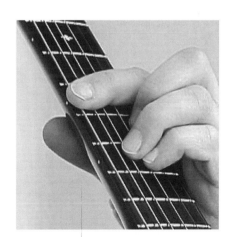

217

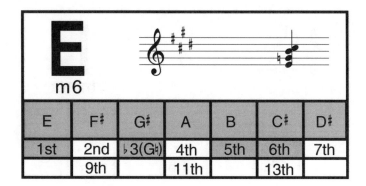

E	F#	G#	A	B	C#	D#
1st	2nd	♭3(G♮)	4th	5th	6th	7th
	9th		11th		13th	

E
m6

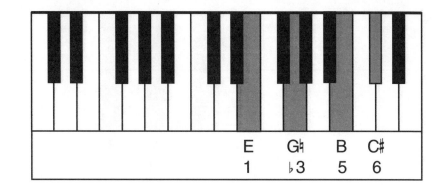

E   G♭   B   C#
1   ♭3   5   6

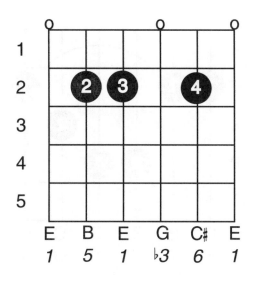

```
1
2
3
4
5
```

E   B   E   G   C# E
1   5   1   ♭3 6   1

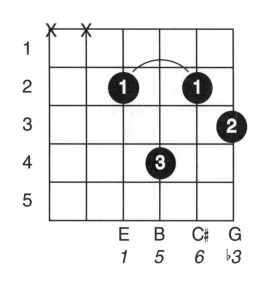

```
1
2
3
4
5
```

E   B   C# G
1   5   6   ♭3

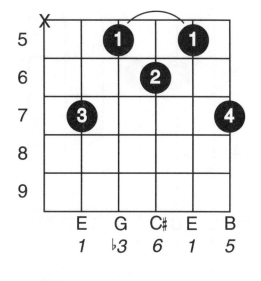

```
5
6
7
8
9
```

E   G   C# E   B
1   ♭3 6   1   5

218

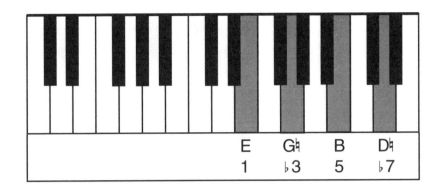

E G♮ B D♮
1 ♭3 5 ♭7

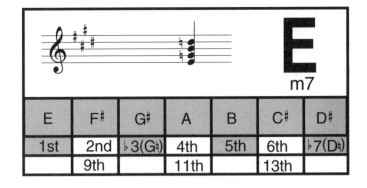

E m7

E	F#	G#	A	B	C#	D#
1st	2nd	♭3(G♮)	4th	5th	6th	♭7(D♮)
	9th		11th		13th	

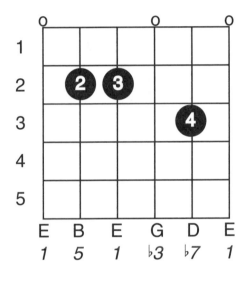

E B E G D E
1 5 1 ♭3 ♭7 1

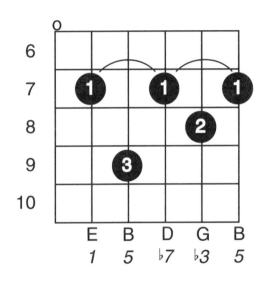

E B D G B
1 5 ♭7 ♭3 5

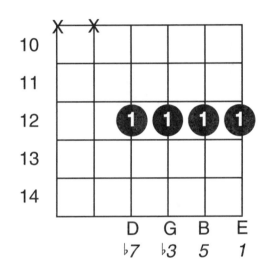

D G B E
♭7 ♭3 5 1

219

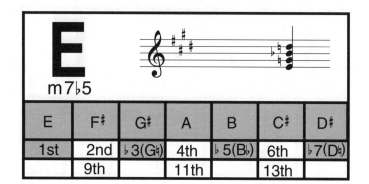

E
m7♭5

E	F#	G#	A	B	C#	D#
1st	2nd	♭3(G♮)	4th	♭5(B♭)	6th	♭7(D♮)
	9th		11th		13th	

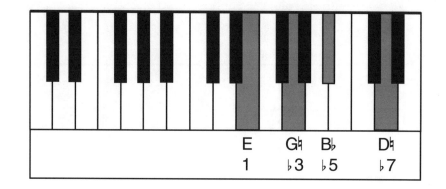

	E	G♮	B♭	D♮
	1	♭3	♭5	♭7

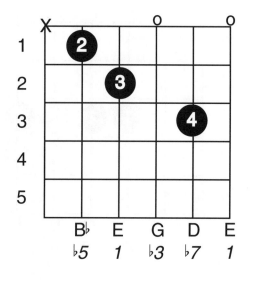

B♭	E	G	D	E
♭5	1	♭3	♭7	1

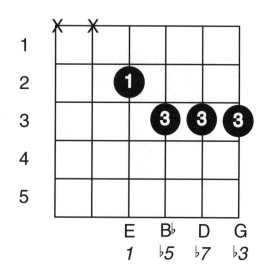

E	B♭	D	G
1	♭5	♭7	♭3

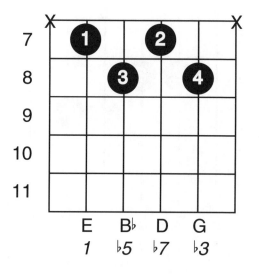

E	B♭	D	G
1	♭5	♭7	♭3

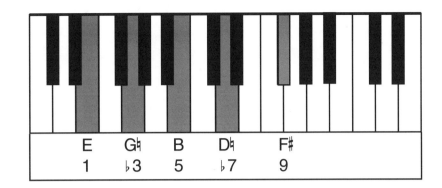

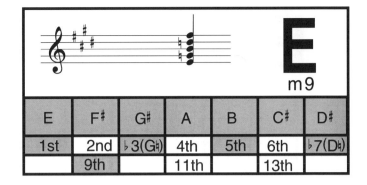

E	F#	G#	A	B	C#	D#
1st	2nd	♭3(G♮)	4th	5th	6th	♭7(D♮)
	9th		11th		13th	

E m9

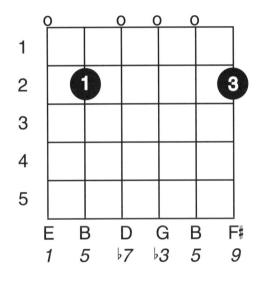

E B D G B F#
1 5 ♭7 ♭3 5 9

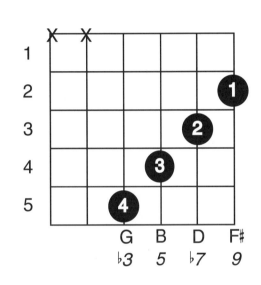

G B D F#
♭3 5 ♭7 9

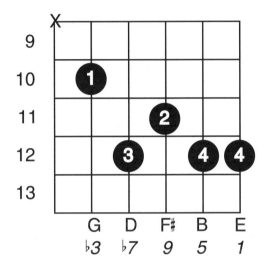

G D F# B E
♭3 ♭7 9 5 1

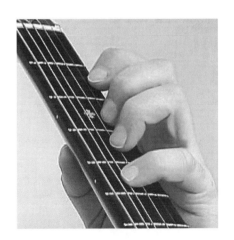

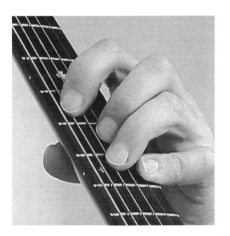

E
dim7

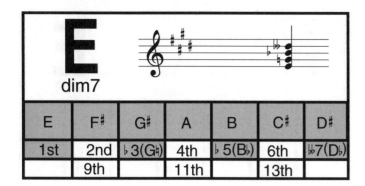

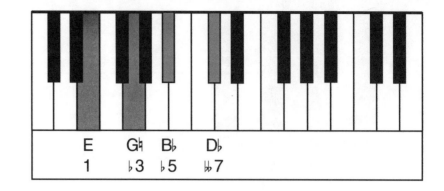

E	F#	G#	A	B	C#	D#
1st	2nd	♭3(G♮)	4th	♭5(B♭)	6th	♭♭7(D♭)
	9th		11th		13th	

Keyboard labels: E (1), G♮ (♭3), B♭ (♭5), D♭ (♭♭7)

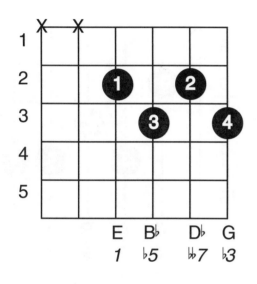

E B♭ D♭ G
1 ♭5 ♭♭7 ♭3

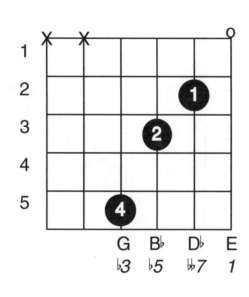

G B♭ D♭ E
♭3 ♭5 ♭♭7 1

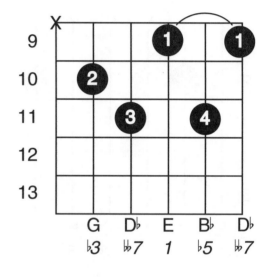

G D♭ E B♭ D♭
♭3 ♭♭7 1 ♭5 ♭♭7

222

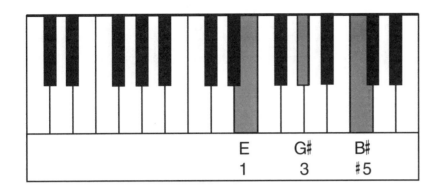

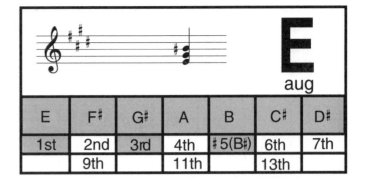

E	F#	G#	A	B	C#	D#
1st	2nd	3rd	4th	#5(B#)	6th	7th
	9th		11th		13th	

E
aug

Keyboard:
E — 1
G# — 3
B# — #5

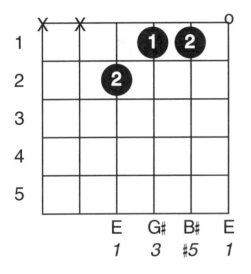

E	G#	B#	E
1	3	#5	1

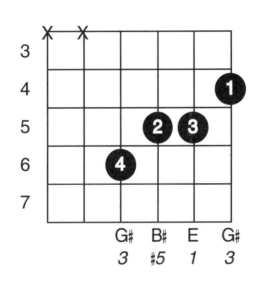

G#	B#	E	G#
3	#5	1	3

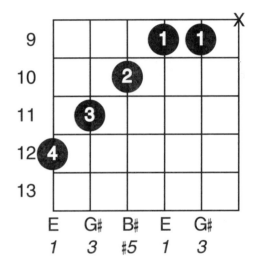

E	G#	B#	E	G#
1	3	#5	1	3

223

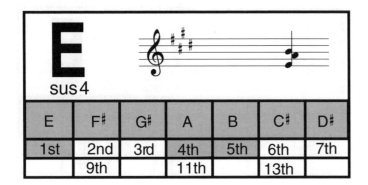

E	F#	G#	A	B	C#	D#
1st	2nd	3rd	4th	5th	6th	7th
	9th		11th		13th	

E sus 4

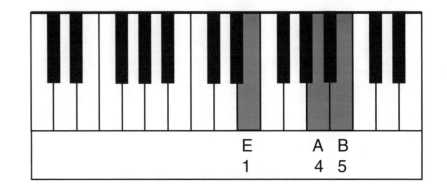

E A B
1 4 5

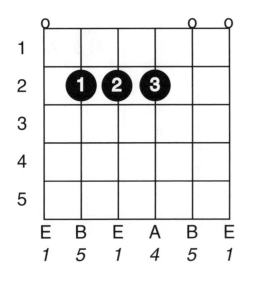

E B E A B E
1 5 1 4 5 1

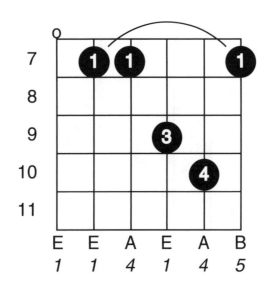

E E A E A B
1 1 4 1 4 5

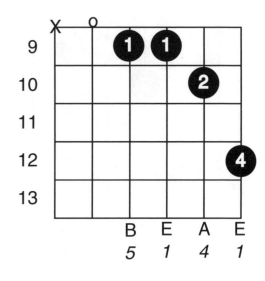

B E A E
5 1 4 1

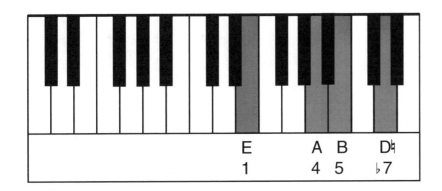

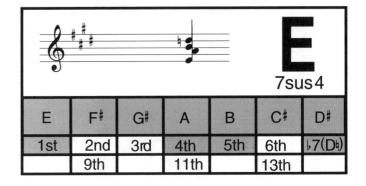

E 7sus4

E	F#	G#	A	B	C#	D#
1st	2nd	3rd	4th	5th	6th	♭7(D♮)
	9th		11th		13th	

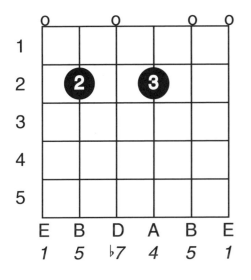

E	B	D	A	B	E
1	5	♭7	4	5	1

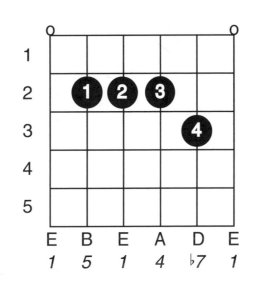

E	B	E	A	D	E
1	5	1	4	♭7	1

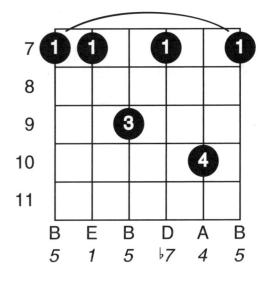

B	E	B	D	A	B
5	1	5	♭7	4	5

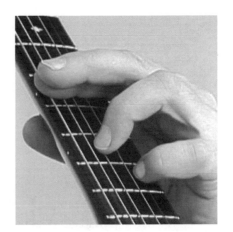

225

F
Major

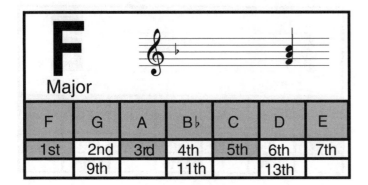

F	G	A	B♭	C	D	E
1st	2nd	3rd	4th	5th	6th	7th
	9th		11th		13th	

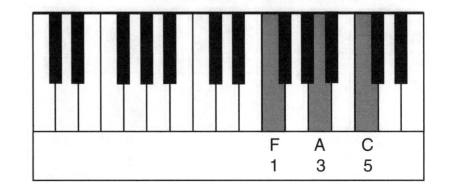

F A C
1 3 5

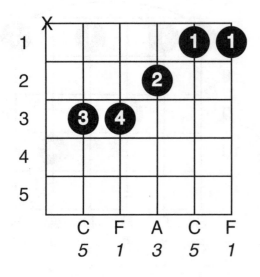

X

1
2
3
4
5

C F A C F
5 1 3 5 1

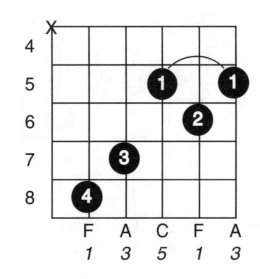

X

4
5
6
7
8

F A C F A
1 3 5 1 3

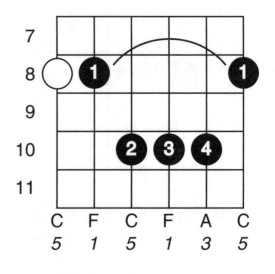

7
8
9
10
11

C F C F A C
5 1 5 1 3 5

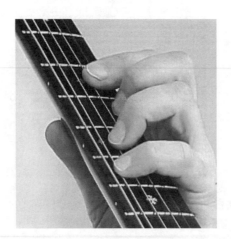

226

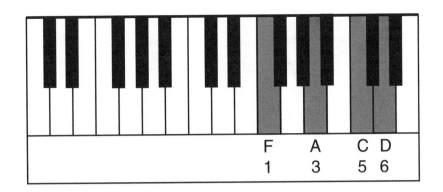

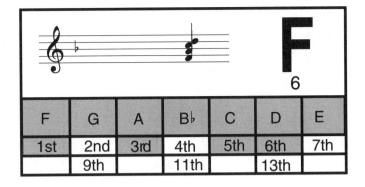

F₆

F	G	A	B♭	C	D	E
1st	2nd	3rd	4th	5th	6th	7th
	9th		11th		13th	

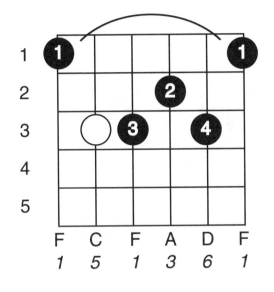

F	C	F	A	D	F
1	*5*	*1*	*3*	*6*	*1*

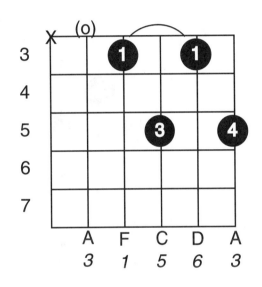

A	F	C	D	A	
3	*1*	*5*	*6*	*3*	

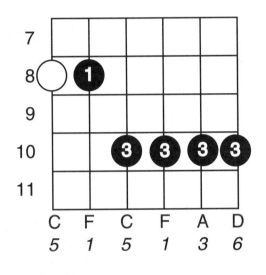

C	F	C	F	A	D
5	*1*	*5*	*1*	*3*	*6*

227

F 6/9

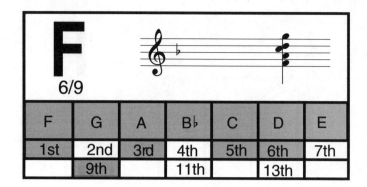

F	G	A	B♭	C	D	E
1st	2nd	3rd	4th	5th	6th	7th
	9th		11th		13th	

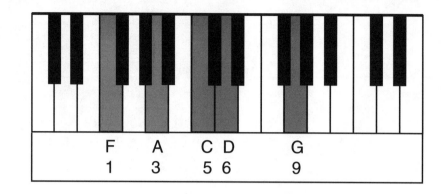

F	A	C	D	G
1	3	5	6	9

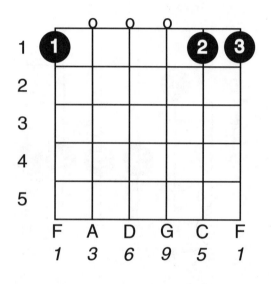

F	A	D	G	C	F
1	*3*	*6*	*9*	*5*	*1*

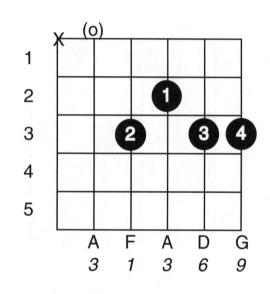

A	F	A	D	G
3	*1*	*3*	*6*	*9*

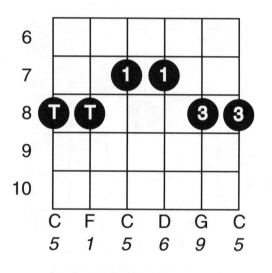

C	F	C	D	G	C
5	*1*	*5*	*6*	*9*	*5*

228

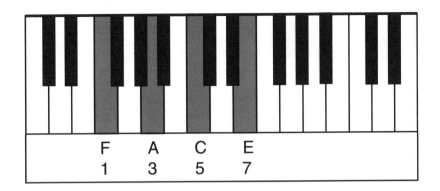

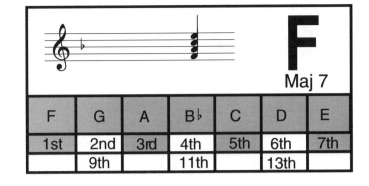

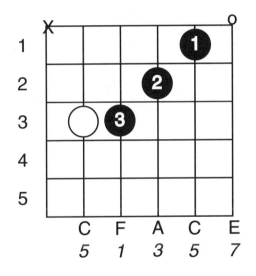

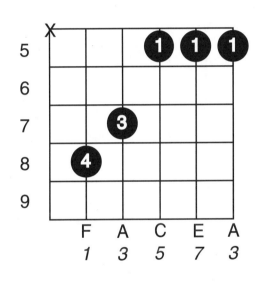

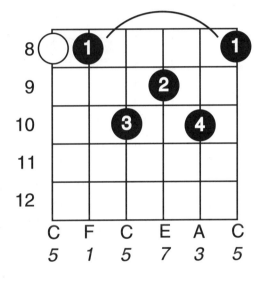

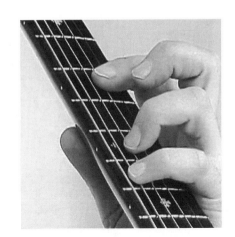

F

mMaj7

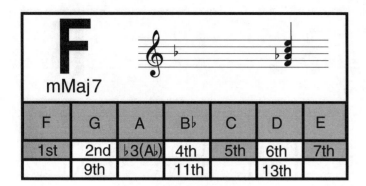

F	G	A	B♭	C	D	E
1st	2nd	♭3(A♭)	4th	5th	6th	7th
	9th		11th		13th	

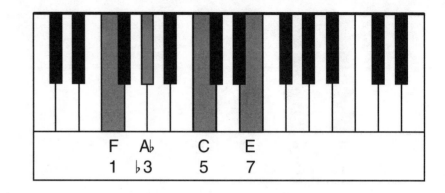

F   A♭   C   E
1   ♭3   5   7

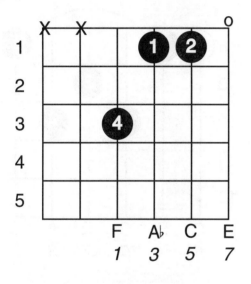

F   A♭   C   E
1   *3*   *5*   *7*

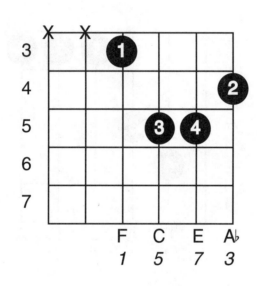

F   C   E   A♭
1   *5*   *7*   *3*

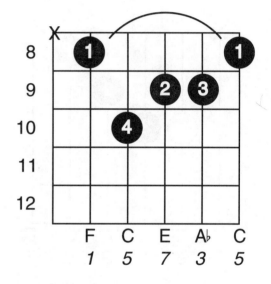

F   C   E   A♭   C
1   *5*   *7*   *3*   *5*

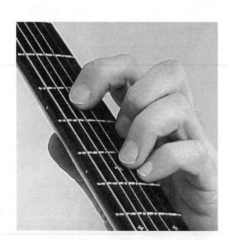

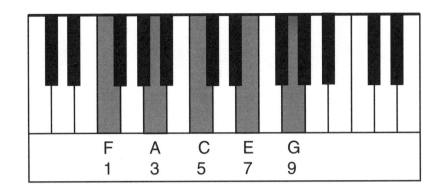

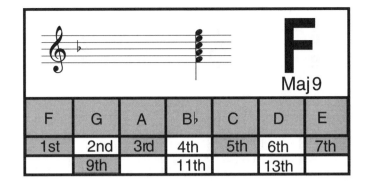

F Maj9

F	G	A	B♭	C	D	E
1st	2nd	3rd	4th	5th	6th	7th
	9th		11th		13th	

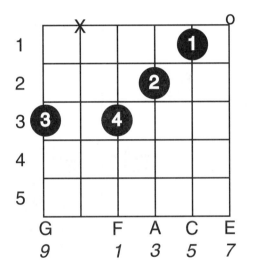

G		F	A	C	E
9		1	3	5	7

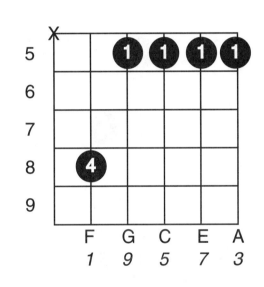

F	G	C	E	A
1	9	5	7	3

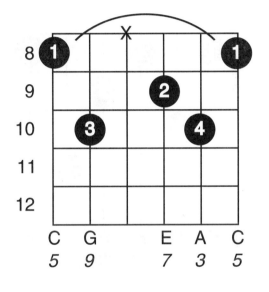

C	G		E	A	C
5	9		7	3	5

F

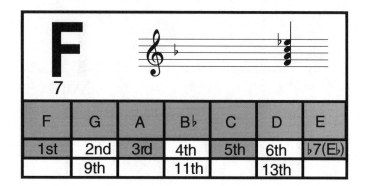

F	G	A	B♭	C	D	E
1st	2nd	3rd	4th	5th	6th	♭7(E♭)
	9th		11th		13th	

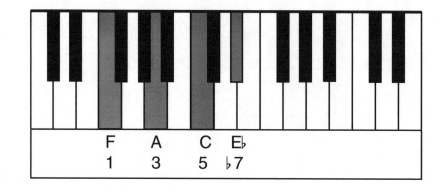

F   A   C   E♭
1   3   5   ♭7

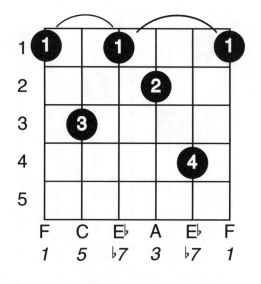

F C E♭ A E♭ F
1 *5* *♭7* *3* *♭7* *1*

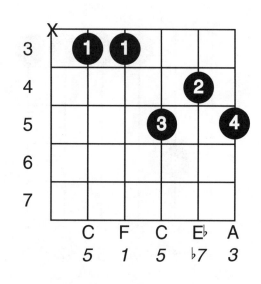

C F C E♭ A
5 *1* *5* *♭7* *3*

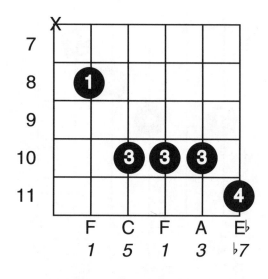

F C F A E♭
1 *5* *1* *3* *♭7*

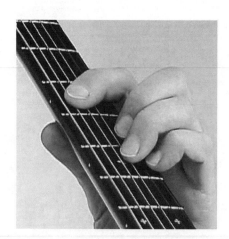

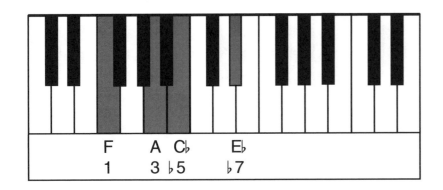

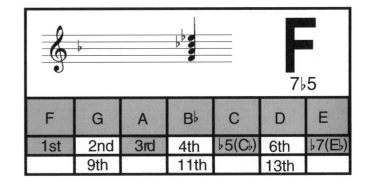

F	G	A	B♭	C	D	E
1st	2nd	3rd	4th	♭5(C♭)	6th	♭7(E♭)
	9th		11th		13th	

F 7♭5

F   A C♭   E♭
1   3 ♭5 ♭7

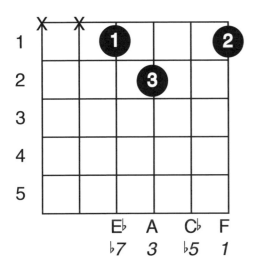

E♭ A C♭ F
♭7 3 ♭5 1

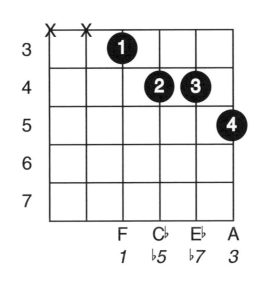

F C♭ E♭ A
1 ♭5 ♭7 3

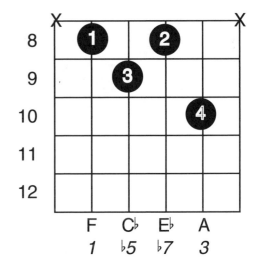

F C♭ E♭ A
1 ♭5 ♭7 3

233

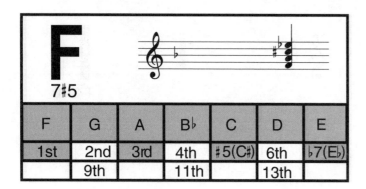

F
7#5

F	G	A	B♭	C	D	E
1st	2nd	3rd	4th	#5(C#)	6th	♭7(E♭)
	9th		11th		13th	

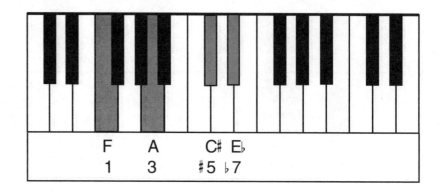

F   A   C#   E♭
1   3   #5   ♭7

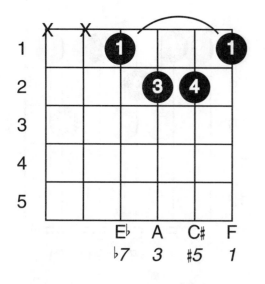

E♭   A   C#   F
♭7   3   #5   1

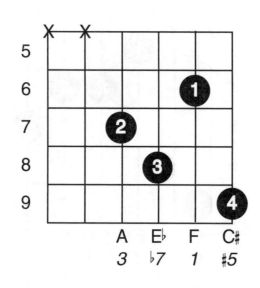

A   E♭   F   C#
3   ♭7   1   #5

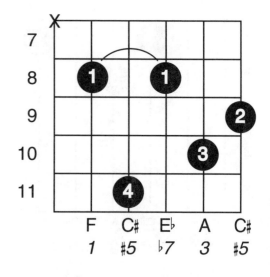

F   C#   E♭   A   C#
1   #5   ♭7   3   #5

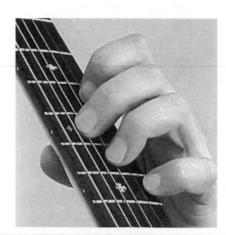

234

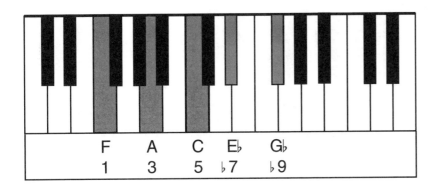

F

E♭ G♭

F A C E♭ G♭
1 3 5 ♭7 ♭9

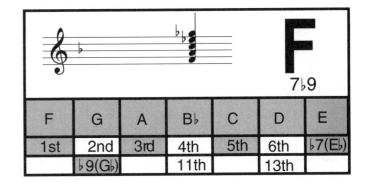

F 7♭9

F	G	A	B♭	C	D	E
1st	2nd	3rd	4th	5th	6th	♭7(E♭)
	♭9(G♭)		11th		13th	

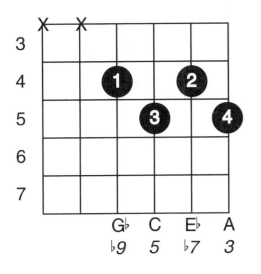

3
4
5
6
7

G♭ C E♭ A
♭9 5 ♭7 3

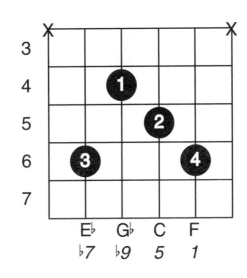

3
4
5
6
7

E♭ G♭ C F
♭7 ♭9 5 1

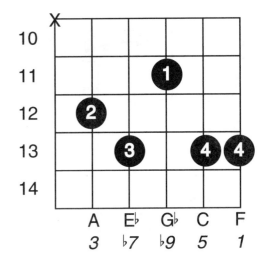

10
11
12
13
14

A E♭ G♭ C F
3 ♭7 ♭9 5 1

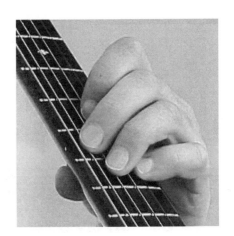

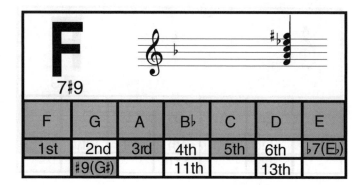

F

7#9

F	G	A	B♭	C	D	E
1st	2nd	3rd	4th	5th	6th	♭7(E♭)
	#9(G#)		11th		13th	

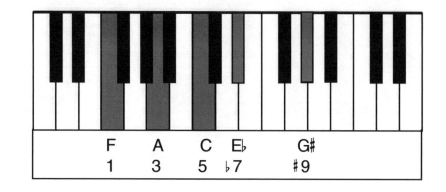

	F	A	C	E♭	G#
	1	3	5	♭7	#9

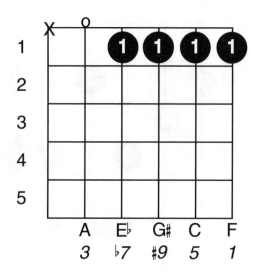

A	E♭	G#	C	F
3	*♭7*	*#9*	*5*	*1*

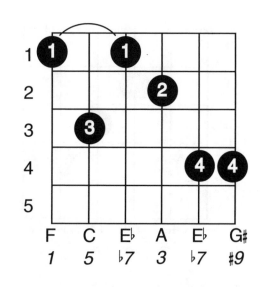

F	C	E♭	A	E♭	G#
1	*5*	*♭7*	*3*	*♭7*	*#9*

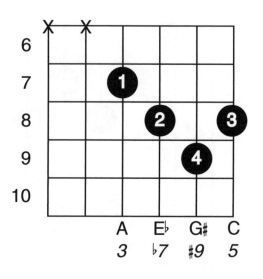

A	E♭	G#	C
3	*♭7*	*#9*	*5*

236

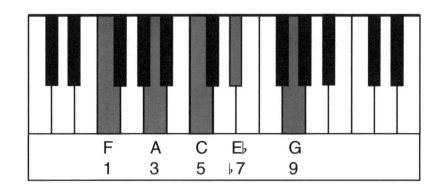

F A C E♭ G
1 3 5 ♭7 9

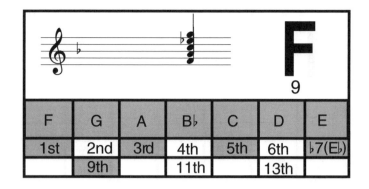

F9

F	G	A	B♭	C	D	E
1st	2nd	3rd	4th	5th	6th	♭7(E♭)
	9th		11th		13th	

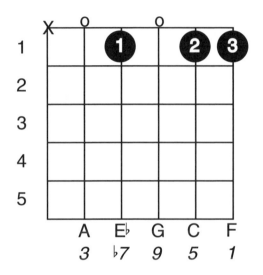

X O O

1
2
3
4
5

A E♭ G C F
3 ♭7 9 5 1

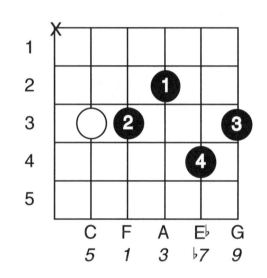

X

1
2
3
4
5

C F A E♭ G
5 1 3 ♭7 9

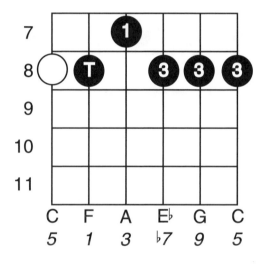

7
8
9
10
11

C F A E♭ G C
5 1 3 ♭7 9 5

237

F

9♭5

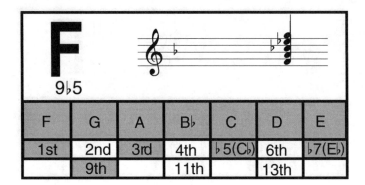

F	G	A	B♭	C	D	E
1st	2nd	3rd	4th	♭5(C♭)	6th	♭7(E♭)
	9th		11th		13th	

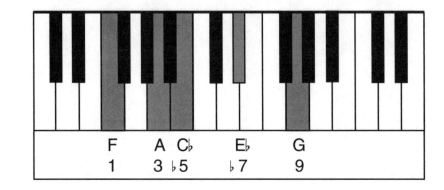

F   A   C♭   E♭   G
1   3   ♭5   ♭7   9

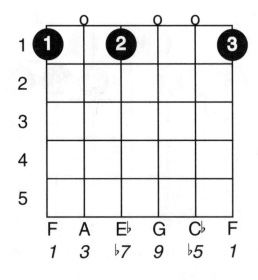

F   A   E♭   G   C♭   F
1   *3*   *♭7*   *9*   *♭5*   *1*

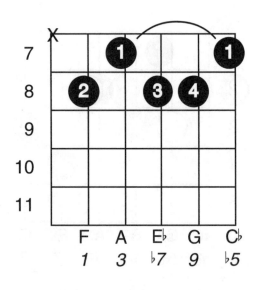

F   A   E♭   G   C♭
1   *3*   *♭7*   *9*   *♭5*

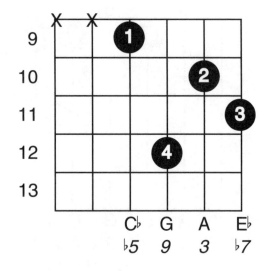

C♭   G   A   E♭
♭5   *9*   *3*   *♭7*

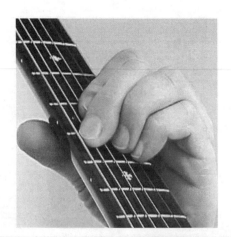

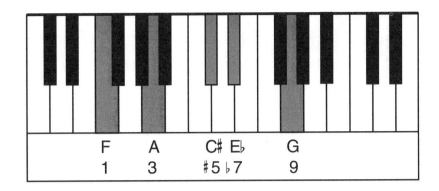

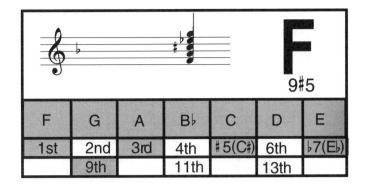

F
9#5

F	G	A	B♭	C	D	E
1st	2nd	3rd	4th	#5(C#)	6th	♭7(E♭)
	9th		11th		13th	

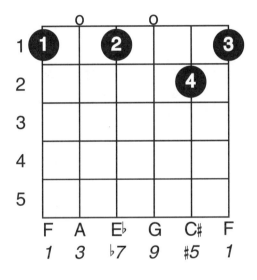

F	A	E♭	G	C#	F
1	*3*	*♭7*	*9*	*#5*	*1*

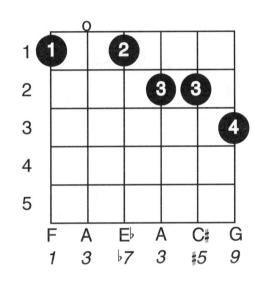

F	A	E♭	A	C#	G
1	*3*	*♭7*	*3*	*#5*	*9*

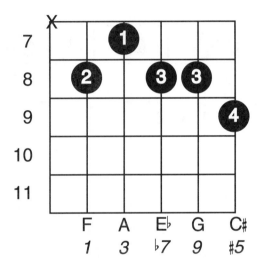

F	A	E♭	G	C#
1	*3*	*♭7*	*9*	*#5*

239

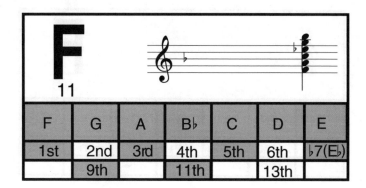

F11

F	G	A	B♭	C	D	E
1st	2nd	3rd	4th	5th	6th	♭7(E♭)
	9th		11th		13th	

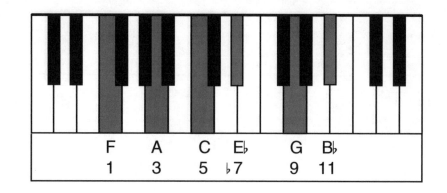

F A C E♭ G B♭
1 3 5 ♭7 9 11

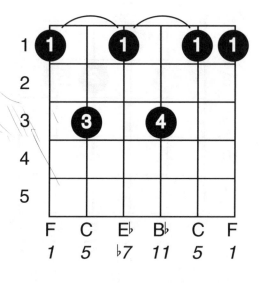

F C E♭ B♭ C F
1 5 ♭7 11 5 1

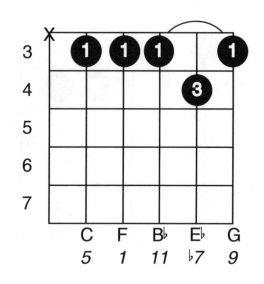

C F B♭ E♭ G
5 1 11 ♭7 9

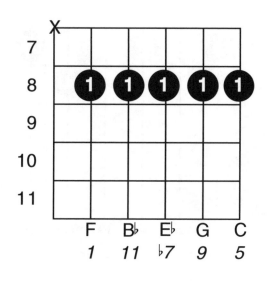

F B♭ E♭ G C
1 11 ♭7 9 5

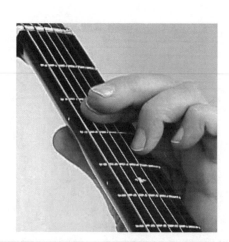

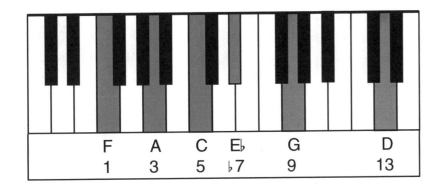

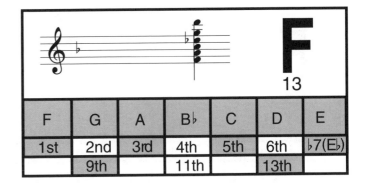

F	G	A	B♭	C	D	E
1st	2nd	3rd	4th	5th	6th	♭7(E♭)
	9th		11th		13th	

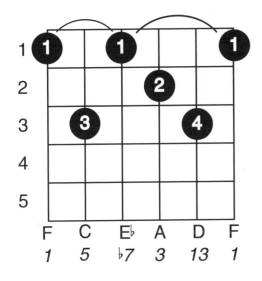

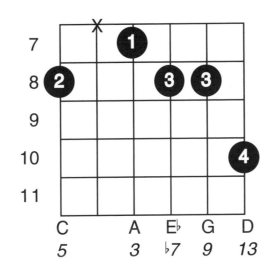

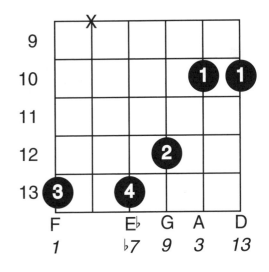

241

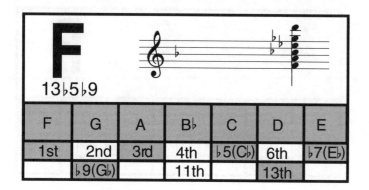

F
13♭5♭9

F	G	A	B♭	C	D	E
1st	2nd	3rd	4th	♭5(C♭)	6th	♭7(E♭)
	♭9(G♭)		11th		13th	

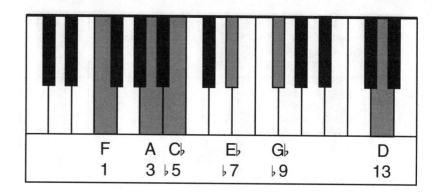

F	A	C♭	E♭	G♭	D
1	3	♭5	♭7	♭9	13

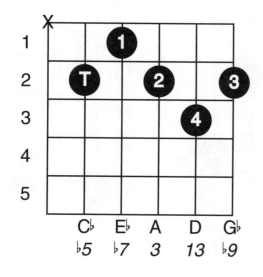

C♭	E♭	A	D	G♭
♭5	♭7	3	13	♭9

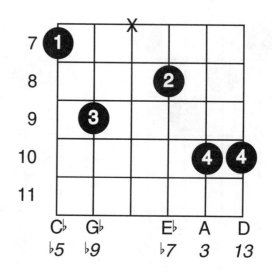

C♭	G♭	E♭	A	D
♭5	♭9	♭7	3	13

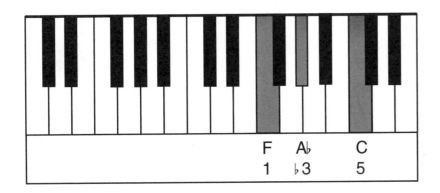

F A♭ C
1 ♭3 5

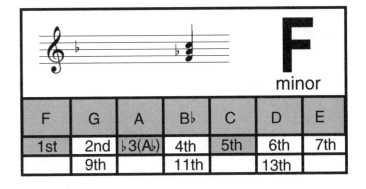

F
minor

F	G	A	B♭	C	D	E
1st	2nd	♭3(A♭)	4th	5th	6th	7th
	9th		11th		13th	

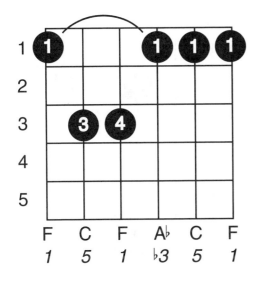

F	C	F	A♭	C	F
1	*5*	*1*	*♭3*	*5*	*1*

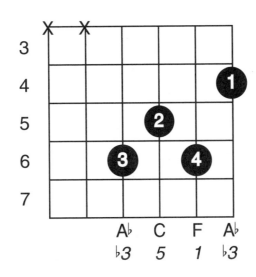

A♭	C	F	A♭
♭3	*5*	*1*	*♭3*

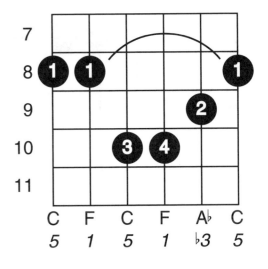

C	F	C	F	A♭	C
5	*1*	*5*	*1*	*♭3*	*5*

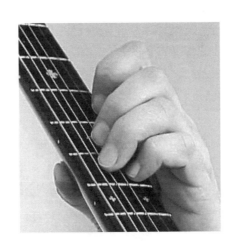

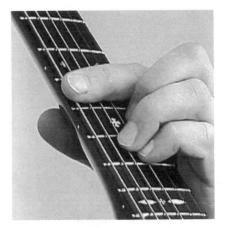

243

F m6

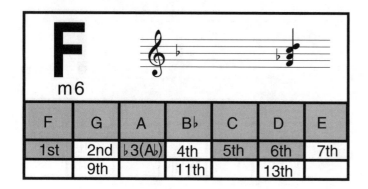

F	G	A	B♭	C	D	E
1st	2nd	♭3(A♭)	4th	5th	6th	7th
	9th		11th		13th	

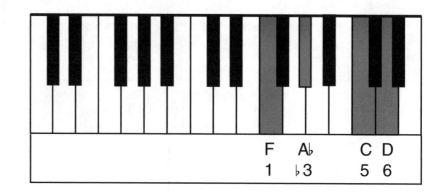

		F	A♭		C	D
		1	♭3		5	6

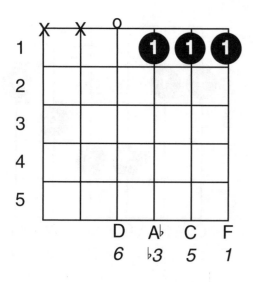

D	A♭	C	F
6	*♭3*	*5*	*1*

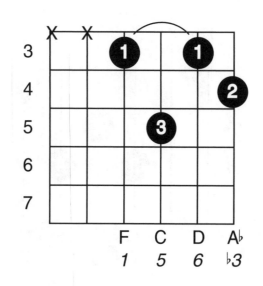

F	C	D	A♭
1	*5*	*6*	*♭3*

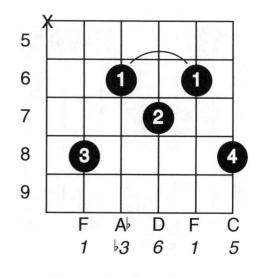

F	A♭	D	F	C
1	*♭3*	*6*	*1*	*5*

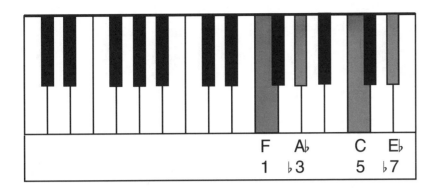

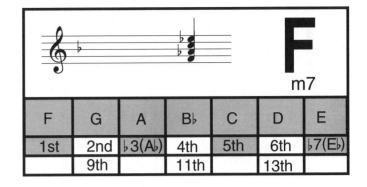

F	G	A	B♭	C	D	E
1st	2nd	♭3(A♭)	4th	5th	6th	♭7(E♭)
	9th		11th		13th	

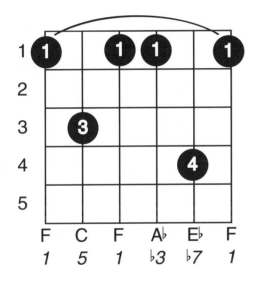

F C F A♭ E♭ F
1 *5* *1* *♭3* *♭7* *1*

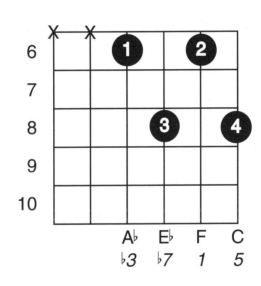

A♭ E♭ F C
♭3 *♭7* *1* *5*

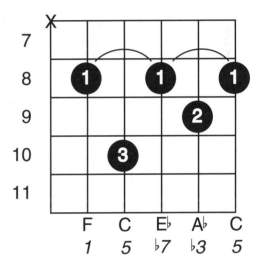

F C E♭ A♭ C
1 *5* *♭7* *♭3* *5*

245

F

m7♭5

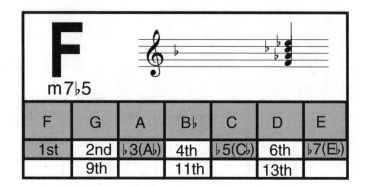

F	G	A	B♭	C	D	E
1st	2nd	♭3(A♭)	4th	♭5(C♭)	6th	♭7(E♭)
	9th		11th		13th	

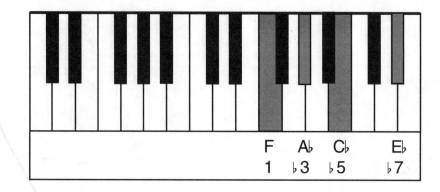

F	A♭	C♭	E♭
1	♭3	♭5	♭7

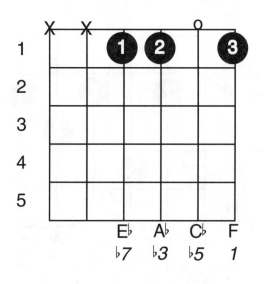

E♭	A♭	C♭	F
♭7	♭3	♭5	1

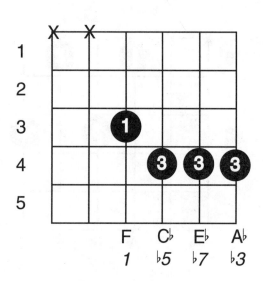

F	C♭	E♭	A♭
1	♭5	♭7	♭3

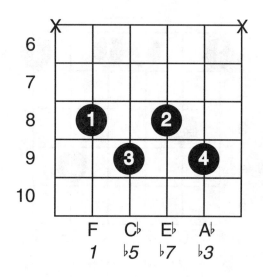

F	C♭	E♭	A♭
1	♭5	♭7	♭3

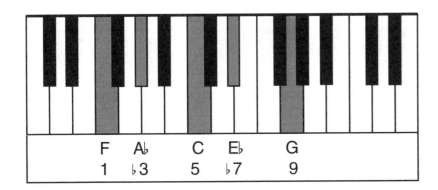

F A♭ C E♭ G
1 ♭3 5 ♭7 9

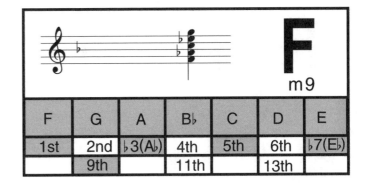

F m9

F	G	A	B♭	C	D	E
1st	2nd	♭3(A♭)	4th	5th	6th	♭7(E♭)
	9th		11th		13th	

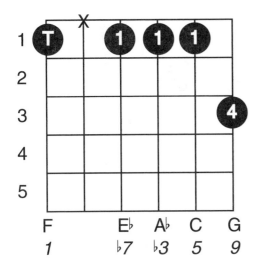

F   E♭ A♭ C G
1   ♭7 ♭3 5 9

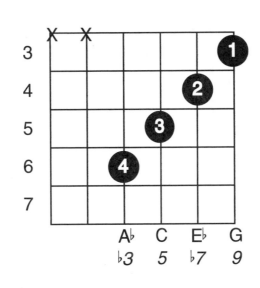

A♭ C E♭ G
♭3 5 ♭7 9

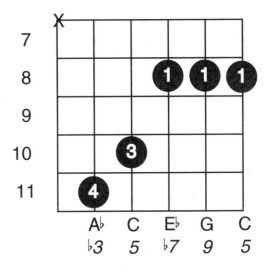

A♭ C E♭ G C
♭3 5 ♭7 9 5

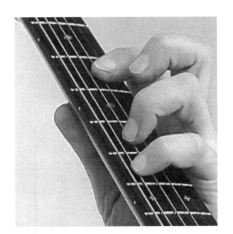

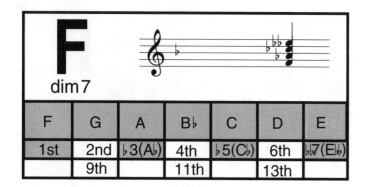

F
dim7

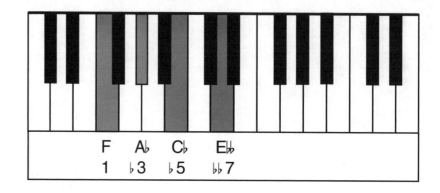

F	G	A	Bb	C	D	E
1st	2nd	b3(Ab)	4th	b5(Cb)	6th	bb7(Ebb)
	9th		11th		13th	

F A♭ C♭ E♭♭
1 ♭3 ♭5 ♭♭7

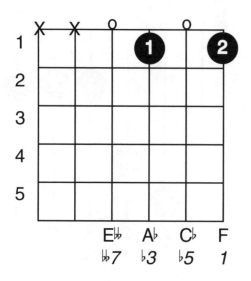

E♭♭ A♭ C♭ F
♭♭7 ♭3 ♭5 1

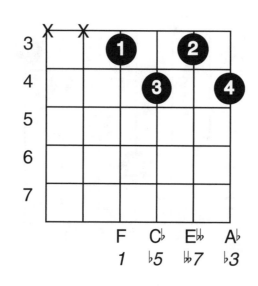

F C♭ E♭♭ A♭
1 ♭5 ♭♭7 ♭3

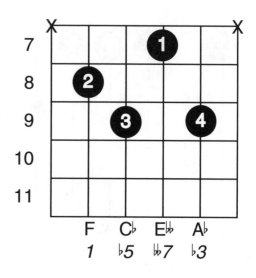

F C♭ E♭♭ A♭
1 ♭5 ♭♭7 ♭3

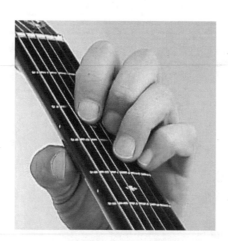

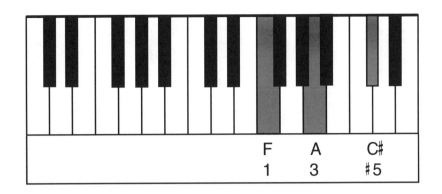

F A C#
1 3 #5

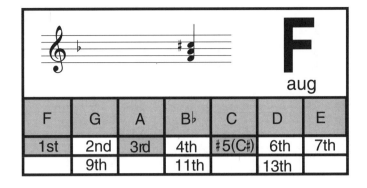

F aug

F	G	A	Bb	C	D	E
1st	2nd	3rd	4th	#5(C#)	6th	7th
	9th		11th		13th	

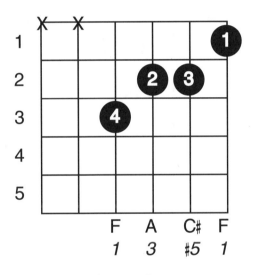

F A C# F
1 *3* *#5* *1*

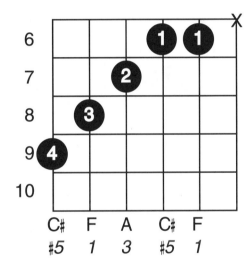

C# F A C# F
#5 *1* *3* *#5* *1*

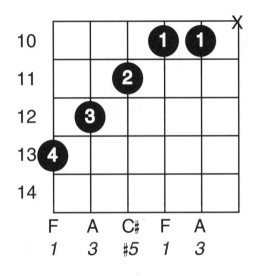

F A C# F A
1 *3* *#5* *1* *3*

249

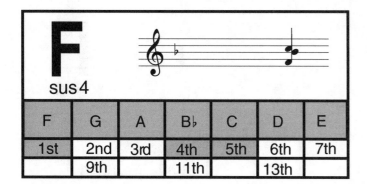

F sus4

F	G	A	B♭	C	D	E
1st	2nd	3rd	4th	5th	6th	7th
	9th		11th		13th	

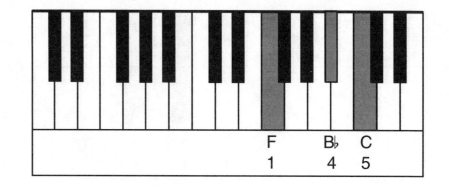

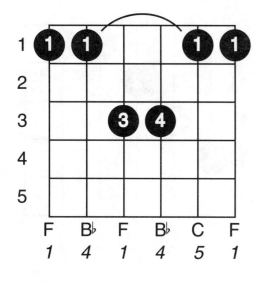

F	B♭	F	B♭	C	F
1	4	1	4	5	1

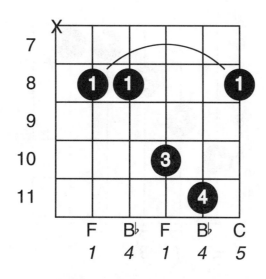

F	B♭	F	B♭	C
1	4	1	4	5

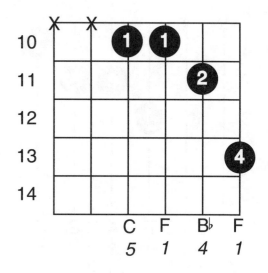

C	F	B♭	F
5	1	4	1

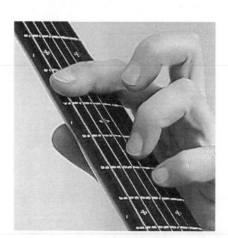

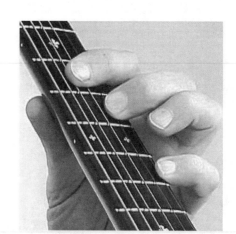

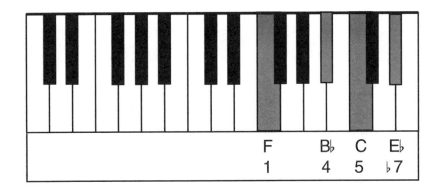

F	Bb	C	Eb
1	4	5	b7

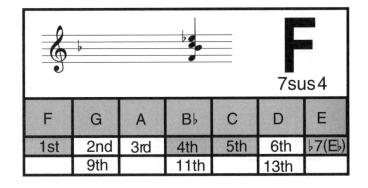

F

7sus4

F	G	A	Bb	C	D	E
1st	2nd	3rd	4th	5th	6th	b7(Eb)
	9th		11th		13th	

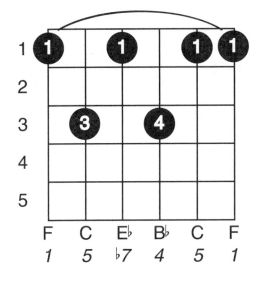

F	C	Eb	Bb	C	F
1	5	b7	4	5	1

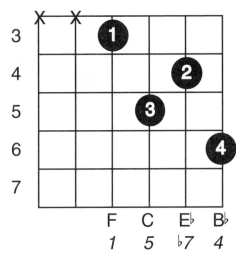

F	C	Eb	Bb
1	5	b7	4

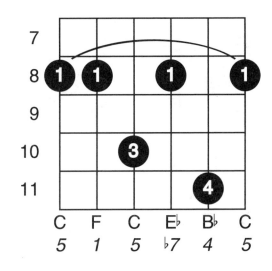

C	F	C	Eb	Bb	C
5	1	5	b7	4	5

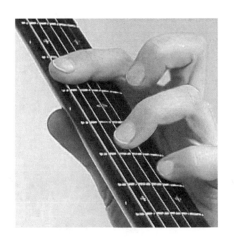

251

F# Major

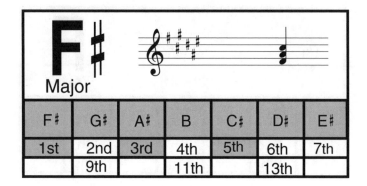

F#	G#	A#	B	C#	D#	E#
1st	2nd	3rd	4th	5th	6th	7th
	9th		11th		13th	

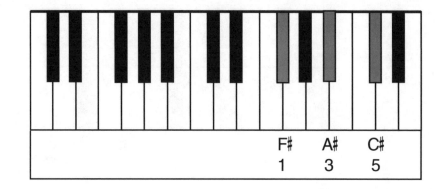

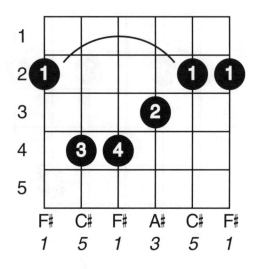

F#	C#	F#	A#	C#	F#
1	*5*	*1*	*3*	*5*	*1*

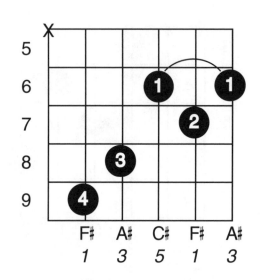

F#	A#	C#	F#	A#
1	*3*	*5*	*1*	*3*

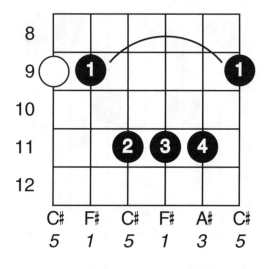

C#	F#	C#	F#	A#	C#
5	*1*	*5*	*1*	*3*	*5*

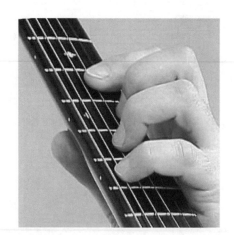

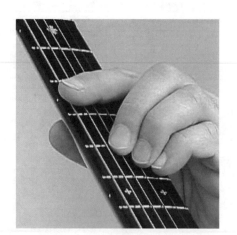

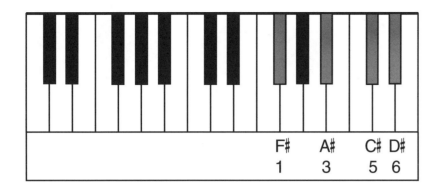

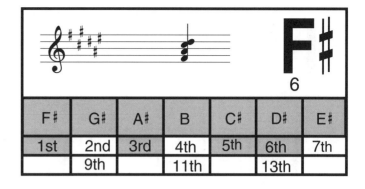

F# 6

F#	G#	A#	B	C#	D#	E#
1st	2nd	3rd	4th	5th	6th	7th
	9th		11th		13th	

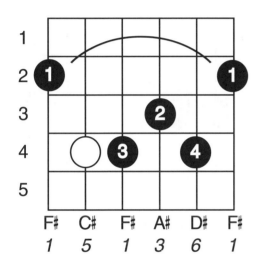

F# C# F# A# D# F#
1   5   1   3   6   1

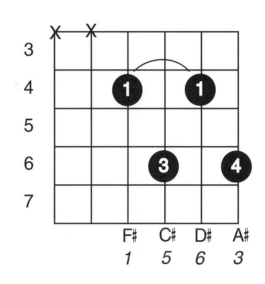

F# C# D# A#
1   5   6   3

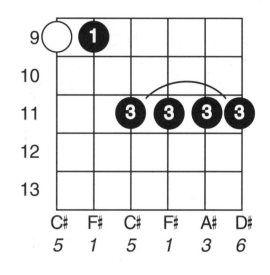

C# F# C# F# A# D#
5   1   5   1   3   6

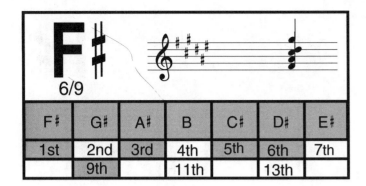

F#
6/9

F#	G#	A#	B	C#	D#	E#
1st	2nd	3rd	4th	5th	6th	7th
	9th		11th		13th	

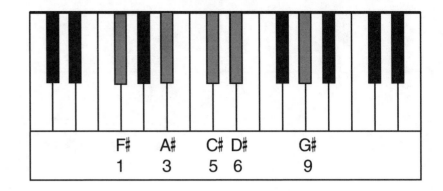

F#	A#	C#	D#	G#
1	3	5	6	9

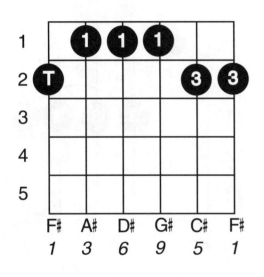

F#	A#	D#	G#	C#	F#
1	3	6	9	5	1

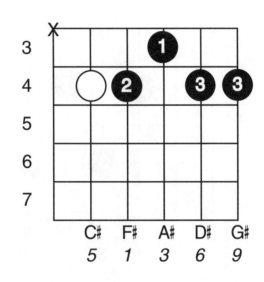

C#	F#	A#	D#	G#
5	1	3	6	9

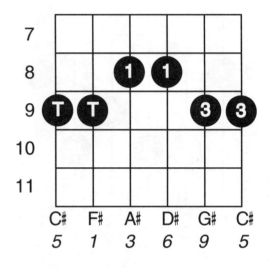

C#	F#	A#	D#	G#	C#
5	1	3	6	9	5

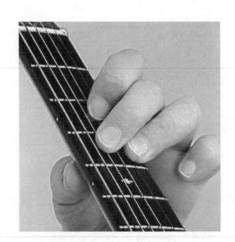

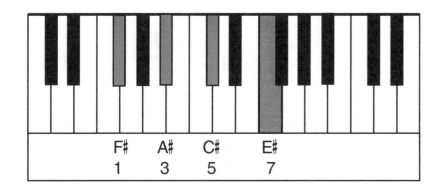

F#
1
A#
3
C#
5
E#
7

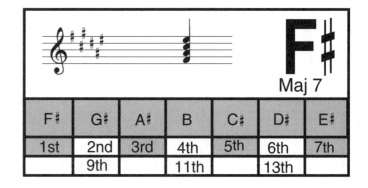

F#
Maj 7

F#	G#	A#	B	C#	D#	E#
1st	2nd	3rd	4th	5th	6th	7th
	9th		11th		13th	

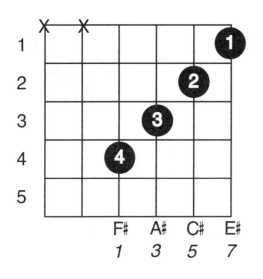

F#   A#   C#   E#
1   *3*   *5*   *7*

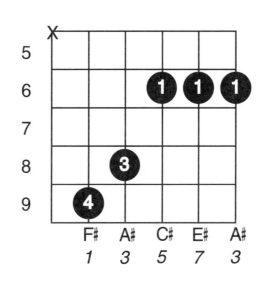

F#   A#   C#   E#   A#
1   *3*   *5*   *7*   *3*

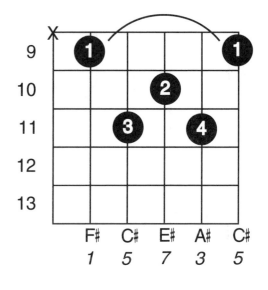

F#   C#   E#   A#   C#
1   *5*   *7*   *3*   *5*

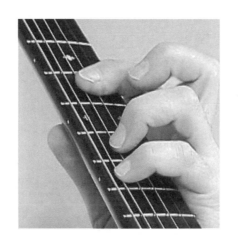

255

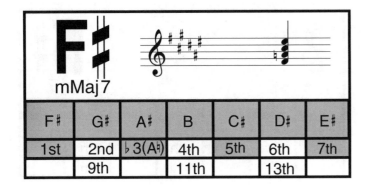

F♯ mMaj7

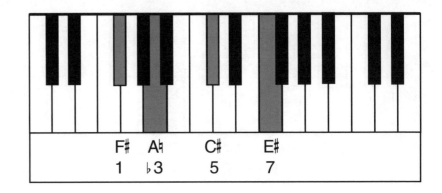

F♯	G♯	A♯	B	C♯	D♯	E♯
1st	2nd	♭3(A♮)	4th	5th	6th	7th
	9th		11th		13th	

F♯   A♮   C♯   E♯
1   ♭3   5   7

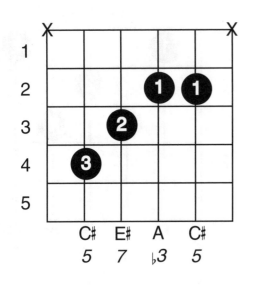

C#   E#   A   C#
5   7   ♭3   5

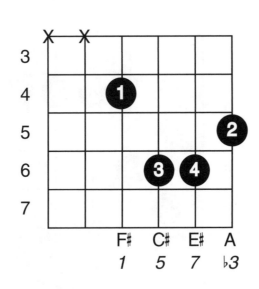

F#   C#   E#   A
1   5   7   ♭3

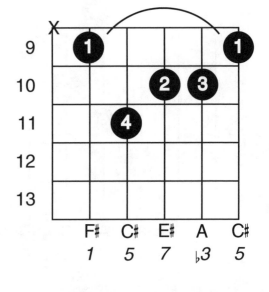

F#   C#   E#   A   C#
1   5   7   ♭3   5

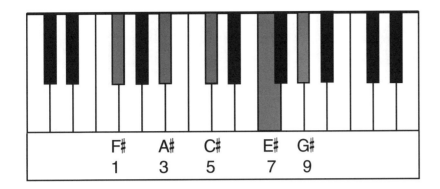

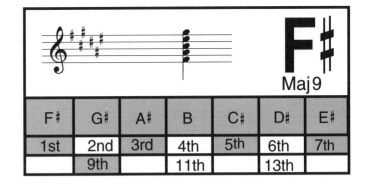

F#	G#	A#	B	C#	D#	E#
1st	2nd	3rd	4th	5th	6th	7th
	9th		11th		13th	

F#
Maj9

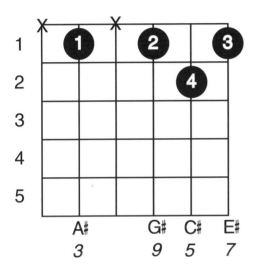

A#   G# C# E#
3   9   5   7

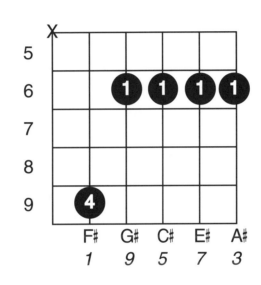

F#   G# C# E# A#
1   9   5   7   3

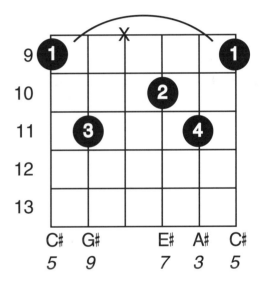

C#   G#   E# A# C#
5   9   7   3   5

257

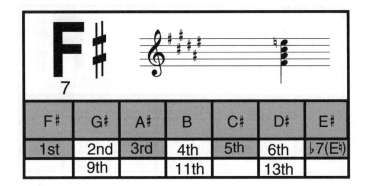

F#7

F#	G#	A#	B	C#	D#	E#
1st	2nd	3rd	4th	5th	6th	♭7(E♮)
	9th		11th		13th	

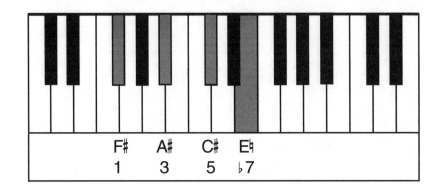

F#	A#	C#	E♮
1	3	5	♭7

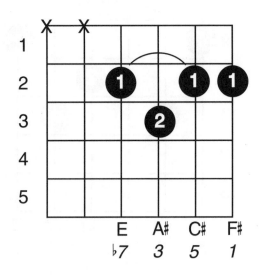

E	A#	C#	F#
♭7	3	5	1

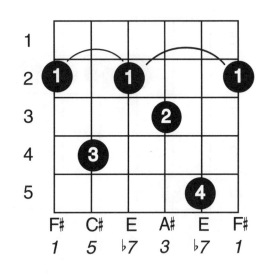

F#	C#	E	A#	E	F#
1	5	♭7	3	♭7	1

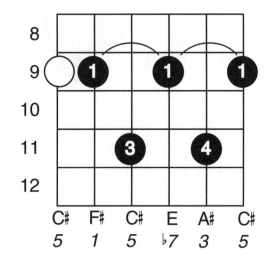

C#	F#	C#	E	A#	C#
5	1	5	♭7	3	5

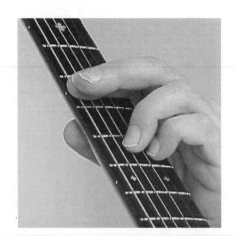

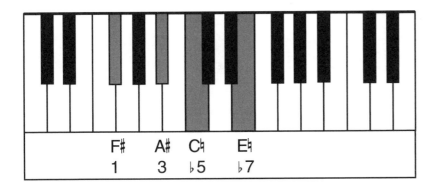

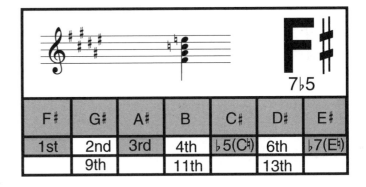

F#

7♭5

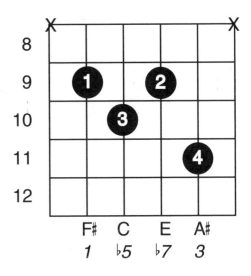

F#	G#	A#	B	C#	D#	E#
1st	2nd	3rd	4th	♭5(C♮)	6th	♭7(E♮)
	9th		11th		13th	

Piano keyboard notes:

F#	A#	C♮	E♮
1	3	♭5	♭7

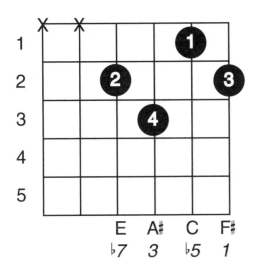

E	A#	C	F#
♭7	3	♭5	1

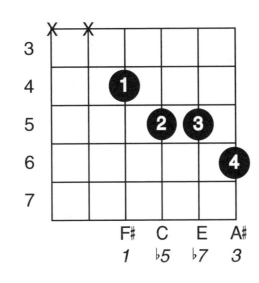

F#	C	E	A#
1	♭5	♭7	3

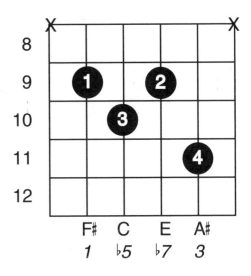

F#	C	E	A#
1	♭5	♭7	3

259

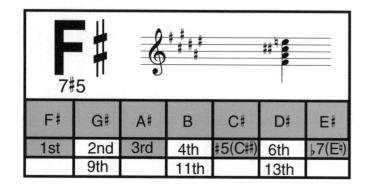

F♯
7♯5

F♯	G♯	A♯	B	C♯	D♯	E♯
1st	2nd	3rd	4th	#5(C##)	6th	♭7(E♮)
	9th		11th		13th	

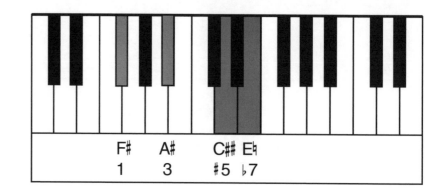

F♯ A♯ C## E♮
1   3   #5   ♭7

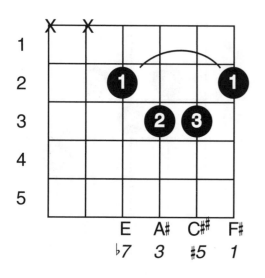

E   A#   C##   F#
♭7   3   #5   1

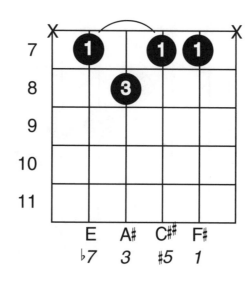

E   A#   C##   F#
♭7   3   #5   1

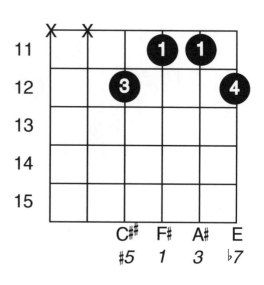

C##   F#   A#   E
#5   1   3   ♭7

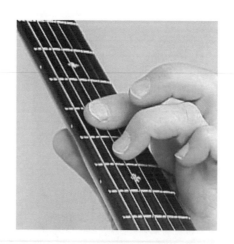

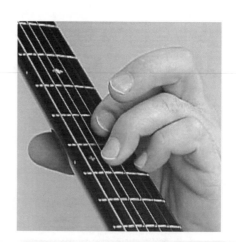

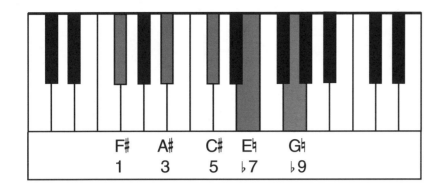

F# (chord notation diagram)
7♭9

F#	G#	A#	B	C#	D#	E#
1st	2nd	3rd	4th	5th	6th	♭7(E♮)
	♭9(G♮)		11th		13th	

Piano keyboard:

F# A# C# E♮ G♮
1 3 5 ♭7 ♭9

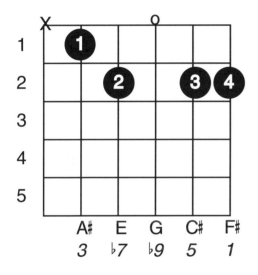

A# E G C# F#
3 ♭7 ♭9 5 1

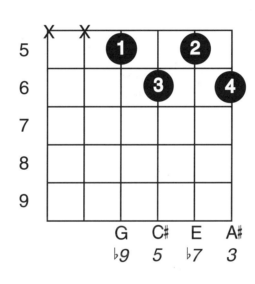

G C# E A#
♭9 5 ♭7 3

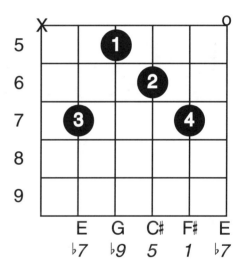

E G C# F# E
♭7 ♭9 5 1 ♭7

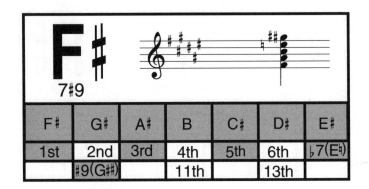

F#
7#9

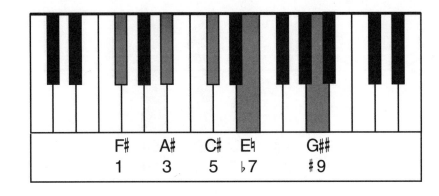

F#	G#	A#	B	C#	D#	E#
1st	2nd	3rd	4th	5th	6th	♭7(E♮)
	#9(G##)		11th		13th	

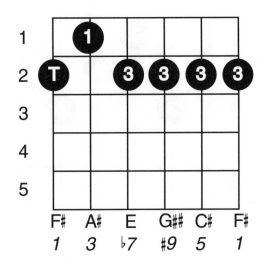

F#	A#	E	G##	C#	F#
1	*3*	*♭7*	*#9*	*5*	*1*

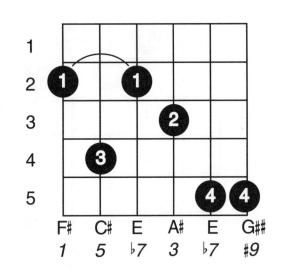

F#	C#	E	A#	E	G##
1	*5*	*♭7*	*3*	*♭7*	*#9*

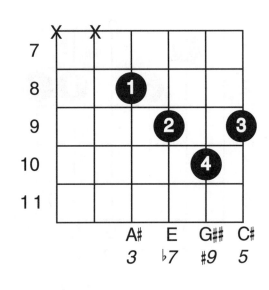

A#	E	G##	C#
3	*♭7*	*#9*	*5*

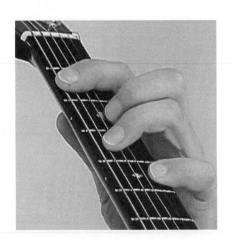

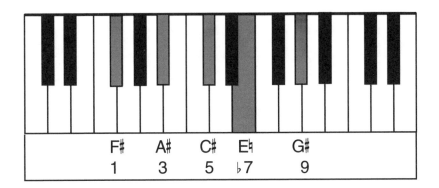

F#
1 3 5 ♭7 9
F# A# C# E♮ G#

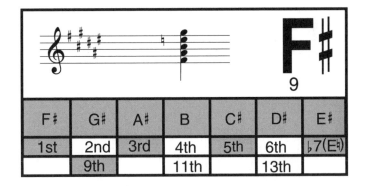

F#
9

F#	G#	A#	B	C#	D#	E#
1st	2nd	3rd	4th	5th	6th	♭7(E♮)
	9th		11th		13th	

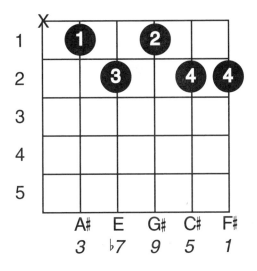

A# E G# C# F#
3 ♭7 9 5 1

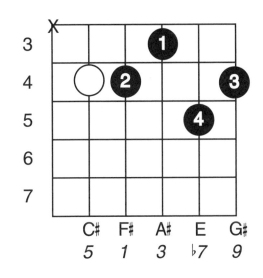

C# F# A# E G#
5 1 3 ♭7 9

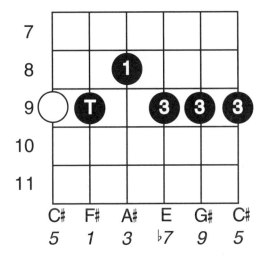

C# F# A# E G# C#
5 1 3 ♭7 9 5

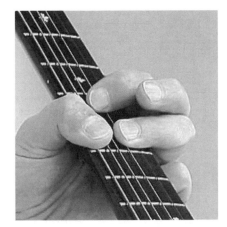

263

F#

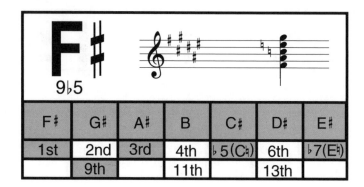

9♭5

F#	G#	A#	B	C#	D#	E#
1st	2nd	3rd	4th	♭5(C♮)	6th	♭7(E♮)
	9th		11th		13th	

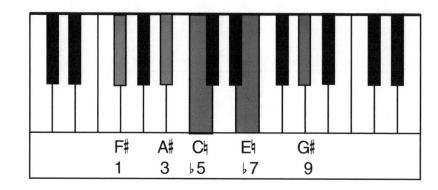

	F#	A#	C♮	E♮	G#	
	1	3	♭5	♭7	9	

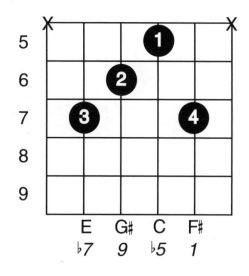

E	G#	C	F#
♭7	9	♭5	1

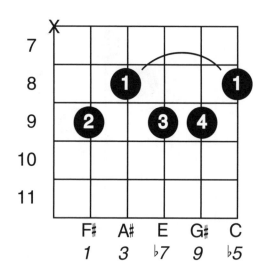

F#	A#	E	G#	C
1	3	♭7	9	♭5

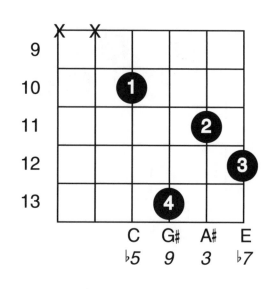

C	G#	A#	E
♭5	9	3	♭7

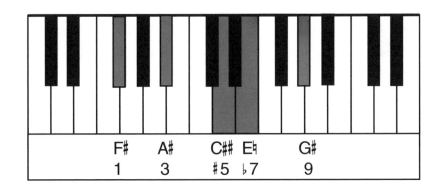

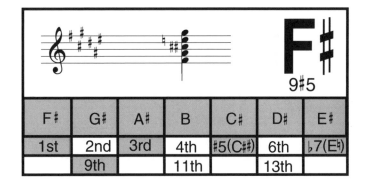

F#

9#5

F#	G#	A#	B	C#	D#	E#
1st	2nd	3rd	4th	#5(C##)	6th	♭7(E♮)
	9th		11th		13th	

Keyboard labels: F# (1), A# (3), C## (#5), E♮ (♭7), G# (9)

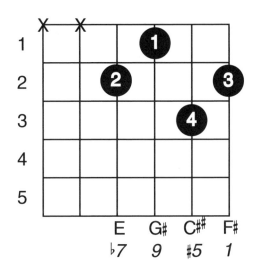

E	G#	C##	F#
♭7	9	#5	1

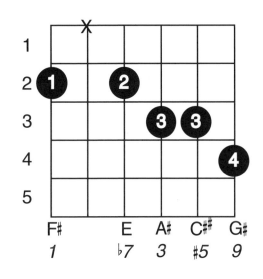

F#		E	A#	C##	G#
1		♭7	3	#5	9

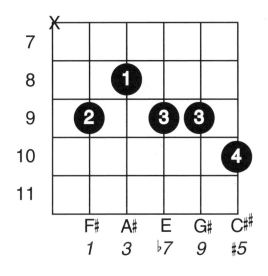

F#	A#	E	G#	C##
1	3	♭7	9	#5

265

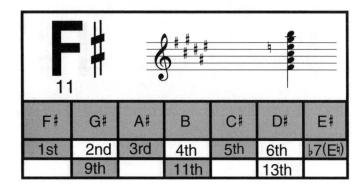

F♯	G♯	A♯	B	C♯	D♯	E♯
1st	2nd	3rd	4th	5th	6th	♭7(E♮)
	9th		11th		13th	

F♯ 11

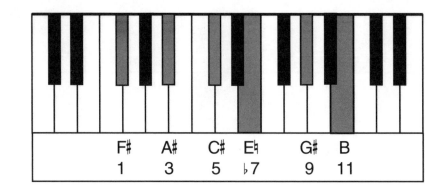

F♯ A♯ C♯ E♮ G♯ B
1   3   5   ♭7   9 11

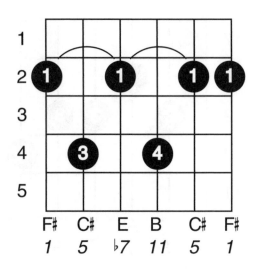

F♯ C♯ E B C♯ F♯
1 *5* *♭7* *11* *5* *1*

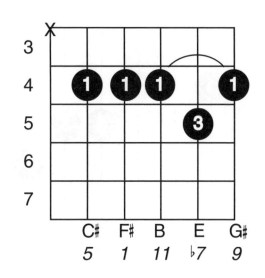

C♯ F♯ B E G♯
5 *1* *11* *♭7* *9*

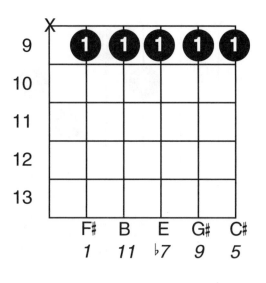

F♯ B E G♯ C♯
1 *11* *♭7* *9* *5*

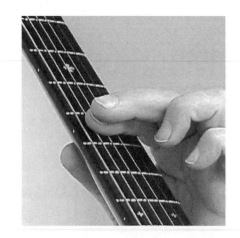

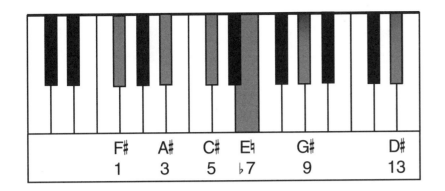

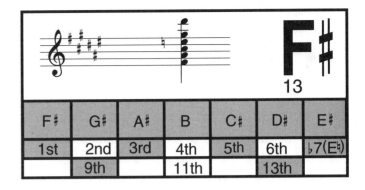

F#	G#	A#	B	C#	D#	E#
1st	2nd	3rd	4th	5th	6th	♭7(E♮)
	9th		11th		13th	

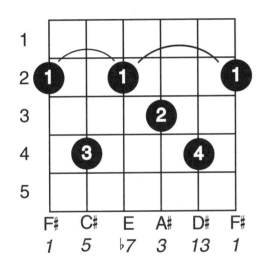

F# C# E A# D# F#
1 5 ♭7 3 13 1

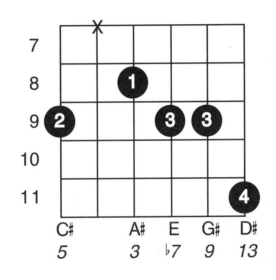

C# A# E G# D#
5 3 ♭7 9 13

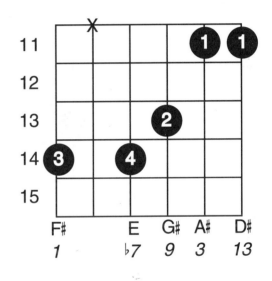

F# E G# A# D#
1 ♭7 9 3 13

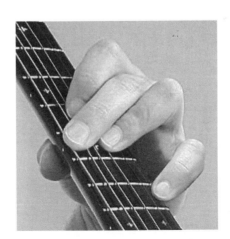

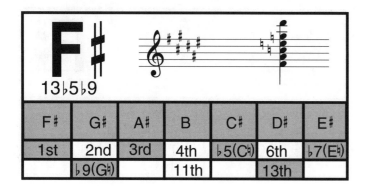

F♯

13♭5♭9

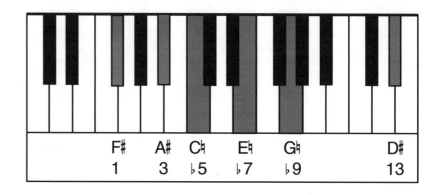

F♯	G♯	A♯	B	C♯	D♯	E♯
1st	2nd	3rd	4th	♭5(C♮)	6th	♭7(E♮)
	♭9(G♮)		11th		13th	

Keyboard notes: F♯ A♯ C♮ E♮ G♮ D♯
1 3 ♭5 ♭7 ♭9 13

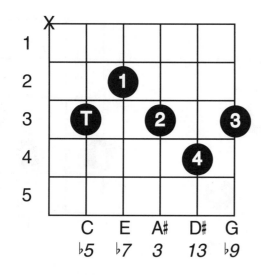

C E A♯ D♯ G
♭5 ♭7 3 13 ♭9

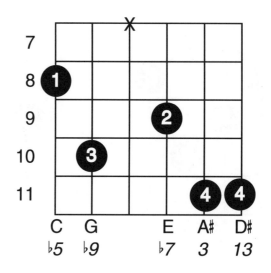

C G E A♯ D♯
♭5 ♭9 ♭7 3 13

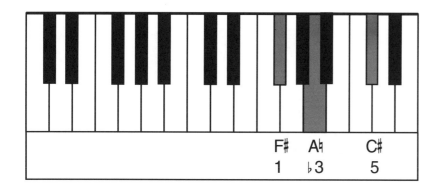

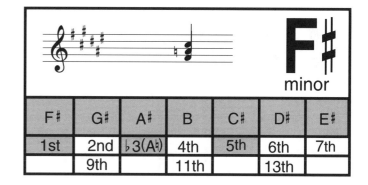

F#
minor

F#	G#	A#	B	C#	D#	E#
1st	2nd	♭3(A♮)	4th	5th	6th	7th
	9th		11th		13th	

Keyboard: F# 1, A♮ ♭3, C# 5

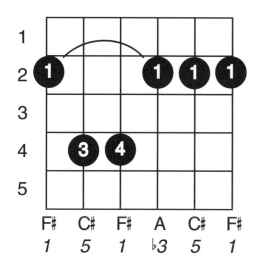

F# C# F# A C# F#
1 5 1 ♭3 5 1

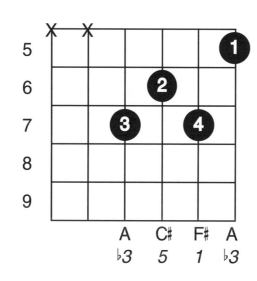

A C# F# A
♭3 5 1 ♭3

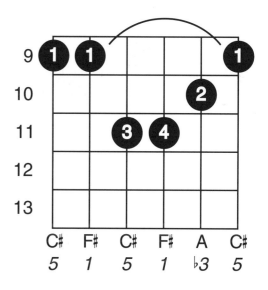

C# F# C# F# A C#
5 1 5 1 ♭3 5

269

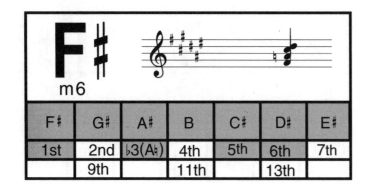

F♯
m6

F♯	G♯	A♯	B	C♯	D♯	E♯
1st	2nd	♭3(A♮)	4th	5th	6th	7th
	9th		11th		13th	

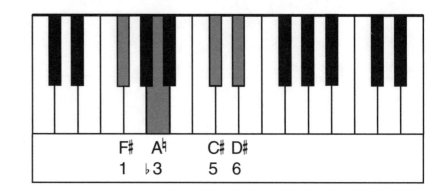

F♯   A♮   C♯ D♯
1   ♭3   5   6

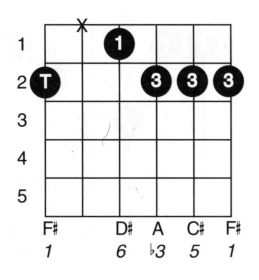

F♯		D♯	A	C♯	F♯
1		*6*	*♭3*	*5*	*1*

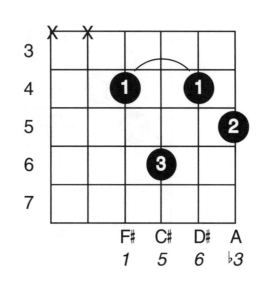

F♯	C♯	D♯	A
1	*5*	*6*	*♭3*

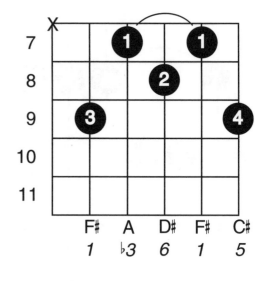

F♯	A	D♯	F♯	C♯
1	*♭3*	*6*	*1*	*5*

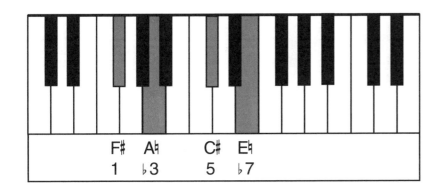

F#, A♮, C#, E♮
1, ♭3, 5, ♭7

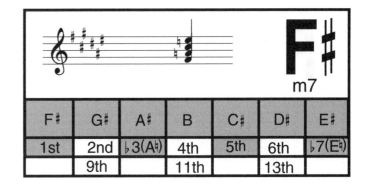

F#
m7

F#	G#	A#	B	C#	D#	E#
1st	2nd	♭3(A♮)	4th	5th	6th	♭7(E♮)
	9th		11th		13th	

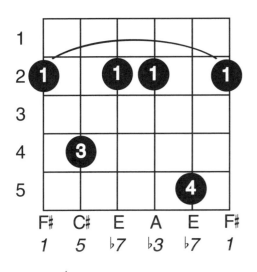

F# C# E A E F#
1   5   ♭7 ♭3 ♭7 1

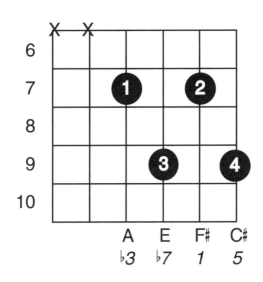

A   E   F# C#
♭3 ♭7 1   5

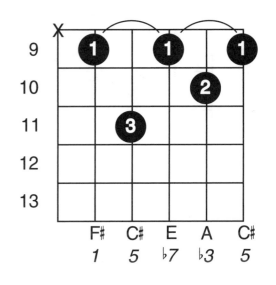

F# C# E   A   C#
1   5   ♭7 ♭3 5

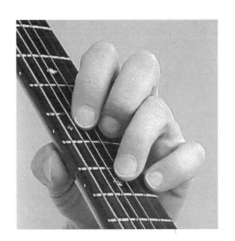

271

F♯

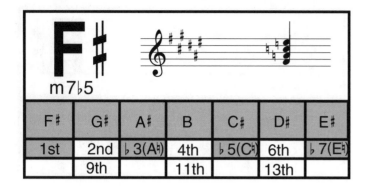

m7♭5

F#	G#	A#	B	C#	D#	E#
1st	2nd	♭3(A♮)	4th	♭5(C♮)	6th	♭7(E♮)
	9th		11th		13th	

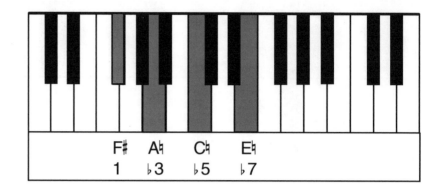

	F#	A♮	C♮	E♮
	1	♭3	♭5	♭7

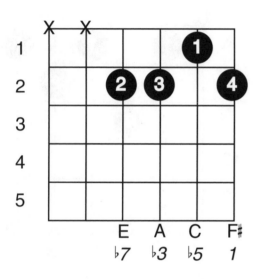

E	A	C	F#
♭7	♭3	♭5	1

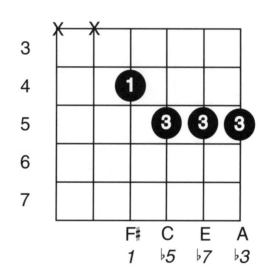

F#	C	E	A
1	♭5	♭7	♭3

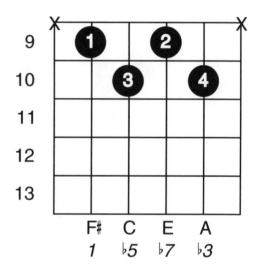

F#	C	E	A
1	♭5	♭7	♭3

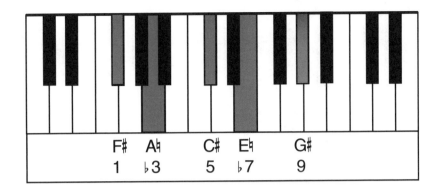

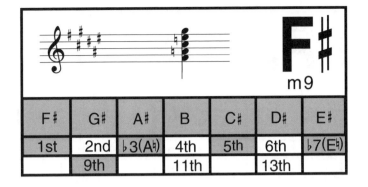

F#	G#	A#	B	C#	D#	E#
1st	2nd	♭3(A♮)	4th	5th	6th	♭7(E♮)
	9th		11th		13th	

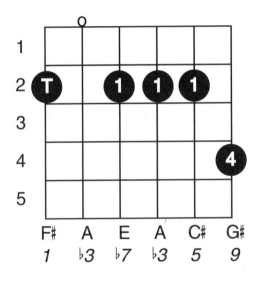

F#	A	E	A	C#	G#
1	*♭3*	*♭7*	*♭3*	*5*	*9*

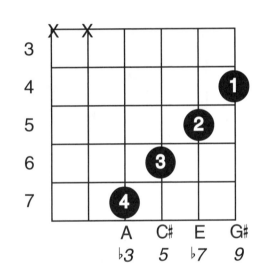

A	C#	E	G#
♭3	*5*	*♭7*	*9*

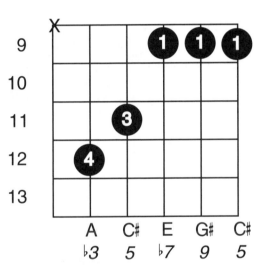

A	C#	E	G#	C#
♭3	*5*	*♭7*	*9*	*5*

273

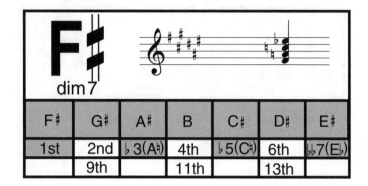

F#
dim 7

F#	G#	A#	B	C#	D#	E#
1st	2nd	♭3(A♮)	4th	♭5(C♮)	6th	♭♭7(E♭)
	9th		11th		13th	

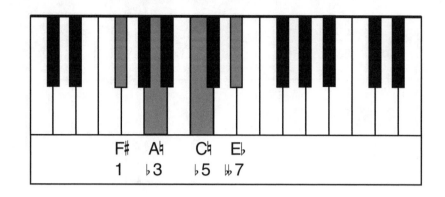

F#   A♮   C♮   E♭
1   ♭3   ♭5 ♭♭7

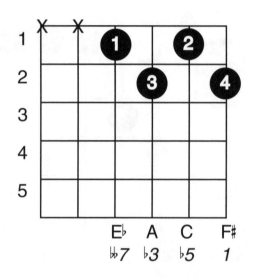

E♭   A   C   F#
♭♭7 ♭3 ♭5 1

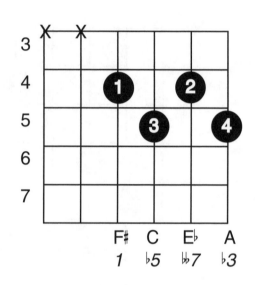

F#   C   E♭   A
1   ♭5 ♭♭7 ♭3

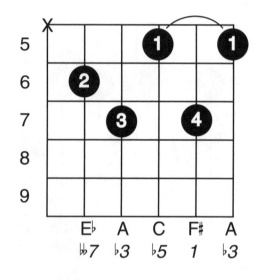

E♭   A   C   F#   A
♭♭7 ♭3 ♭5 1 ♭3

274

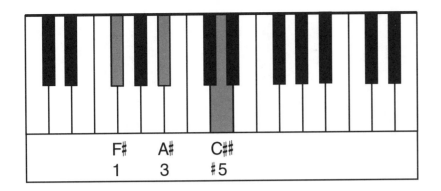

F# 1 A# 3 C## #5

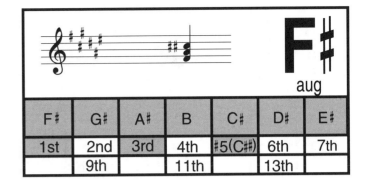

F#
aug

F#	G#	A#	B	C#	D#	E#
1st	2nd	3rd	4th	#5(C##)	6th	7th
	9th		11th		13th	

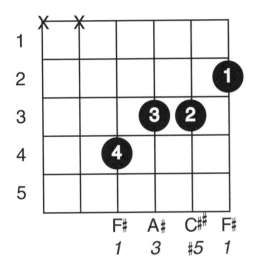

F# A# C## F#
1 *3* *#5* *1*

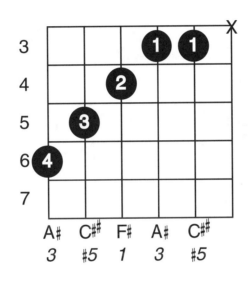

A# C## F# A# C##
3 *#5* *1* *3* *#5*

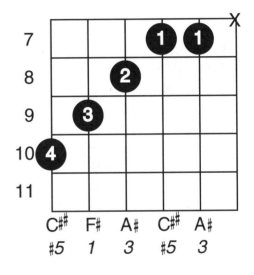

C## F# A# C## A#
#5 *1* *3* *#5* *3*

275

F♯

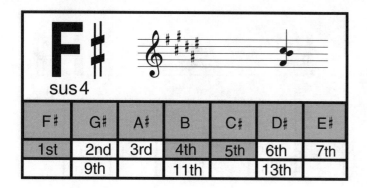

sus4

F#	G#	A#	B	C#	D#	E#
1st	2nd	3rd	4th	5th	6th	7th
	9th		11th		13th	

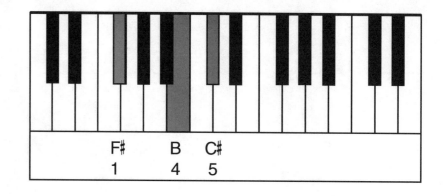

	F#		B	C#
	1		4	5

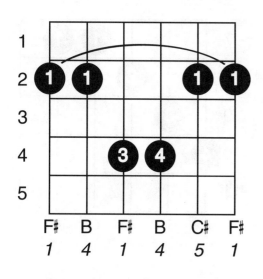

F#	B	F#	B	C#	F#
1	4	1	4	5	1

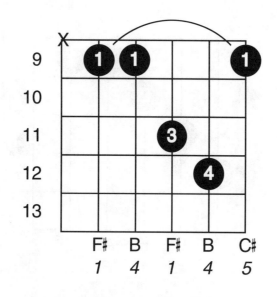

F#	B	F#	B	C#
1	4	1	4	5

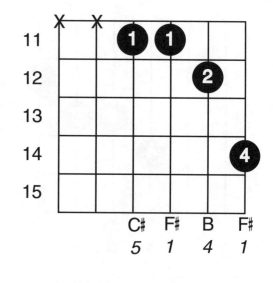

C#	F#	B	F#
5	1	4	1

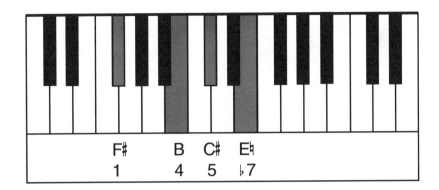

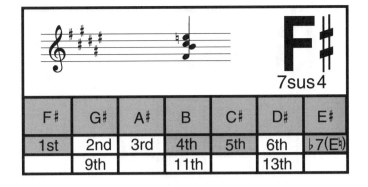

F#
7sus4

F#	G#	A#	B	C#	D#	E#
1st	2nd	3rd	4th	5th	6th	♭7(E♮)
	9th		11th		13th	

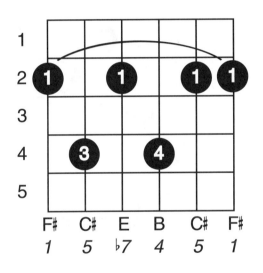

F# C# E B C# F#
1 5 ♭7 4 5 1

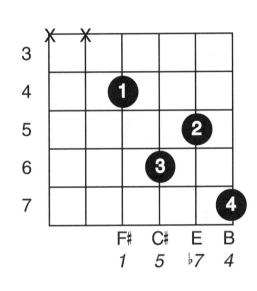

F# C# E B
1 5 ♭7 4

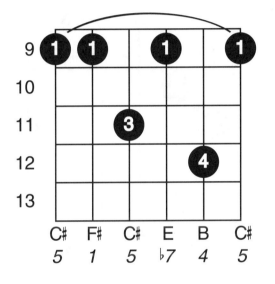

C# F# C# E B C#
5 1 5 ♭7 4 5

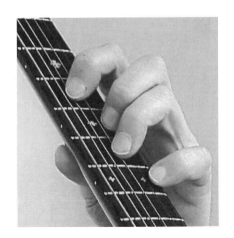

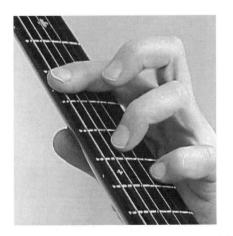

G
Major

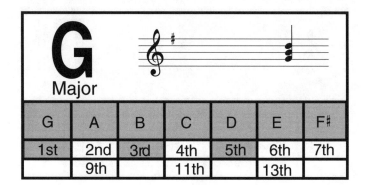

G	A	B	C	D	E	F#
1st	2nd	3rd	4th	5th	6th	7th
	9th		11th		13th	

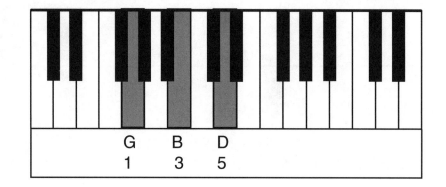

G 1
B 3
D 5

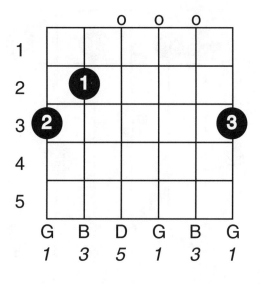

G	B	D	G	B	G
1	3	5	1	3	1

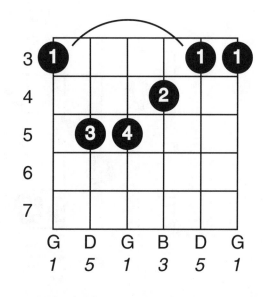

G	D	G	B	D	G
1	5	1	3	5	1

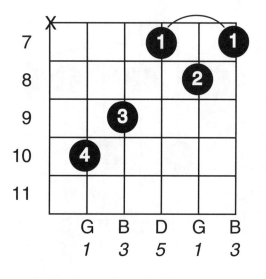

G	B	D	G	B
1	3	5	1	3

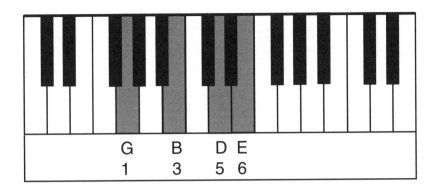

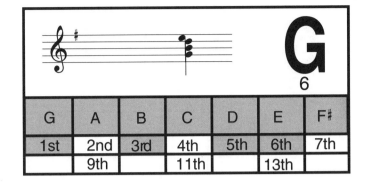

G	A	B	C	D	E	F#
1st	2nd	3rd	4th	5th	6th	7th
	9th		11th		13th	

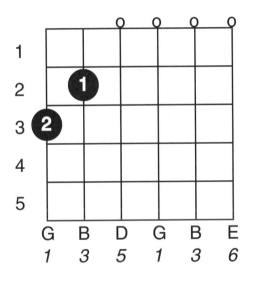

G B D G B E
1 *3* *5* *1* *3* *6*

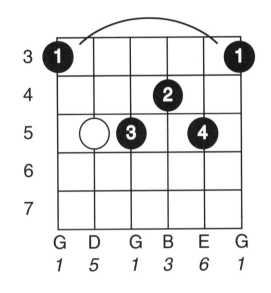

G D G B E G
1 *5* *1* *3* *6* *1*

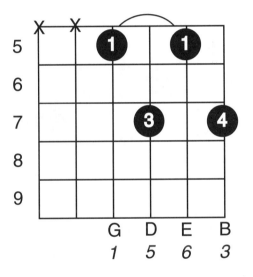

G D E B
1 *5* *6* *3*

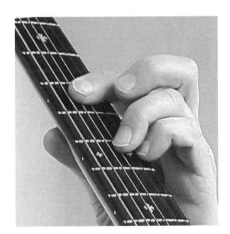

279

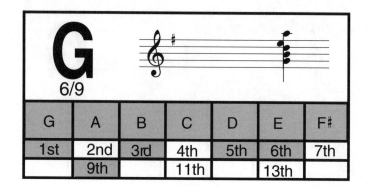

G
6/9

G	A	B	C	D	E	F#
1st	2nd	3rd	4th	5th	6th	7th
	9th		11th		13th	

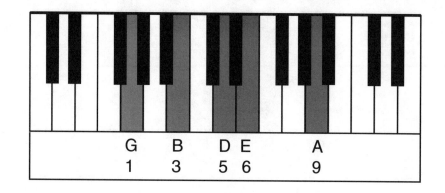

G B D E   A
1 3 5 6   9

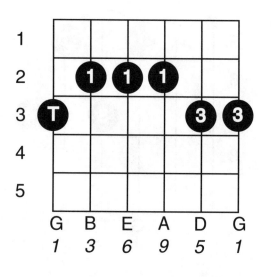

G   B   E   A   D   G
1   3   6   9   5   1

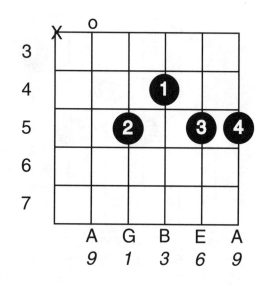

A   G   B   E   A
9   1   3   6   9

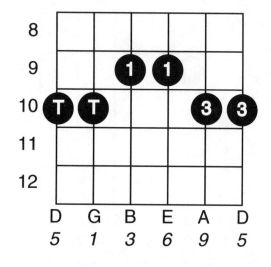

D   G   B   E   A   D
5   1   3   6   9   5

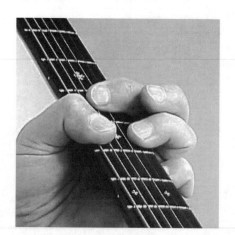

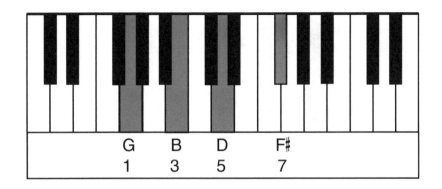

G B D F#
1 3 5 7

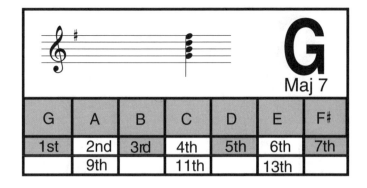

G
Maj 7

G	A	B	C	D	E	F#
1st	2nd	3rd	4th	5th	6th	7th
	9th		11th		13th	

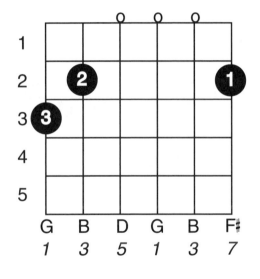

| | | o | o | o | |

1

2 — 2 — 1

3 — 3

4

5

G B D G B F#
1 3 5 1 3 7

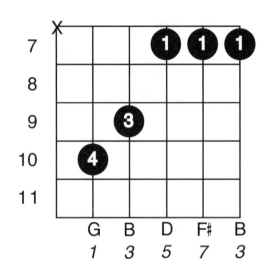

x

7 — 1 1 1

8

9 — 3

10 — 4

11

G B D F# B
1 3 5 7 3

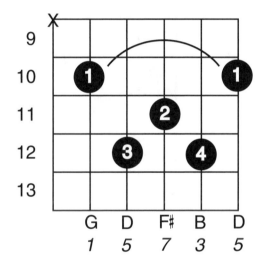

x

9

10 — 1 — 1

11 — 2

12 — 3 — 4

13

G D F# B D
1 5 7 3 5

G
mMaj7

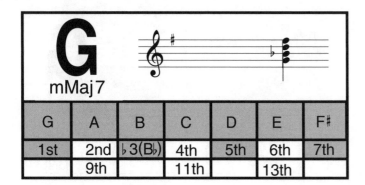

G	A	B	C	D	E	F#
1st	2nd	♭3(B♭)	4th	5th	6th	7th
	9th		11th		13th	

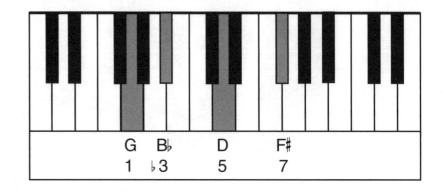

G   B♭   D   F#
1   ♭3   5   7

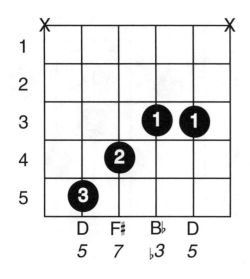

D   F#   B♭   D
5   *7*   *♭3*   *5*

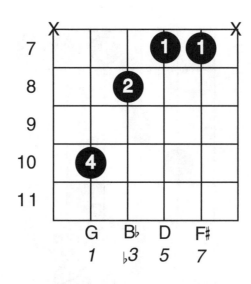

G   B♭   D   F#
1   *♭3*   *5*   *7*

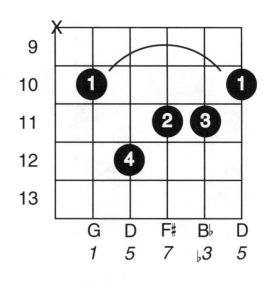

G   D   F#   B♭   D
1   *5*   *7*   *♭3*   *5*

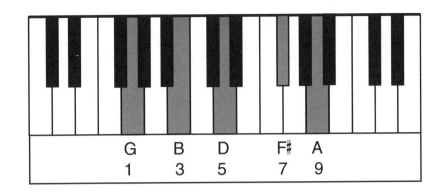

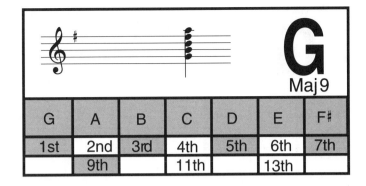

G Maj9

G	A	B	C	D	E	F#
1st	2nd	3rd	4th	5th	6th	7th
	9th		11th		13th	

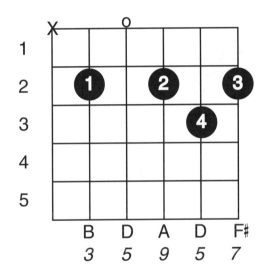

B	D	A	D	F#
3	*5*	*9*	*5*	*7*

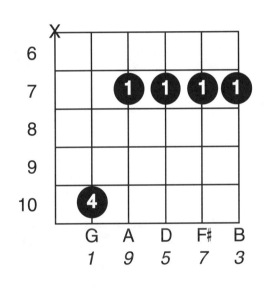

G	A	D	F#	B
1	*9*	*5*	*7*	*3*

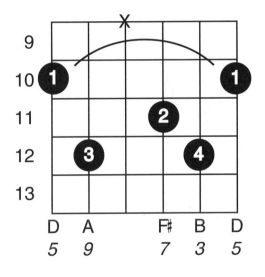

D	A		F#	B	D
5	*9*		*7*	*3*	*5*

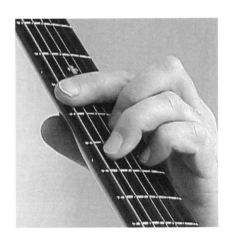

283

G

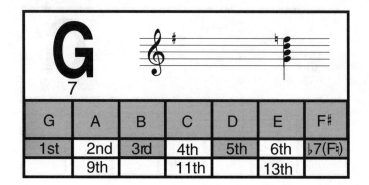

G	A	B	C	D	E	F#
1st	2nd	3rd	4th	5th	6th	♭7(F♮)
	9th		11th		13th	

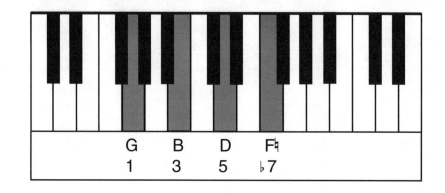

G   B   D   F♮
1   3   5   ♭7

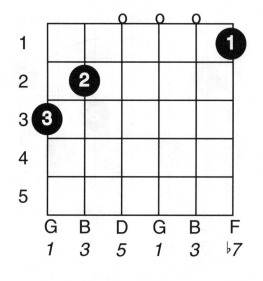

G   B   D   G   B   F
1   *3*   *5*   *1*   *3*   *♭7*

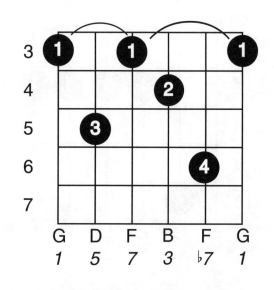

G   D   F   B   F   G
1   *5*   *7*   *3*   *♭7*   *1*

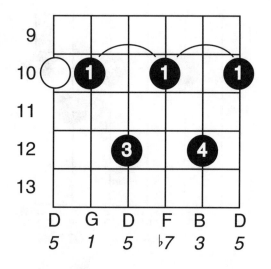

D   G   D   F   B   D
5   *1*   *5*   *♭7*   *3*   *5*

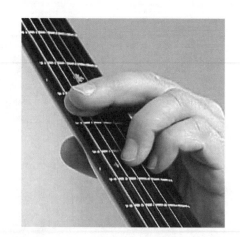

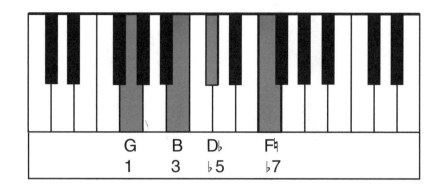

G B D♭ F♮
1 3 ♭5 ♭7

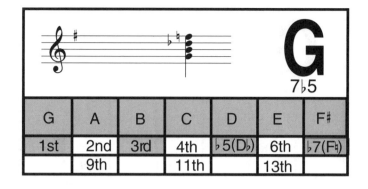

G 7♭5

G	A	B	C	D	E	F#
1st	2nd	3rd	4th	♭5(D♭)	6th	♭7(F♮)
	9th		11th		13th	

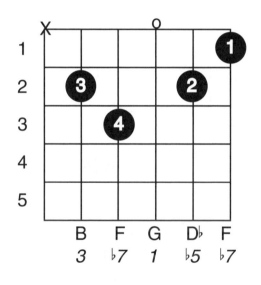

B F G D♭ F
3 ♭7 1 ♭5 ♭7

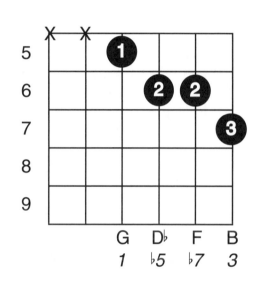

G D♭ F B
1 ♭5 ♭7 3

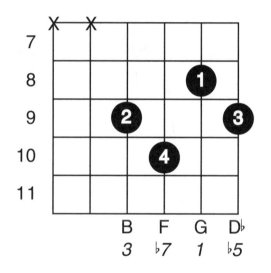

B F G D♭
3 ♭7 1 ♭5

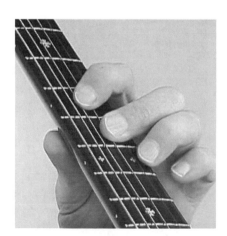

G

7♯5

G	A	B	C	D	E	F♯
1st	2nd	3rd	4th	♯5(D♯)	6th	♭7(F♮)
	9th		11th		13th	

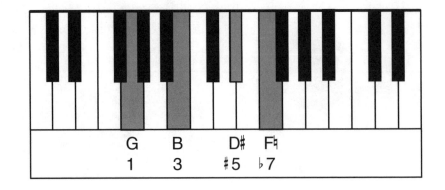

G   B   D♯   F♮
1   3   ♯5   ♭7

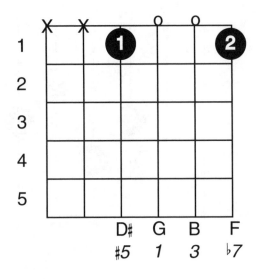

D♯   G   B   F
♯5   1   3   ♭7

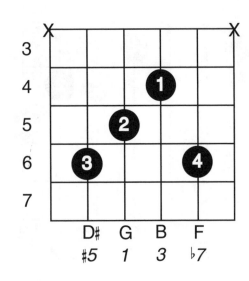

D♯   G   B   F
♯5   1   3   ♭7

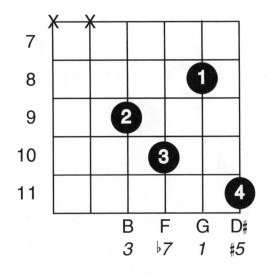

B   F   G   D♯
3   ♭7   1   ♯5

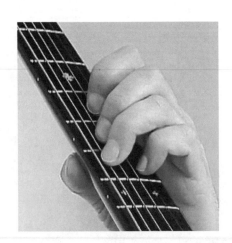

286

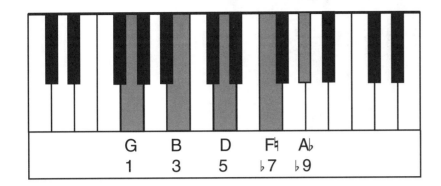

G B D F♮ A♭
1 3 5 ♭7 ♭9

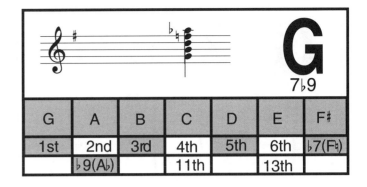

G
7♭9

G	A	B	C	D	E	F#
1st	2nd	3rd	4th	5th	6th	♭7(F♮)
	♭9(A♭)		11th		13th	

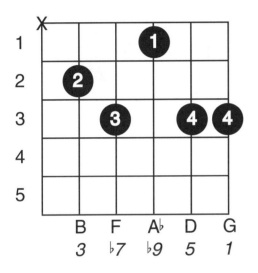

B F A♭ D G
3 ♭7 ♭9 5 1

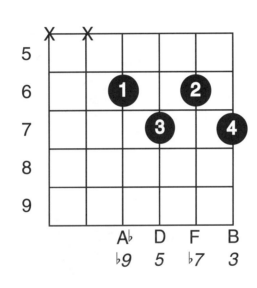

A♭ D F B
♭9 5 ♭7 3

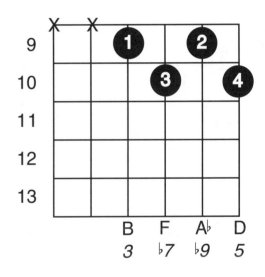

B F A♭ D
3 ♭7 ♭9 5

287

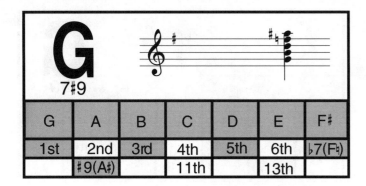

G
7#9

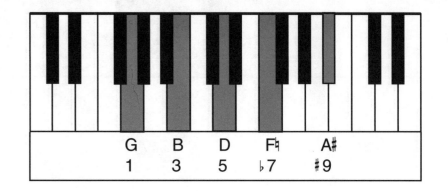

G	A	B	C	D	E	F#
1st	2nd	3rd	4th	5th	6th	♭7(F♮)
	#9(A#)		11th		13th	

Piano keyboard:

G	B	D	F♮	A#
1	3	5	♭7	#9

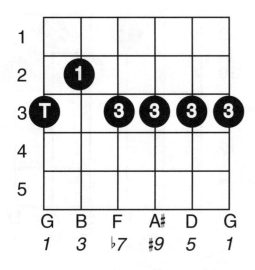

G	B	F	A#	D	G
1	3	♭7	#9	5	1

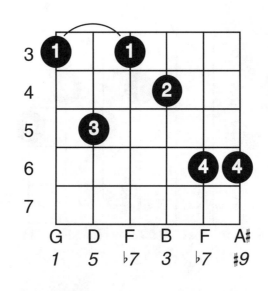

G	D	F	B	F	A#
1	5	♭7	3	♭7	#9

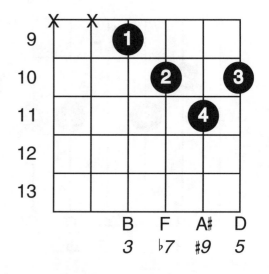

B	F	A#	D
3	♭7	#9	5

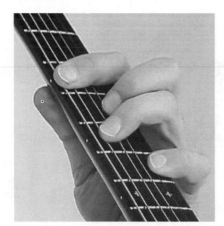

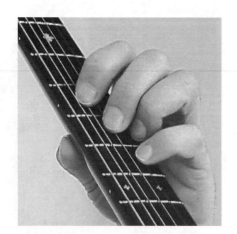

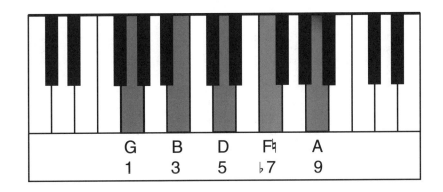

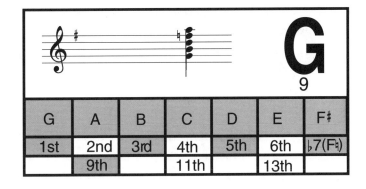

G
9

G	A	B	C	D	E	F#
1st	2nd	3rd	4th	5th	6th	♭7(F♮)
	9th		11th		13th	

Keyboard:
G B D F♮ A
1 3 5 ♭7 9

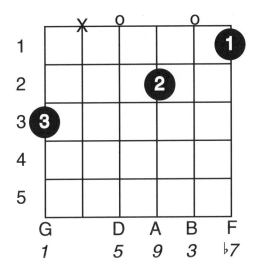

```
      x    o         o
1                         (1)
2              (2)
3  (3)
4
5
   G      D    A    B    F
   1      5    9    3    ♭7
```

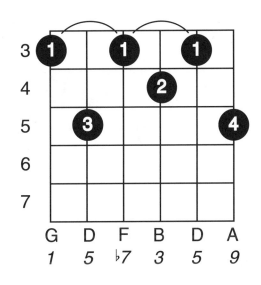

```
3  (1)      (1)        (1)
4              (2)
5       (3)            (4)
6
7
   G    D    F    B    D    A
   1    5   ♭7    3    5    9
```

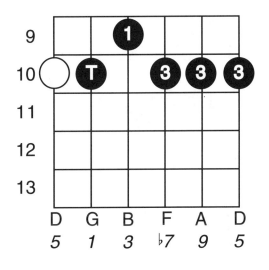

```
9            (1)
10  ( )  (T)      (3) (3) (3)
11
12
13
    D    G    B    F    A    D
    5    1    3   ♭7    9    5
```

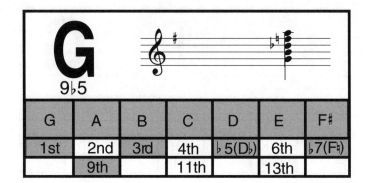

G
9♭5

G	A	B	C	D	E	F#
1st	2nd	3rd	4th	♭5(D♭)	6th	♭7(F♮)
	9th		11th		13th	

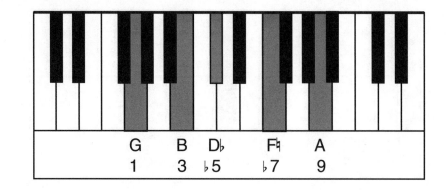

G	B	D♭	F♮	A
1	3	♭5	♭7	9

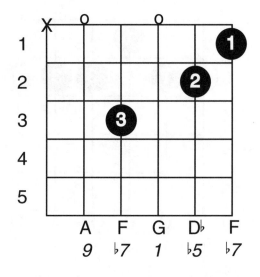

A	F	G	D♭	F
9	♭7	1	♭5	♭7

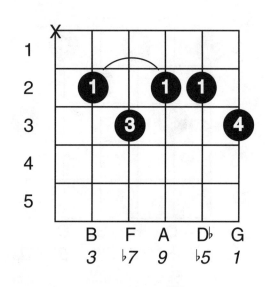

B	F	A	D♭	G
3	♭7	9	♭5	1

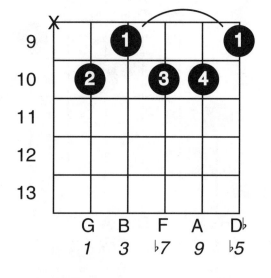

G	B	F	A	D♭
1	3	♭7	9	♭5

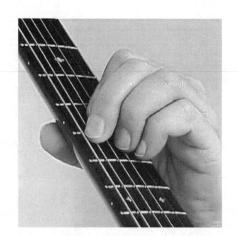

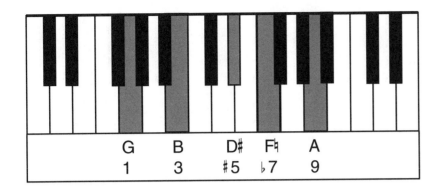

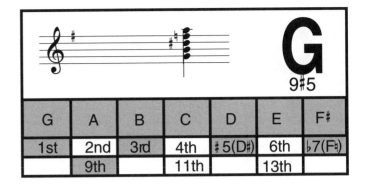

G	A	B	C	D	E	F#
1st	2nd	3rd	4th	#5(D#)	6th	b7(F#)
	9th		11th		13th	

G9#5

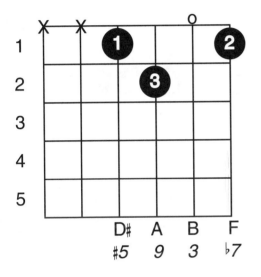

D#   A   B   F
#5   9   3   b7

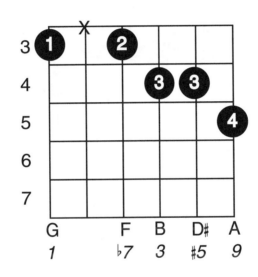

G   F   B   D#   A
1   b7   3   #5   9

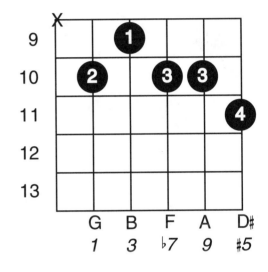

G   B   F   A   D#
1   3   b7   9   #5

G
11

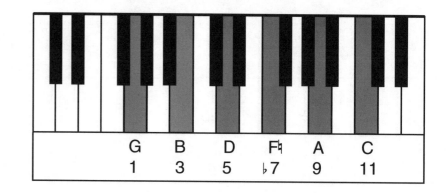

G	A	B	C	D	E	F#
1st	2nd	3rd	4th	5th	6th	♭7(F♮)
	9th		11th		13th	

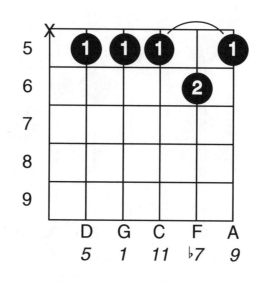

G | B | D | F♮ | A | C
1 | 3 | 5 | ♭7 | 9 | 11

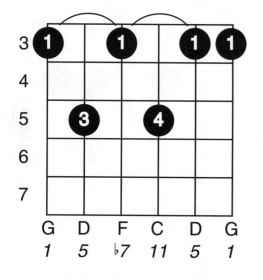

3 **1** — **1** — **1** **1**
4
5 **3** **4**
6
7

G | D | F | C | D | G
1 | *5* | *♭7* | *11* | *5* | *1*

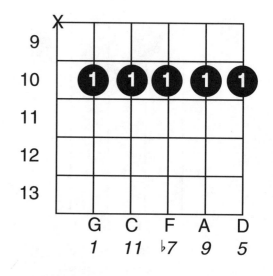

X
5 **1** **1** **1** **1**
6 **2**
7
8
9

D | G | C | F | A
5 | *1* | *11* | *♭7* | *9*

X
9
10 **1** **1** **1** **1** **1**
11
12
13

G | C | F | A | D
1 | *11* | *♭7* | *9* | *5*

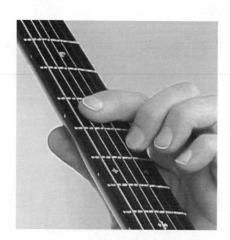

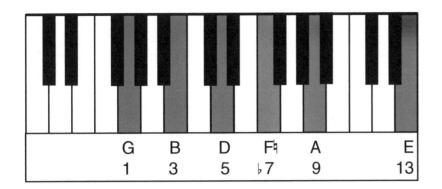

G B D F♮ A E
1 3 5 ♭7 9 13

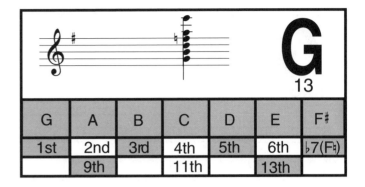

G
13

G	A	B	C	D	E	F#
1st	2nd	3rd	4th	5th	6th	♭7(F♮)
	9th		11th		13th	

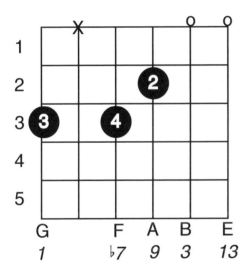

1
2
3
4
5

G   F A B E
1   ♭7 9 3 13

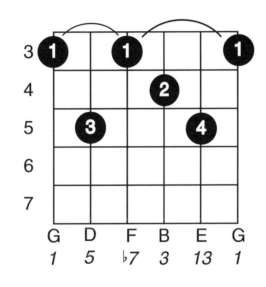

3
4
5
6
7

G D F B E G
1 5 ♭7 3 13 1

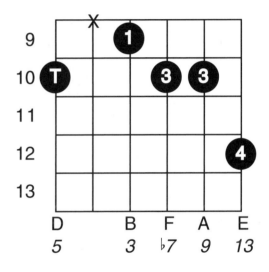

9
10
11
12
13

D   B F A E
5   3 ♭7 9 13

293

G

13♭5♭9

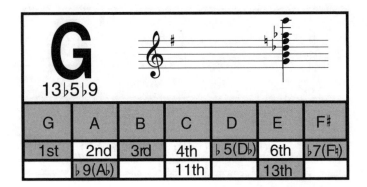

G	A	B	C	D	E	F♯
1st	2nd	3rd	4th	♭5(D♭)	6th	♭7(F♮)
	♭9(A♭)		11th		13th	

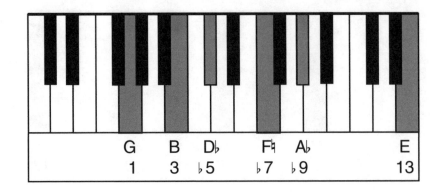

G · B · D♭ · F♮ · A♭ · E
1 · 3 · ♭5 · ♭7 · ♭9 · 13

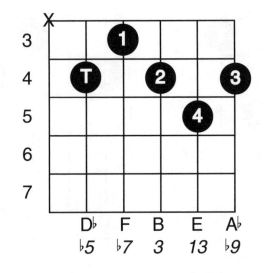

D♭ · F · B · E · A♭
♭5 · ♭7 · 3 · 13 · ♭9

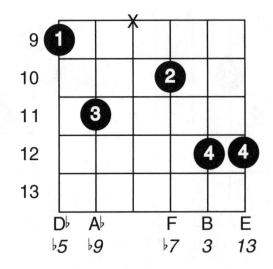

D♭ · A♭ · F · B · E
♭5 · ♭9 · ♭7 · 3 · 13

294

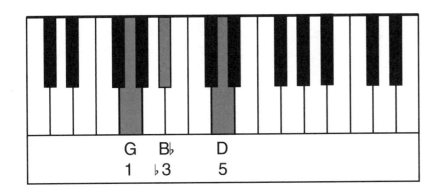

G
B♭
D

G   B♭   D
1   ♭3   5

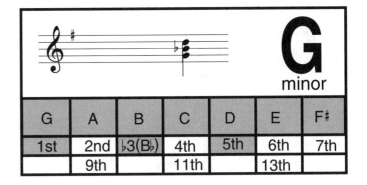

G
minor

G	A	B	C	D	E	F♯
1st	2nd	♭3(B♭)	4th	5th	6th	7th
	9th		11th		13th	

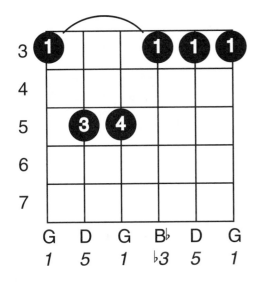

3
4
5
6
7

G   D   G   B♭   D   G
1   5   1   ♭3   5   1

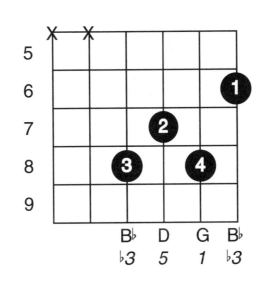

5
6
7
8
9

B♭   D   G   B♭
♭3   5   1   ♭3

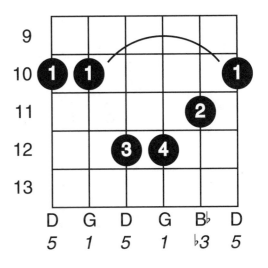

9
10
11
12
13

D   G   D   G   B♭   D
5   1   5   1   ♭3   5

G
m6

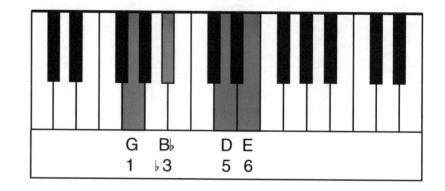

G	A	B	C	D	E	F#
1st	2nd	♭3(B♭)	4th	5th	6th	7th
	9th		11th		13th	

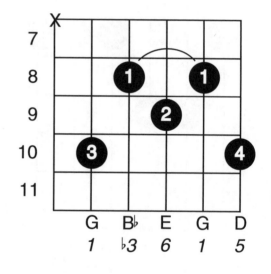

G B♭ D E
1 ♭3 5 6

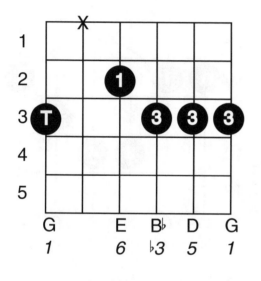

G   E B♭ D G
1   6 ♭3 5 1

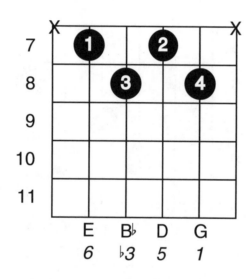

E B♭ D G
6 ♭3 5 1

G B♭ E G D
1 ♭3 6 1 5

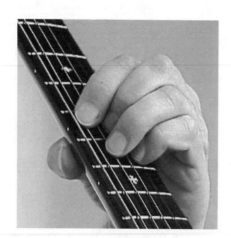

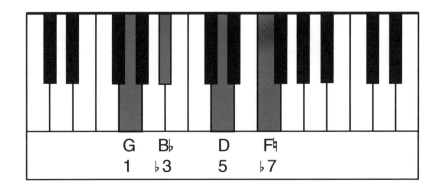

G Bb D F♮
1 ♭3 5 ♭7

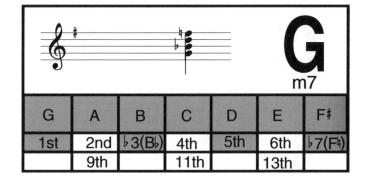

G m7

G	A	B	C	D	E	F#
1st	2nd	♭3(B♭)	4th	5th	6th	♭7(F♮)
	9th		11th		13th	

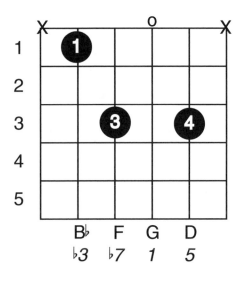

Bb F G D
♭3 ♭7 1 5

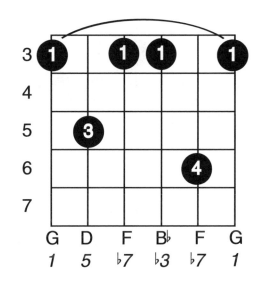

G D F Bb F G
1 5 ♭7 ♭3 ♭7 1

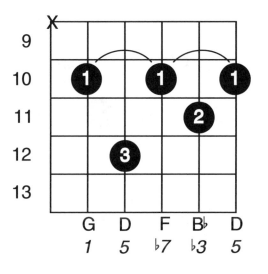

G D F Bb D
1 5 ♭7 ♭3 5

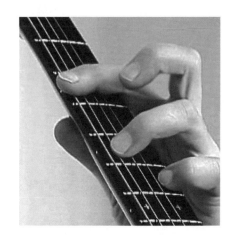

297

G
m7♭5

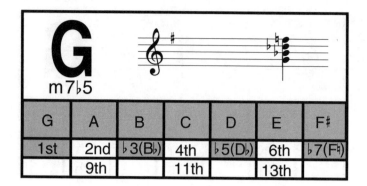

G	A	B	C	D	E	F#
1st	2nd	♭3(B♭)	4th	♭5(D♭)	6th	♭7(F♮)
	9th		11th		13th	

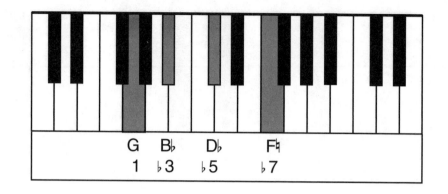

G　B♭　D♭　F♮
1　♭3　♭5　♭7

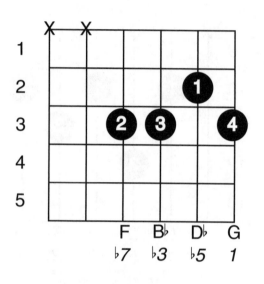

F　B♭　D♭　G
♭7　♭3　♭5　1

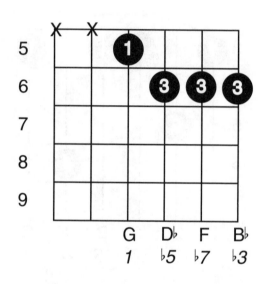

G　D♭　F　B♭
1　♭5　♭7　♭3

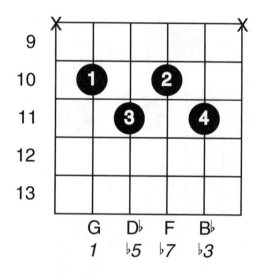

G　D♭　F　B♭
1　♭5　♭7　♭3

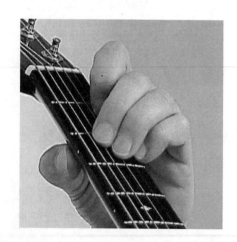

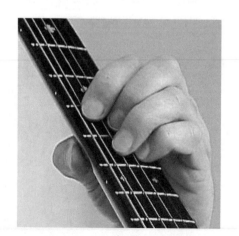

298

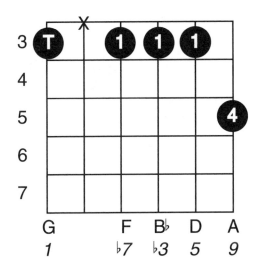

G   B♭   D   F♮   A
1   ♭3   5   ♭7   9

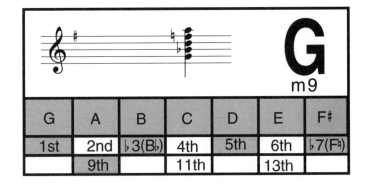

G
m9

	G	A	B	C	D	E	F#
1st		2nd	♭3(B♭)	4th	5th	6th	♭7(F#)
		9th		11th		13th	

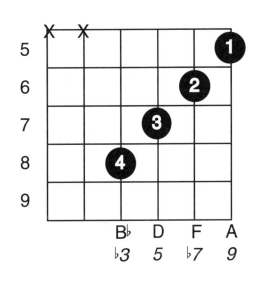

3 ⊗ ① ① ①
4
5   ④
6
7

G   F   B♭   D   A
1   ♭7   ♭3   5   9

5 ✗ ✗   ①
6   ②
7   ③
8   ④
9

B♭   D   F   A
♭3   5   ♭7   9

9 ✗
10   ① ① ①
11
12   ③
13   ④

B♭   D   F   A   D
♭3   5   ♭7   9   5

299

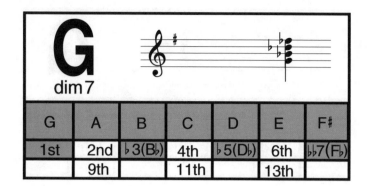

G
dim7

G	A	B	C	D	E	F#
1st	2nd	♭3(B♭)	4th	♭5(D♭)	6th	♭♭7(F♭)
	9th		11th		13th	

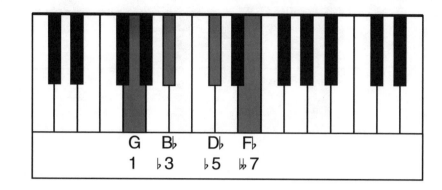

G   B♭   D♭   F♭
1   ♭3   ♭5   ♭♭7

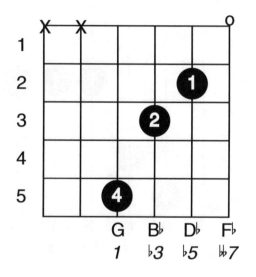

G   B♭   D♭   F♭
1   *♭3*   *♭5*   *♭♭7*

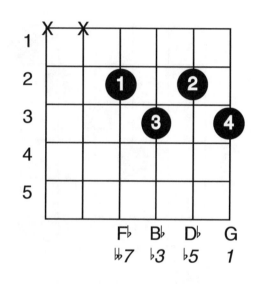

F♭   B♭   D♭   G
♭♭7   *♭3*   *♭5*   *1*

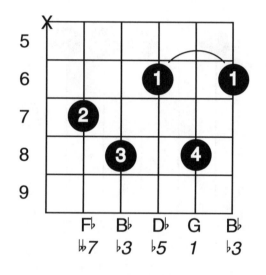

F♭   B♭   D♭   G   B♭
♭♭7   *♭3*   *♭5*   *1*   *♭3*

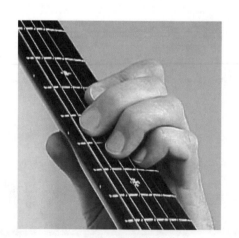

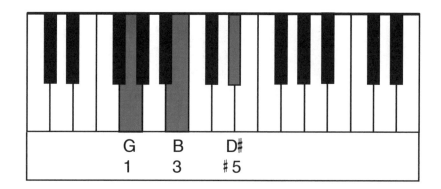

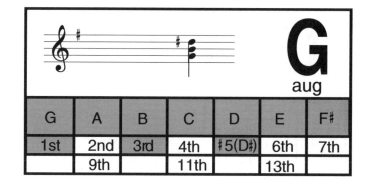

G	A	B	C	D	E	F#
1st	2nd	3rd	4th	#5(D#)	6th	7th
	9th		11th		13th	

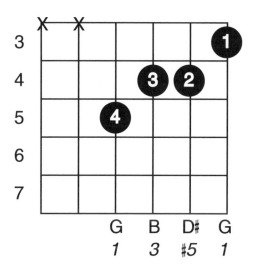

G	B	D#	G
1	3	#5	1

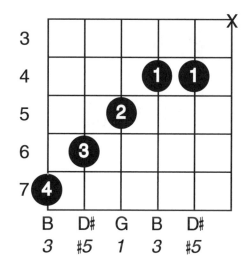

B	D#	G	B	D#
3	#5	1	3	#5

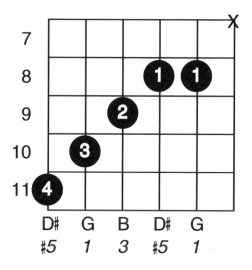

D#	G	B	D#	G
#5	1	3	#5	1

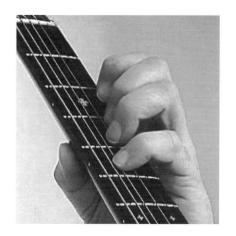

301

G
sus4

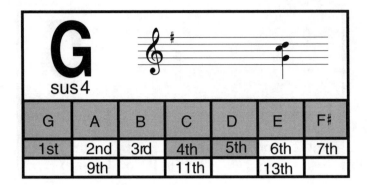

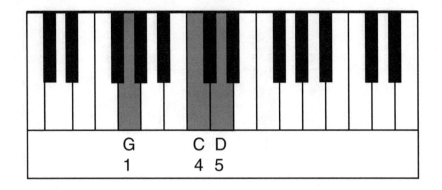

G	A	B	C	D	E	F#
1st	2nd	3rd	4th	5th	6th	7th
	9th		11th		13th	

G
1

C
4

D
5

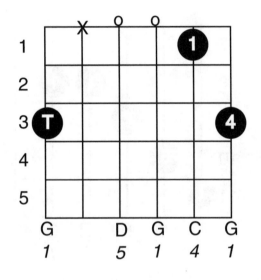

```
x   o   o
            1


T           4



G   D   G   C   G
1   5   1   4   1
```

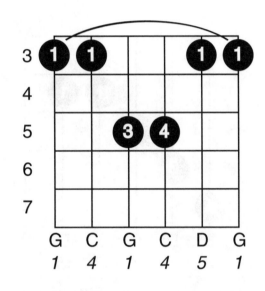

```
  1   1           1   1


        3   4


G   C   G   C   D   G
1   4   1   4   5   1
```

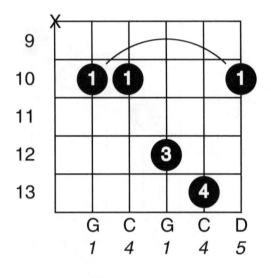

```
x
    1   1           1


            3

                4
G   C   G   C   D
1   4   1   4   5
```

302

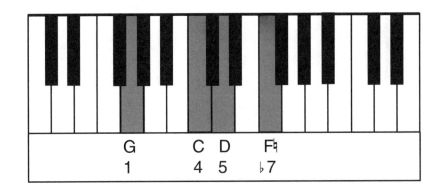
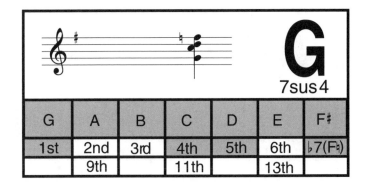

G
7sus4

G	A	B	C	D	E	F#
1st	2nd	3rd	4th	5th	6th	♭7(F♮)
	9th		11th		13th	

Keyboard:

G — 1, C — 4, D — 5, F♮ — ♭7

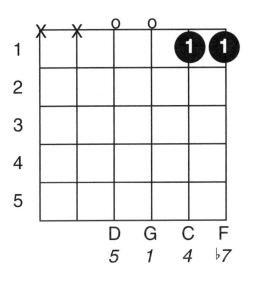

X X o o

D G C F
5 1 4 ♭7

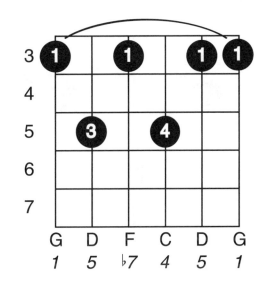

G D F C D G
1 5 ♭7 4 5 1

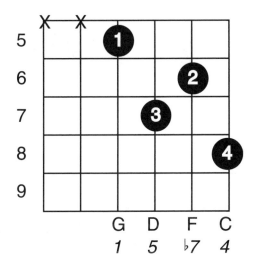

X X

G D F C
1 5 ♭7 4

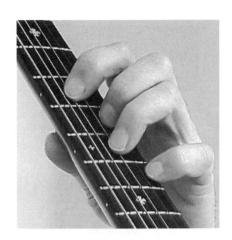

303

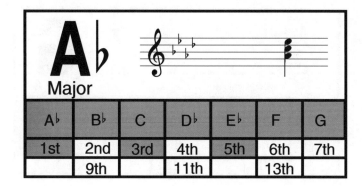

A♭	B♭	C	D♭	E♭	F	G
1st	2nd	3rd	4th	5th	6th	7th
	9th		11th		13th	

Major

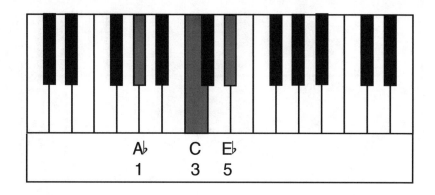

A♭ C E♭
1   3   5

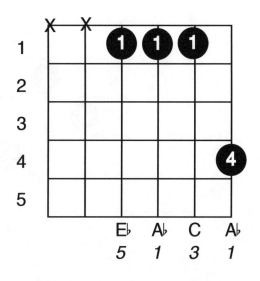

E♭ A♭ C A♭
5   1   3   1

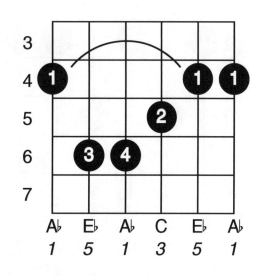

A♭ E♭ A♭ C E♭ A♭
1   5   1   3   5   1

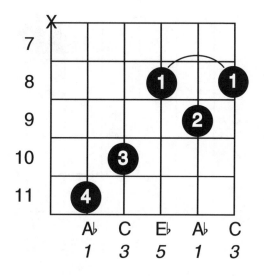

A♭ C E♭ A♭ C
1   3   5   1   3

304

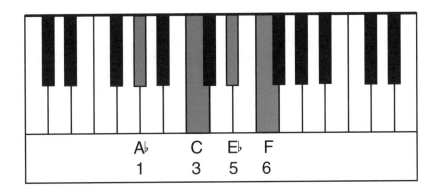

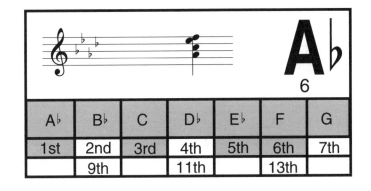

A♭	B♭	C	D♭	E♭	F	G
1st	2nd	3rd	4th	5th	6th	7th
	9th		11th		13th	

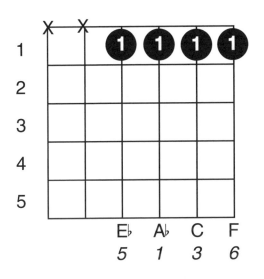

E♭　A♭　C　F
5　　1　　3　　6

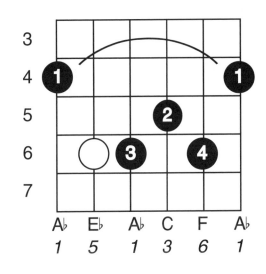

A♭　E♭　A♭　C　F　A♭
1　　5　　1　　3　　6　　1

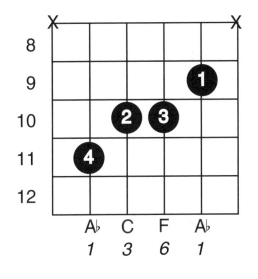

A♭　C　F　A♭
1　　3　　6　　1

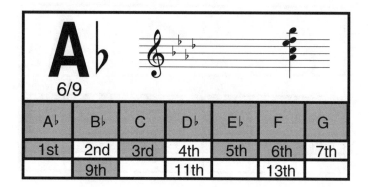

A♭

6/9

A♭	B♭	C	D♭	E♭	F	G
1st	2nd	3rd	4th	5th	6th	7th
	9th		11th		13th	

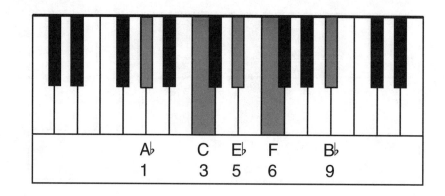

A♭	C	E♭	F	B♭
1	3	5	6	9

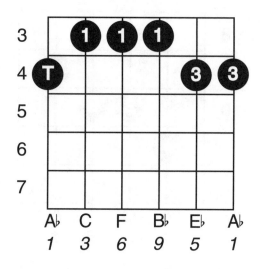

A♭	C	F	B♭	E♭	A♭
1	*3*	*6*	*9*	*5*	*1*

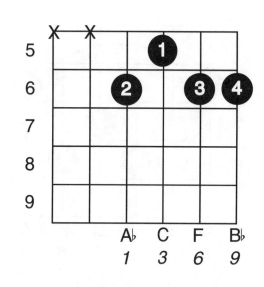

A♭	C	F	B♭
1	*3*	*6*	*9*

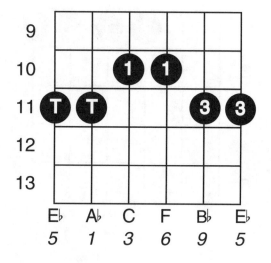

E♭	A♭	C	F	B♭	E♭
5	*1*	*3*	*6*	*9*	*5*

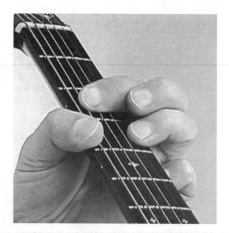

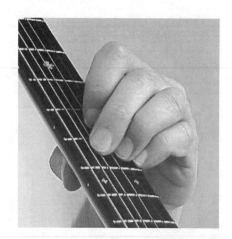

306

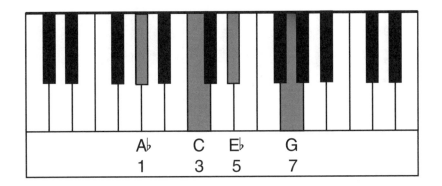

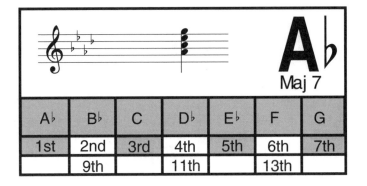

A♭	B♭	C	D♭	E♭	F	G
1st	2nd	3rd	4th	5th	6th	7th
	9th		11th		13th	

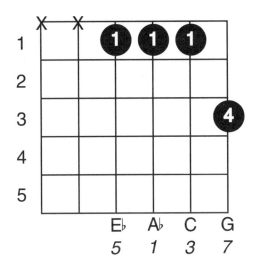

E♭ A♭ C G
5   1   3 7

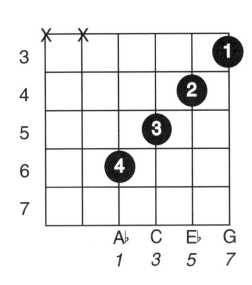

A♭ C E♭ G
1   3 5   7

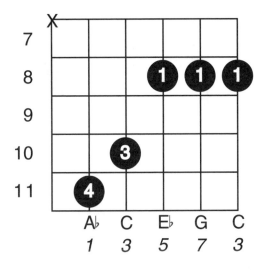

A♭ C E♭ G C
1   3 5   7 3

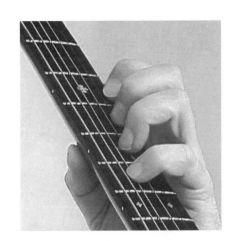

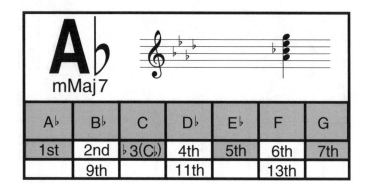

A♭	B♭	C	D♭	E♭	F	G
1st	2nd	♭3(C♭)	4th	5th	6th	7th
	9th		11th		13th	

mMaj7

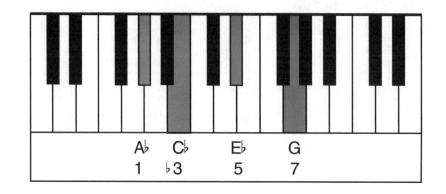

A♭ C♭ E♭ G
1 ♭3 5 7

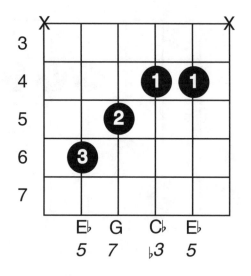

E♭ G C♭ E♭
5 *7* *♭3* *5*

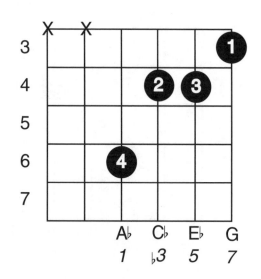

A♭ C♭ E♭ G
1 *♭3* *5* *7*

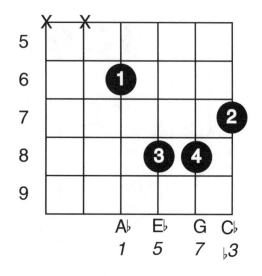

A♭ E♭ G C♭
1 *5* *7* *♭3*

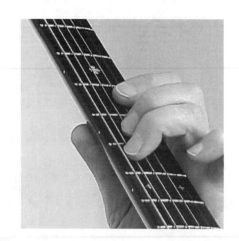

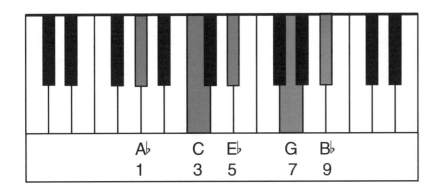

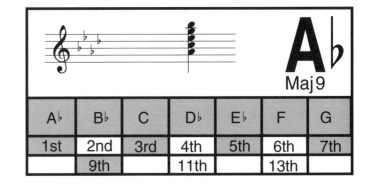

A♭	B♭	C	D♭	E♭	F	G
1st	2nd	3rd	4th	5th	6th	7th
	9th		11th		13th	

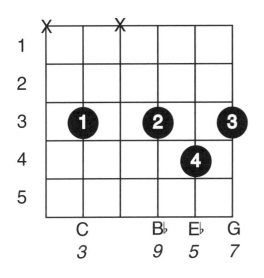

C   B♭   E♭   G
3   9   5   7

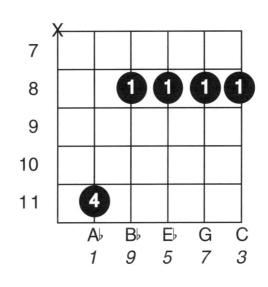

A♭   B♭   E♭   G   C
1   9   5   7   3

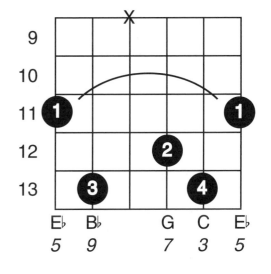

E♭   B♭   G   C   E♭
5   9   7   3   5

309

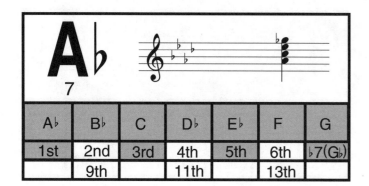

A♭	B♭	C	D♭	E♭	F	G
1st	2nd	3rd	4th	5th	6th	♭7(G♭)
	9th		11th		13th	

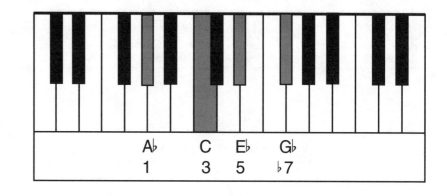

A♭   C   E♭   G♭
1   3   5   ♭7

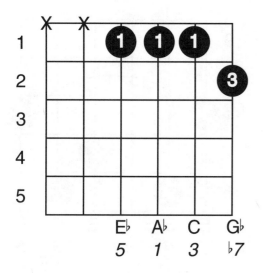

E♭ A♭ C G♭
5 1 3 ♭7

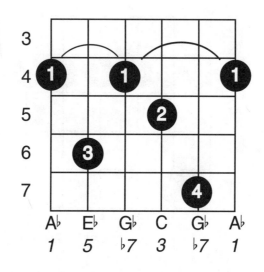

A♭ E♭ G♭ C G♭ A♭
1 5 ♭7 3 ♭7 1

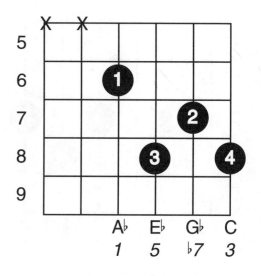

A♭ E♭ G♭ C
1 5 ♭7 3

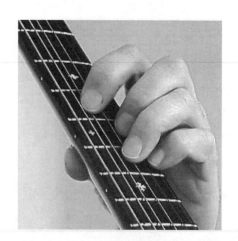

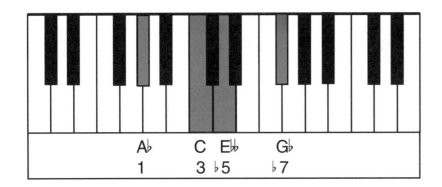

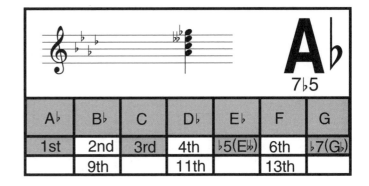

A♭	B♭	C	D♭	E♭	F	G
1st	2nd	3rd	4th	♭5(E♭♭)	6th	♭7(G♭)
	9th		11th		13th	

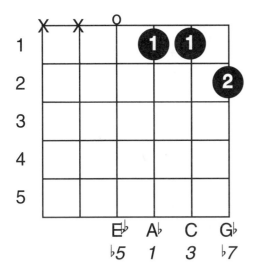

E♭♭   A♭   C   G♭
♭5   1   3   ♭7

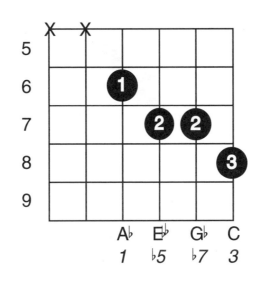

A♭   E♭♭   G♭   C
1   ♭5   ♭7   3

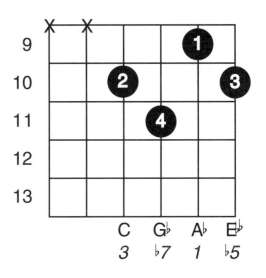

C   G♭   A♭   E♭♭
3   ♭7   1   ♭5

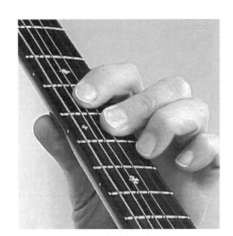

311

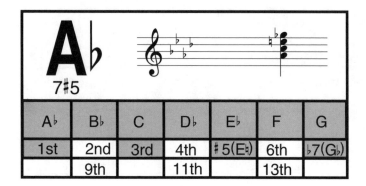

A♭
7♯5

A♭	B♭	C	D♭	E♭	F	G
1st	2nd	3rd	4th	♯5(E♮)	6th	♭7(G♭)
	9th		11th		13th	

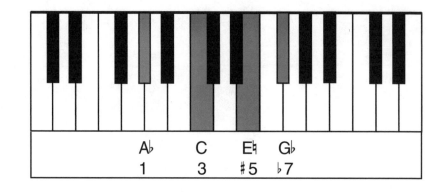

A♭   C   E♮   G♭
1   3   ♯5   ♭7

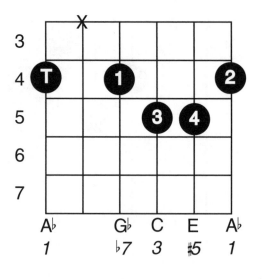

A♭   G♭ C E A♭
1   *♭7* *3* *♯5* *1*

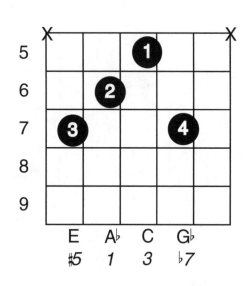

E A♭ C G♭
♯5 *1* *3* *♭7*

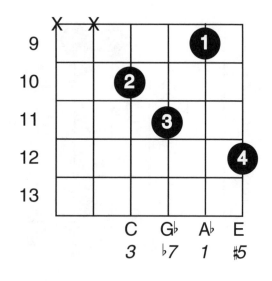

C G♭ A♭ E
3 *♭7* *1* *♯5*

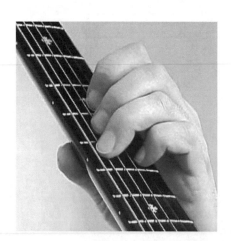

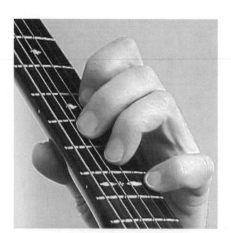

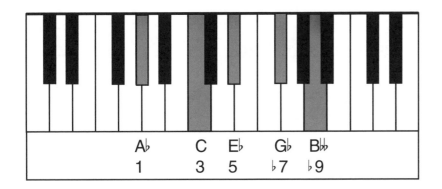

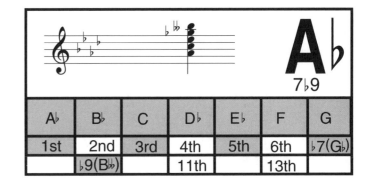

A♭	B♭	C	D♭	E♭	F	G
1st	2nd	3rd	4th	5th	6th	♭7(G♭)
	♭9(B♭♭)		11th		13th	

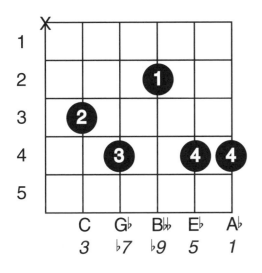

C G♭ B♭♭ E♭ A♭
3 ♭7 ♭9 5 1

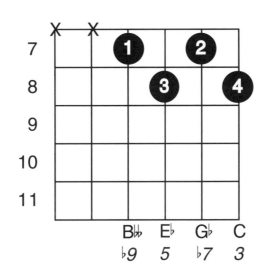

B♭♭ E♭ G♭ C
♭9 5 ♭7 3

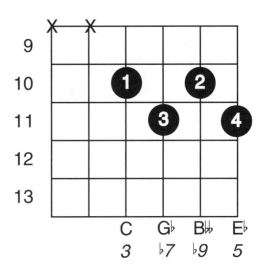

C G♭ B♭♭ E♭
3 ♭7 ♭9 5

313

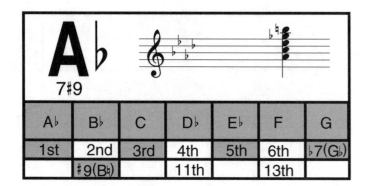

A♭
7#9

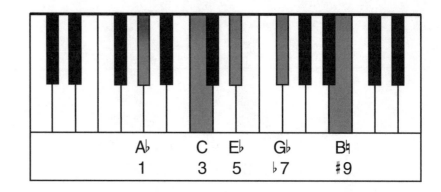

A♭	B♭	C	D♭	E♭	F	G
1st	2nd	3rd	4th	5th	6th	♭7(G♭)
	#9(B♮)		11th		13th	

Keyboard: A♭ C E♭ G♭ B♮
1 3 5 ♭7 #9

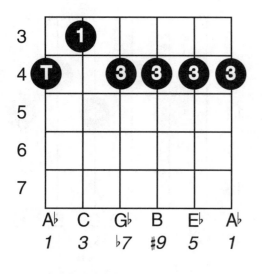

A♭	C	G♭	B	E♭	A♭
1	3	♭7	#9	5	1

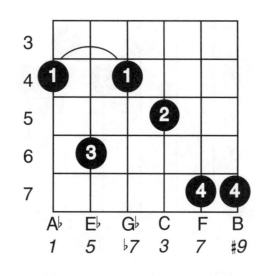

A♭	E♭	G♭	C	F	B
1	5	♭7	3	7	#9

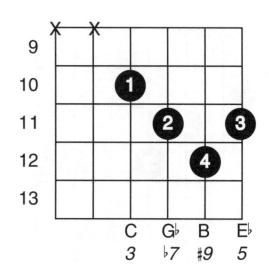

C	G♭	B	E♭
3	♭7	#9	5

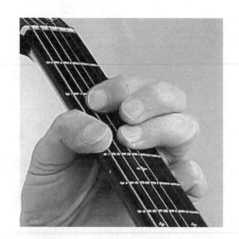

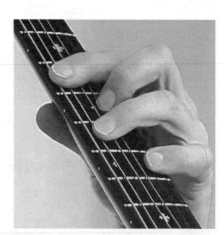

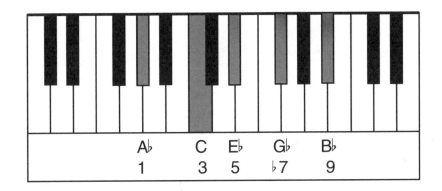

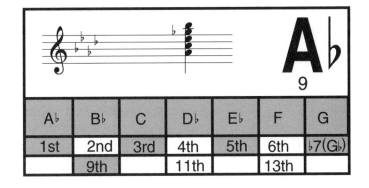

A♭	B♭	C	D♭	E♭	F	G
1st	2nd	3rd	4th	5th	6th	♭7(G♭)
	9th		11th		13th	

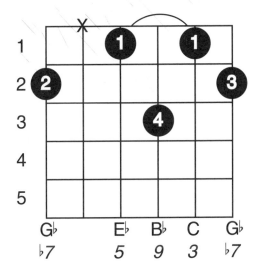

G♭		E♭	B♭	C	G♭
♭7		5	9	3	♭7

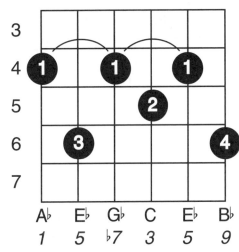

A♭	E♭	G♭	C	E♭	B♭
1	5	♭7	3	5	9

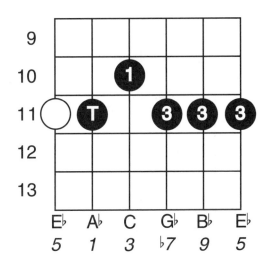

E♭	A♭	C	G♭	B♭	E♭
5	1	3	♭7	9	5

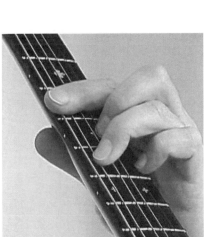

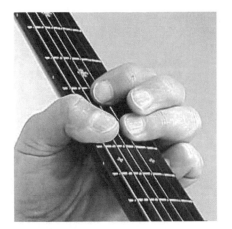

315

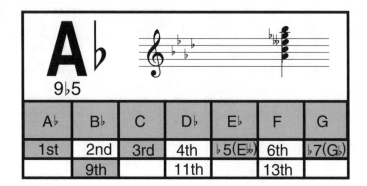

A♭ 9♭5

A♭	B♭	C	D♭	E♭	F	G
1st	2nd	3rd	4th	♭5(E♭♭)	6th	♭7(G♭)
	9th		11th		13th	

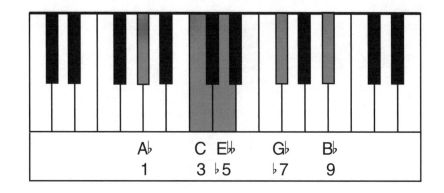

A♭   C   E♭♭   G♭   B♭
1   3   ♭5   ♭7   9

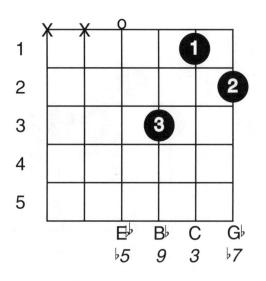

E♭   B♭   C   G♭
♭5   9   3   ♭7

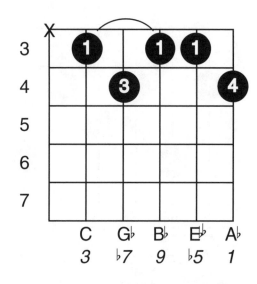

C   G♭   B♭   E♭   A♭
3   ♭7   9   ♭5   1

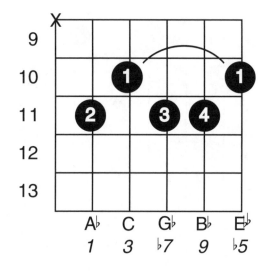

A♭   C   G♭   B♭   E♭
1   3   ♭7   9   ♭5

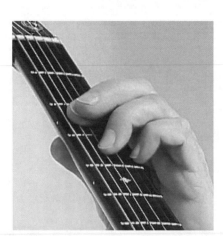

316

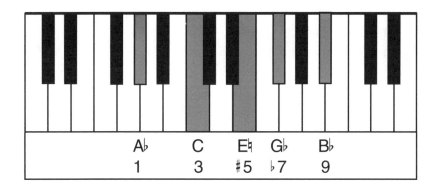

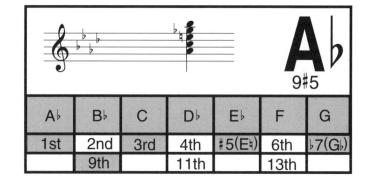

A♭	B♭	C	D♭	E♭	F	G
1st	2nd	3rd	4th	#5(E♮)	6th	♭7(G♭)
	9th		11th		13th	

A♭ 9#5

Keyboard notes: A♭ (1), C (3), E♮ (#5), G♭ (♭7), B♭ (9)

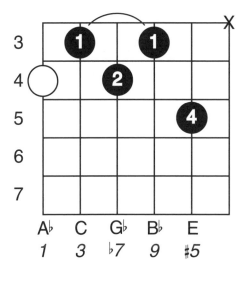

A♭ C G♭ B♭ E
1 3 ♭7 9 #5

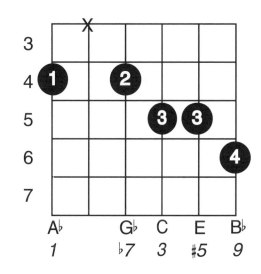

A♭ G♭ C E B♭
1 ♭7 3 #5 9

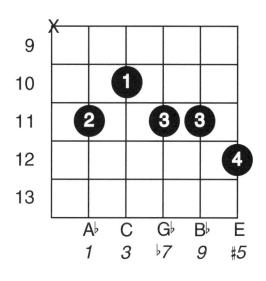

A♭ C G♭ B♭ E
1 3 ♭7 9 #5

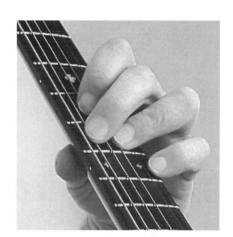

317

A♭

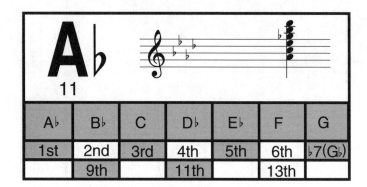

11

A♭	B♭	C	D♭	E♭	F	G
1st	2nd	3rd	4th	5th	6th	♭7(G♭)
	9th		11th		13th	

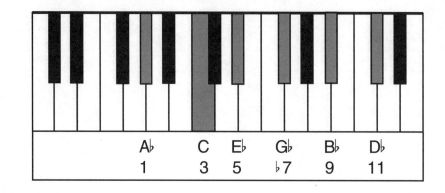

	A♭	C	E♭	G♭	B♭	D♭
	1	3	5	♭7	9	11

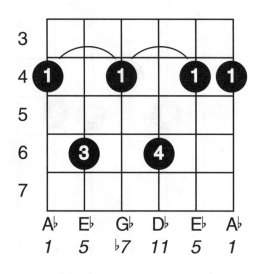

A♭	E♭	G♭	D♭	E♭	A♭
1	5	♭7	11	5	1

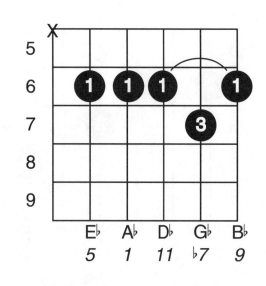

E♭	A♭	D♭	G♭	B♭
5	1	11	♭7	9

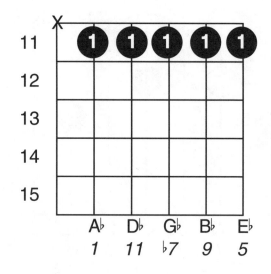

A♭	D♭	G♭	B♭	E♭
1	11	♭7	9	5

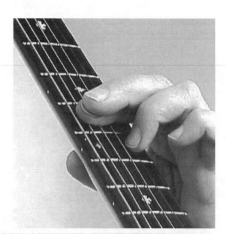

318

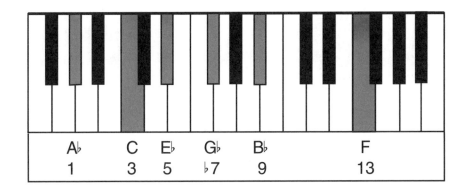

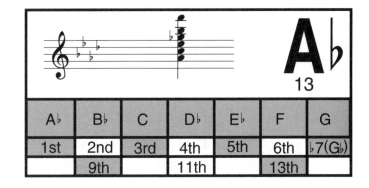

A♭	B♭	C	D♭	E♭	F	G
1st	2nd	3rd	4th	5th	6th	♭7(G♭)
	9th		11th		13th	

A♭13

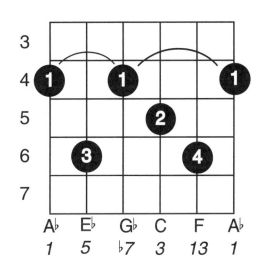

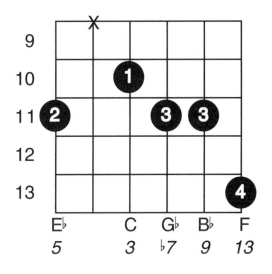

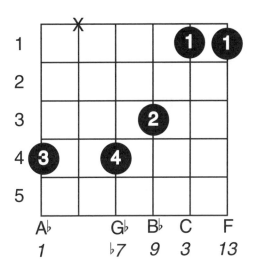

319

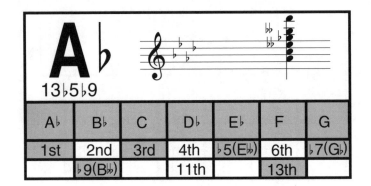

A♭

13♭5♭9

A♭	B♭	C	D♭	E♭	F	G
1st	2nd	3rd	4th	♭5(E♭♭)	6th	♭7(G♭)
	♭9(B♭♭)		11th		13th	

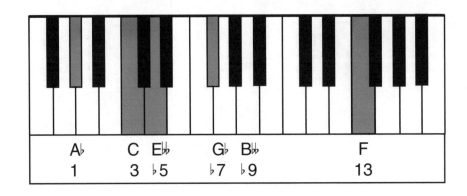

A♭   C   E♭♭   G♭   B♭♭   F
1   3   ♭5   ♭7   ♭9   13

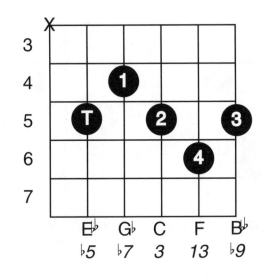

E♭   G♭   C   F   B♭
♭5   ♭7   3   13   ♭9

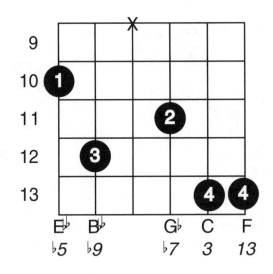

E♭   B♭   G♭   C   F
♭5   ♭9   ♭7   3   13

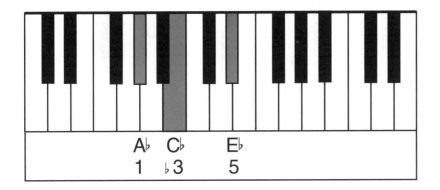

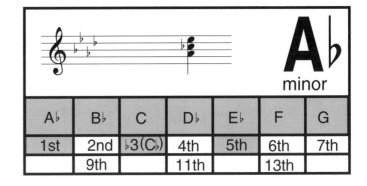

A♭ minor

A♭	B♭	C	D♭	E♭	F	G
1st	2nd	♭3(C♭)	4th	5th	6th	7th
	9th		11th		13th	

Keyboard notes:

A♭ C♭ E♭
1 ♭3 5

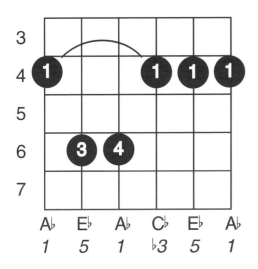

A♭	E♭	A♭	C♭	E♭	A♭
1	*5*	*1*	*♭3*	*5*	*1*

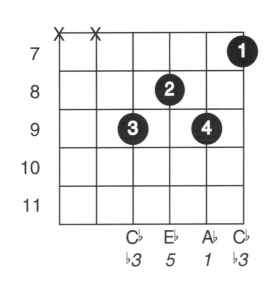

C♭	E♭	A♭	C♭
♭3	*5*	*1*	*♭3*

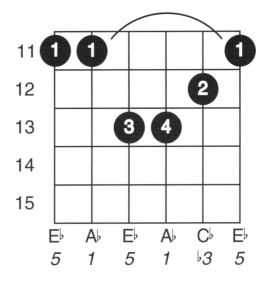

E♭	A♭	E♭	A♭	C♭	E♭
5	*1*	*5*	*1*	*♭3*	*5*

A♭

m6

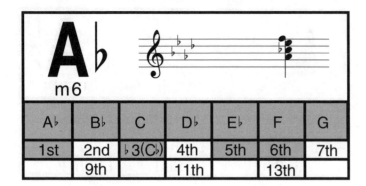

A♭	B♭	C	D♭	E♭	F	G
1st	2nd	♭3(C♭)	4th	5th	6th	7th
	9th		11th		13th	

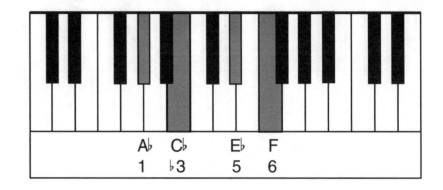

A♭ C♭ E♭ F
1 ♭3 5 6

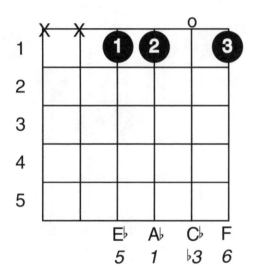

E♭ A♭ C♭ F
5 1 ♭3 6

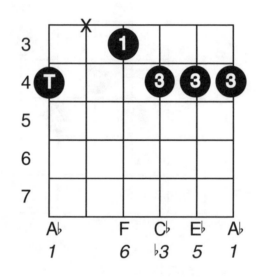

A♭ F C♭ E♭ A♭
1 6 ♭3 5 1

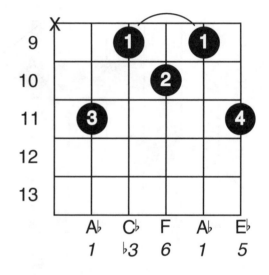

A♭ C♭ F A♭ E♭
1 ♭3 6 1 5

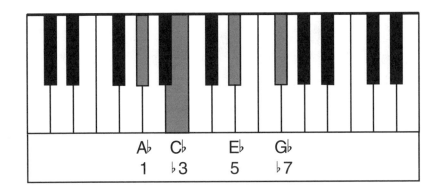

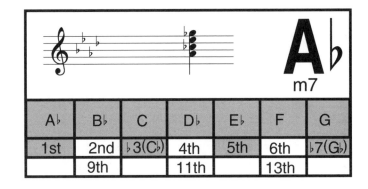

A♭m7

A♭	B♭	C	D♭	E♭	F	G
1st	2nd	♭3(C♭)	4th	5th	6th	♭7(G♭)
	9th		11th		13th	

Keyboard labels:
A♭ C♭   E♭ G♭
1   ♭3   5   ♭7

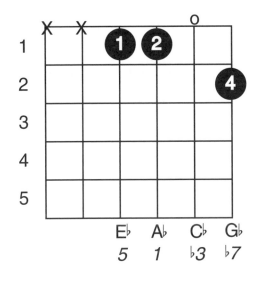

	E♭	A♭	C♭	G♭
	5	1	♭3	♭7

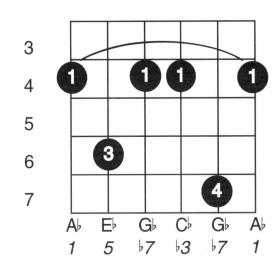

A♭	E♭	G♭	C♭	G♭	A♭
1	5	♭7	♭3	♭7	1

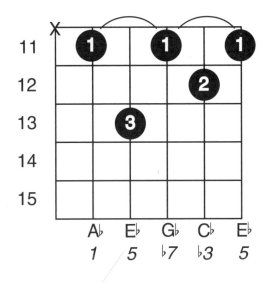

A♭	E♭	G♭	C♭	E♭
1	5	♭7	♭3	5

323

A♭

m7♭5

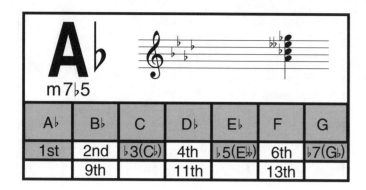

A♭	B♭	C	D♭	E♭	F	G
1st	2nd	♭3(C♭)	4th	♭5(E♭♭)	6th	♭7(G♭)
	9th		11th		13th	

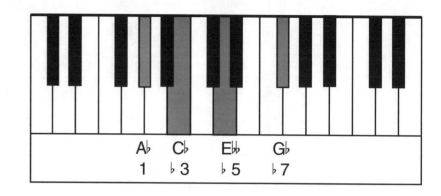

A♭ C♭ E♭♭ G♭
1   ♭3   ♭5   ♭7

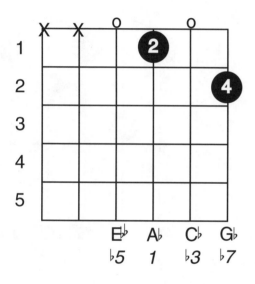

E♭ A♭ C♭ G♭
♭5   1   ♭3   ♭7

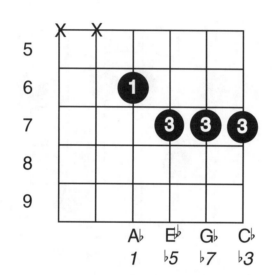

A♭ E♭ G♭ C♭
1   ♭5   ♭7   ♭3

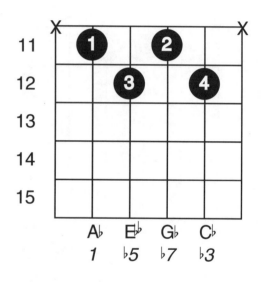

A♭ E♭ G♭ C♭
1   ♭5   ♭7   ♭3

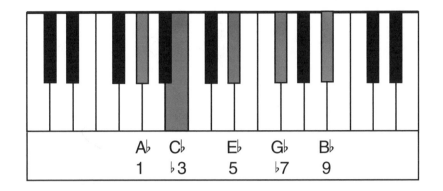

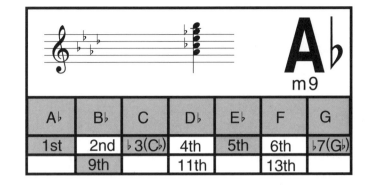

A♭m9

A♭	B♭	C	D♭	E♭	F	G
1st	2nd	♭3(C♭)	4th	5th	6th	♭7(G♭)
	9th		11th		13th	

Keyboard

A♭ C♭ E♭ G♭ B♭
1   ♭3 5   ♭7 9

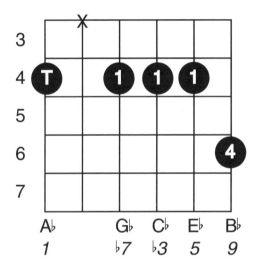

A♭   G♭ C♭ E♭ B♭
1   ♭7 ♭3 5   9

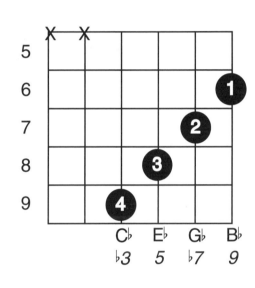

C♭ E♭ G♭ B♭
♭3 5   ♭7 9

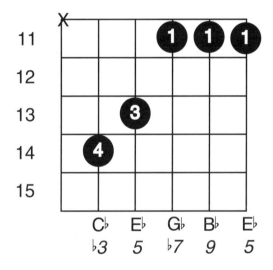

C♭ E♭ G♭ B♭ E♭
♭3 5   ♭7 9   5

A♭ dim 7

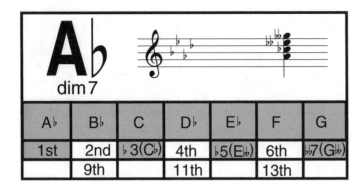

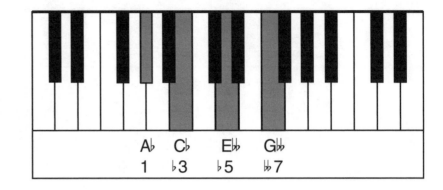

A♭	B♭	C	D♭	E♭	F	G
1st	2nd	♭3(C♭)	4th	♭5(E♭♭)	6th	♭♭7(G♭♭)
	9th		11th		13th	

A♭   C♭   E♭♭   G♭♭
1   ♭3   ♭5   ♭♭7

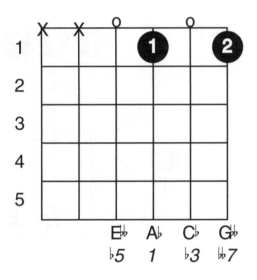

E♭ A♭ C♭ G♭♭
♭5 1 ♭3 ♭♭7

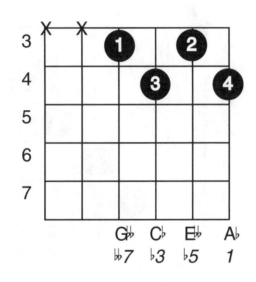

G♭♭ C♭ E♭♭ A♭
♭♭7 ♭3 ♭5 1

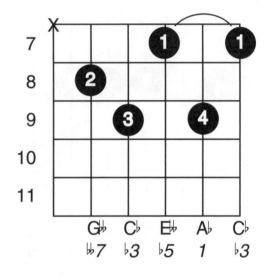

G♭♭ C♭ E♭♭ A♭ C♭
♭♭7 ♭3 ♭5 1 ♭3

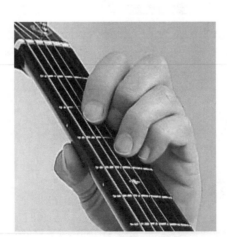

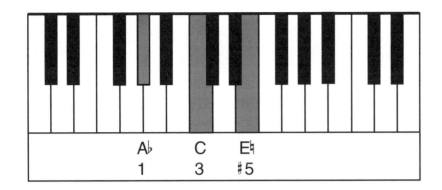

A♭   C   E♮
1   3   #5

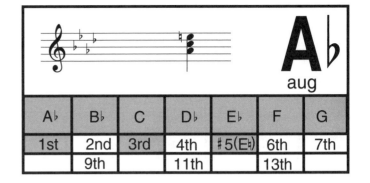

A♭
aug

A♭	B♭	C	D♭	E♭	F	G
1st	2nd	3rd	4th	#5(E♮)	6th	7th
	9th		11th		13th	

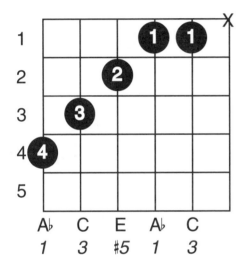

A♭   C   E   A♭   C
1   *3*   *#5*   *1*   *3*

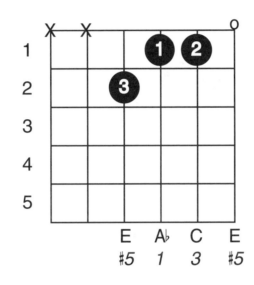

E   A♭   C   E
#5   *1*   *3*   *#5*

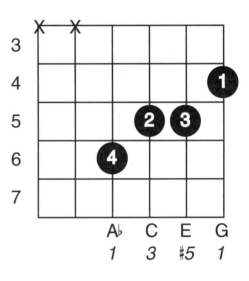

A♭   C   E   G
1   *3*   *#5*   *1*

A♭

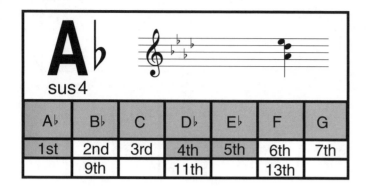

sus4

A♭	B♭	C	D♭	E♭	F	G
1st	2nd	3rd	4th	5th	6th	7th
	9th		11th		13th	

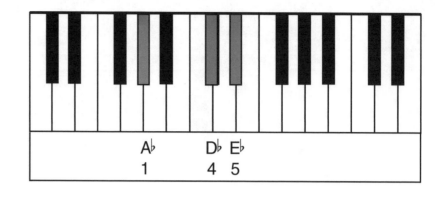

A♭   D♭ E♭
1   4   5

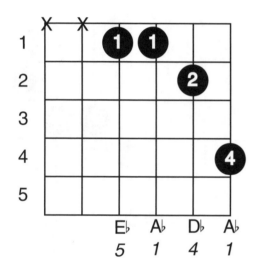

E♭   A♭   D♭   A♭
5   1   4   1

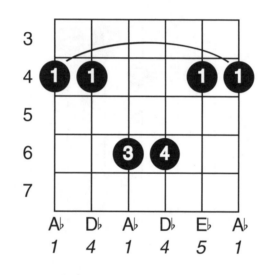

A♭   D♭   A♭   D♭   E♭   A♭
1   4   1   4   5   1

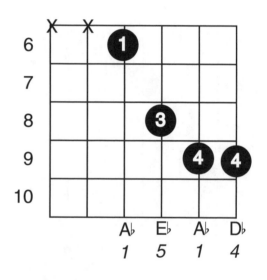

A♭   E♭   A♭   D♭
1   5   1   4

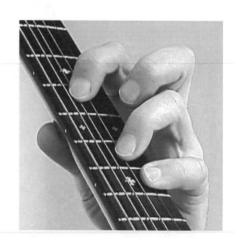

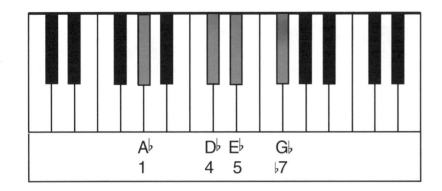

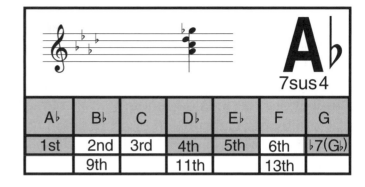

A♭ 7sus4

A♭	B♭	C	D♭	E♭	F	G
1st	2nd	3rd	4th	5th	6th	♭7(G♭)
	9th		11th		13th	

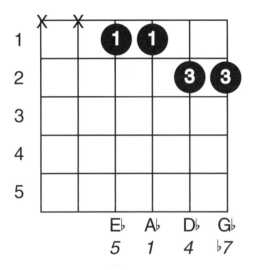

E♭ A♭ D♭ G♭
5 1 4 ♭7

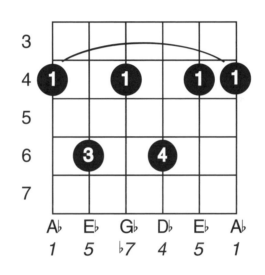

A♭ E♭ G♭ D♭ E♭ A♭
1 5 ♭7 4 5 1

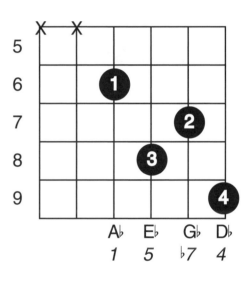

A♭ E♭ G♭ D♭
1 5 ♭7 4

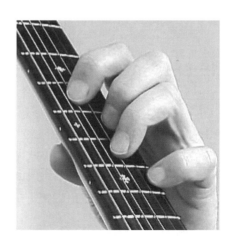

329

FIVE BASIC CHORD FORMS

A good deal of the chords you will use as a guitarist will evolve from the five basic forms illustrated below. One would be wise to learn these before all others. Forms display the fingering of the chord in open position. The actual chord name is dependent on the fret location of the first finger barre. ⌒

Notice only the C form is in open position (no barre.) The others are in positions named after the fret number of the 1st finger barre location. If they each were in the open position they each would reflect a chord name (as the C form does) the same as the "Form".

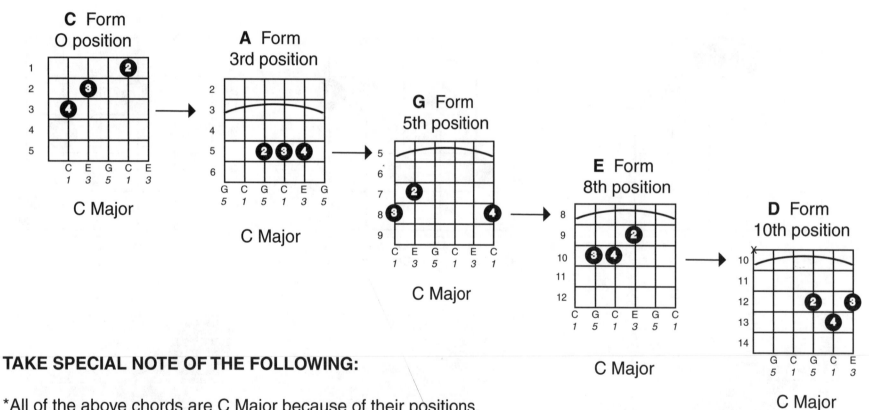

TAKE SPECIAL NOTE OF THE FOLLOWING:

*All of the above chords are C Major because of their positions.

* The form positions travel up the neck in the following order, **C,A,G,E,D** and continually repeat themselves.

* The position of the form is determined by the highest fretted note of the form before it (except from D to C.)
   (for ex. If the G form's highest fretted note is on the 8th fret, then the E form's 1st finger barre is on the 8th fret. If the E form's highest fretted note is on the 10th, then the D form's 1st finger barre is on the 10th fret.)

FIVE BASIC CHORD FORMS (cont.)

*The sequence can begin with **any** of the open chord forms (see illustration below) and as noted previously the positions travel up the neck in the order of **C,A,G,E,D** and continually repeat themselves.

As stated the position of each individual form is determined by the highest fretted note of the form before it. (except from D to C.)

* The **D to C EXCEPTION**-To begin the cycle over again one must travel from the D form to the C form. Here the first finger barre is determined by the highest fretted note minus one.

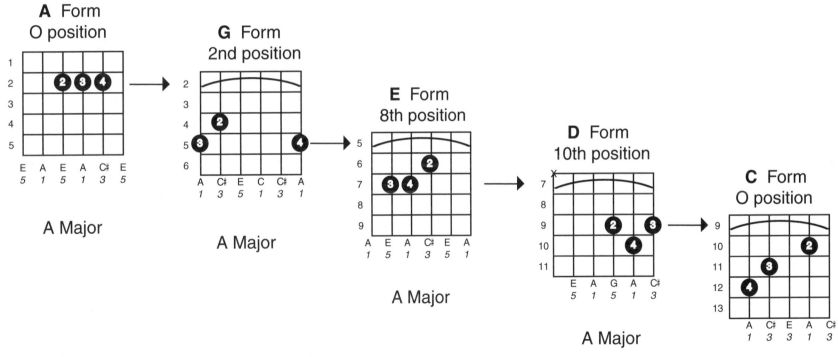

A Form
O position

A Major

G Form
2nd position

A Major

E Form
8th position

A Major

D Form
10th position

A Major

C Form
O position

A Major

*All of the chords will have the name of the open chord beginning the sequence.

KEY SIGNATURES

C

(no sharps or flats)

Starting on C and moving to the 5th degree
will bring you to the key of 1 sharp "G".

Starting on C and moving to the 4th degree
will bring you to the key of 1 flat "F".

G
(1 sharp)

F
(1 flat)

Starting on G and moving to the 5th degree
will bring you to the key of 2 sharps "D".

Starting on F and moving to the 4th degree
will bring you to the key of 2 flats "B♭".

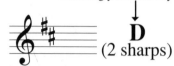

D
(2 sharps)

B♭
(2 flats)

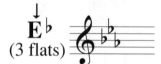

Starting on D and moving to the 5th degree
will bring you to the key of 3 sharps "A".

Starting on B♭and moving to the 4th degree
will bring you to the key of 3 flats "E♭".

A
(3 sharps)

E♭
(3 flats)

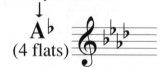

Starting on A and moving to the 5th degree
will bring you to the key of 4 sharps "E".

Starting on E♭and moving to the 4th degree
will bring you to the key of 4 flats "A♭".

E
(4 sharps)

A♭
(4 flats)

Starting on E and moving to the 5th degree
will bring you to the key of 5 sharps "B".

Starting on A♭and moving to the 4th degree
will bring you to the key of 5 flats "D♭".

B
(5 sharps)

D♭
(5 flats)

Starting on B and moving to the 5th degree
will bring you to the key of 6 sharps "F♯".

Starting on D♭and moving to the 4th degree
will bring you to the key of 6 flats "G♭".

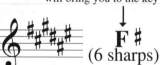

F♯
(6 sharps)

Traveling across the
fretboard in this direction
yields 5ths (Excep.B string)

Traveling across the
fretboard in this direction
yields 4ths (Execp.B string)

G♭
(6 flats)

Starting on F♯and moving to the 5th degree
will bring you to the key of 7 sharps "C♯".

Starting on G♭and moving to the 4th degree
will bring you to the key of 7 flats "C♭".

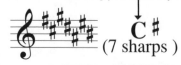

C♯
(7 sharps)

C♭
(7 flats)

Fretboard diagram (strings E A D G):

E	A	D	G
F	B♭	E♭	A♭
F♯/G♭	B	E	A
G	C	F	B♭
A♭	C♯	F♯/G♭	B

MODAL CHORD & SCALE CHART

	I	II	III	IV	V	VI	VII
IONIAN	**M** IONIAN	**m** DORIAN	**m** PHRYGIAN	**M** LYDIAN	**M** MIXOLYDIAN	**m** AEOLIAN	**dim.** LOCRIAN
DORIAN	**m** DORIAN	**m** PHRYGIAN	**M** LYDIAN	**M** MIXOLYDIAN	**m** AEOLIAN	**dim.** LOCRIAN	**M** IONIAN
PHRYGIAN	**m** PHRYGIAN	**M** LYDIAN	**M** MIXOLYDIAN	**m** AEOLIAN	**dim.** LOCRIAN	**M** IONIAN	**m** DORIAN
LYDIAN	**M** LYDIAN	**M** MIXOLYDIAN	**m** AEOLIAN	**dim.** LOCRIAN	**M** IONIAN	**m** DORIAN	**m** PHRYGIAN
MIXOLYDIAN	**M** MIXOLYDIAN	**m** AEOLIAN	**dim.** LOCRIAN	**M** IONIAN	**m** DORIAN	**m** PHRYGIAN	**M** LYDIAN
AEOLIAN	**m** AEOLIAN	**dim.** LOCRIAN	**M** IONIAN	**m** DORIAN	**m** PHRYGIAN	**M** LYDIAN	**M** MIXOLYDIAN
LOCRIAN	**dim.** LOCRIAN	**M** IONIAN	**m** DORIAN	**m** PHRYGIAN	**M** LYDIAN	**M** MIXOLYDIAN	**m** AEOLIAN

*This chart is diatonic and based on the seven chords which are built from the seven scale degrees (notes) found within a key. (The 8th note is the octave.)

*The correct chord type and modal scale are listed below each numerical scale position displayed across the top of the chart. Simply matching your progression with the numerals reveals the correct chord type with its associated mode scale.

Chord Key

M	Major
m	minor
dim.	diminished

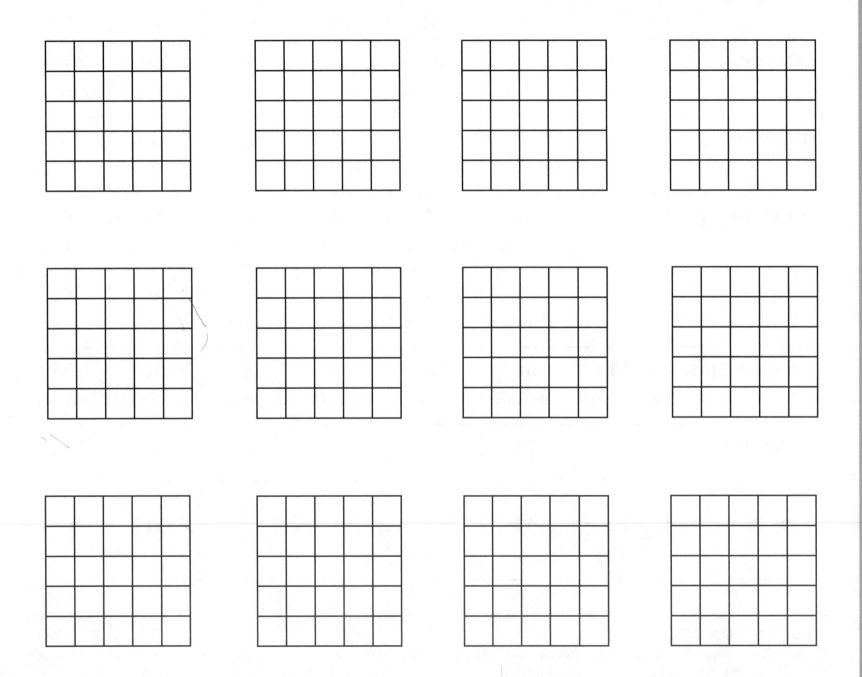

334

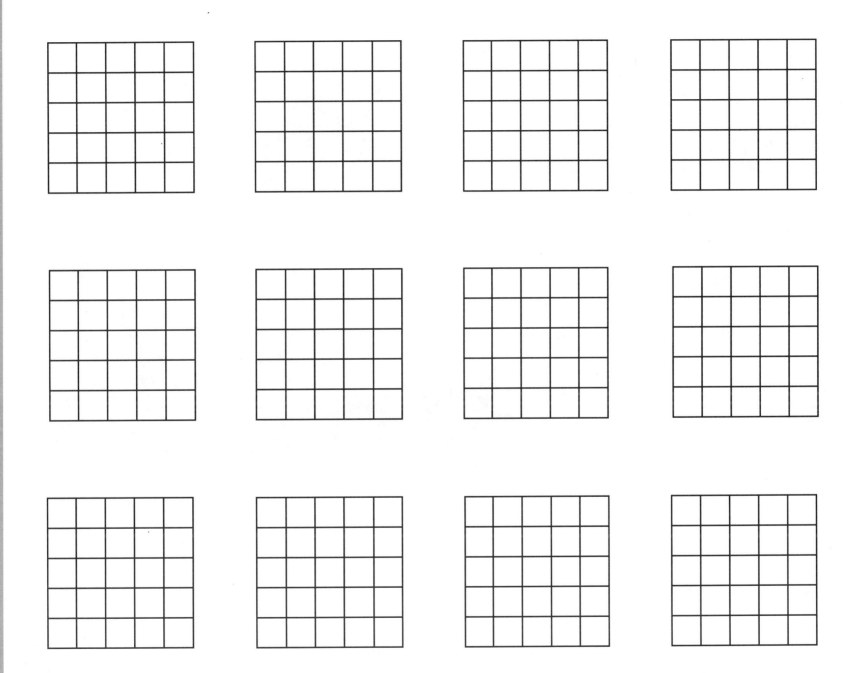

about the author...

David Atkinson owns and operates Kevin's Heaven Studios in New Kensington, Pennsylvania, a suburb of Pittsburgh. Kevin's Heaven Studios is a state of the art digital multitrack recording studio that gives musicians an opportunity to create audio and video recordings. The facility provides music instruction as well. David, an active bassist and guitarist, is the primary children's instructor of both disciplines at the studio. He has authored instructional courses that run the gamut from elementary guitar and bass to engineering a recording session. Within the music industry, David has found the opportunity to demonstrate his analytical ability to dissect a potentially complex subject and present it in a simple, no-nonsense manner.